Olivier Urbain is Director of the Toda Institute
Research, Tokyo and Honolulu, and holds doctor
(University of Southern California) and peace stud... ...., ...
He edited *Music and Conflict Transformation: Harmonies and Dissonances in Geopolitics*
(I.B.Tauris, 2008), and has contributed articles to many learned journals.

'This is a timely and penetrating assessment of Daisaku Ikeda's philosophy of
peace. Though Ikeda's writings, including his dialogues and peace proposals,
constitute a noteworthy contribution to the literature, they have not until now
received the attention they deserve. Urbain's study admirably fills this gap.
First, he draws attention to the decisive influence exerted by Nichiren's teachings and Toda's peace leadership on Ikeda's thought and practice. Secondly, he
brings together in original and thought-provoking fashion Ikeda's understanding
of peace and that of leading contemporary peace researchers, notably Galtung.
Thirdly, and most importantly, he distils the coherence and uniqueness of what
Ikeda has to say by connecting three persistent themes in his intellectual engagement, namely "inner transformation," "dialogue," and "global citizenship."
Urbain is at his most insightful when he juxtaposes these with the contributions
of "humanistic psychology," "communicative rationality," and "cosmopolitan
democracy." In this profound sense Ikeda emerges as a significant synthesizer of
some of the most promising leaps in contemporary human reflexivity.'

– Joseph A. Camilleri, Professor of International Relations,
Director, Centre for Dialogue, La Trobe University.

'This study offers a valuable overview of Daisaku Ikeda's contribution to a philosophy of peace and compares it to that of other pioneering thinkers. It helps us
advance towards a global civilization free from misery and war.'

– Dietrich Fischer, Academic Director,
World Peace Academy, Basel, Switzerland.

'Olivier Urbain has done the world in general, peace in particular, and peace
research even more specifically a major favor. He has made the depth of a great
thinker on peace, Daisaku Ikeda, available outside Soka Gakkai International, the
huge secular Buddhist organization founded by Ikeda in 1975.'

– Johan Galtung, Founder, TRANSCEND International,
from the preface to this volume.

'Olivier Urbain's study of Daisaku Ikeda's philosophy of peace is a remarkably
erudite analysis of a major modern peace thinker. It goes well beyond conventional
biography by showing how Ikeda's views mesh with those of other modern peace
theorists. Urbain is well equipped to bridge Eastern and Western thought on the
issue of peace. He transcends differences, and thus acts out the principles advocated
by Daisaku Ikeda and other creative modern peace theorists and practitioners.'

– George Kent, Professor, Department of Political Science,
University of Hawaii.

'A fascinating, learned exposé of Daisaku Ikeda's way of thinking, believing and acting for peace over a lifetime; but not only that – it highlights his dependence on peace people before him and those of his contemporaries and visionaries of his own calibre.

Olivier Urbain's comparative analysis of Ikeda and Galtung is not only pioneering a field we need much more studies in, it is also highly relevant for anyone who grapples with the essential, even existential, dimension of the overarching question for us all: How to bring about individual-to-global change to save our world before it's too late. I wholeheartedly recommend this book because it tells us that there are lots of lights at the end of the tunnel we are presently in.'

— Jan Øberg, Director, Transnational Foundation
for Peace and Future Research.

'Urbain makes an original contribution to the comparative study of peace theory with implications for global peace action.'

— Glenn D. Paige, author of *Nonkilling Global Political Science*.

'Olivier Urbain has accomplished something with this book on Ikeda's philosophy of peace that few intellectual biographers do with grace and intellectual depth – and that is to place the contribution of his subject into a larger historical context. Urbain has exposed the intellectual roots of Ikeda's philosophy of peace by describing and elucidating upon the historical setting in which the Japan of the 1930s and 1940s found itself. In so doing, he has put flesh on Ikeda's perspectives, philosophy and discourse by tracing how a nation transformed itself from emperor worship and the cult of militarism into a culture that would come to govern itself under a constitution that renounced investment in weapons and militaristic solutions. Out of this matrix, Ikeda's emphasis on inner transformation and self-realization as foundational to the cause of peace makes more sense as a starting point for dialogue between peoples and the evolution of our planetary life toward a culture of peace within the context of a truly global civilization. Urbain's book connects the dots. In so doing, he has laid the groundwork for sharing Ikeda's idealistic and practical path toward peace both within peoples, between cultures, and through an emerging global civilization dedicated to the realization of peace and the renunciation of war.'

— Terrence E. Paupp, author of *Achieving Inclusionary Governance*,
Exodus from Empire and *The Future of Global Relations*. He is a Senior Fellow at
the Council on Hemispheric Affairs, Washington D.C. and serves as
Vice-President of North America for an NGO called the
International Association of Educators for World Peace (IAEWP).

DAISAKU IKEDA'S PHILOSOPHY OF PEACE

DIALOGUE, TRANSFORMATION
AND GLOBAL CITIZENSHIP

Olivier Urbain

in association with
The Toda Institute for Global Peace and Policy Research

Published in 2010 by I.B.Tauris & Co Ltd
6 Salem Road, London W2 4BU
175 Fifth Avenue, New York NY 10010
www.ibtauris.com

Distributed in the United States and Canada Exclusively by Palgrave Macmillan
175 Fifth Avenue, New York NY 10010

Toda Institute book series on Global Peace and Policy

ISBN: 978 1 84885 304 1 (pb)
ISBN: 978 1 84885 303 4 (hb)

A full CIP record for this book is available from the British Library
A full CIP record is available from the Library of Congress

Library of Congress Catalog Card Number: available

Typeset in Garamond by Initial Typesetting Services, Edinburgh
Printed and bound in Great Britain by CPI Antony Rowe, Chippenham

FSC
Mixed Sources
Product group from well-managed
forests and other controlled sources
Cert no. SGS-COC-002953
www.fsc.org
© 1996 Forest Stewardship Council

Contents

Note on proper names and spelling

Proper names follow the English order, given name first and family name last, for instance Mikhail Gorbachev and Josei Toda. When a Japanese name in quoted text was written with family name first in the traditional Japanese style, this order has been preserved in the excerpt. Chinese proper names are always written family name first, for instance Zhou Enlai.

Diacritical marks have been avoided in all languages, except in the case of proper names.

Preface

Olivier Urbain has done the world in general, peace in particular and peace research even more specifically a major favor. He has made the depth of a great thinker on peace, Daisaku Ikeda, available outside Soka Gakkai International, the huge secular Buddhist organization founded by Ikeda in 1975. The reader will be introduced, by a professional well rooted both in SGI and peace theory and practice, to the historical-philosophical background to Nichiren Buddhism, the thought and practice of the founders of Soka Gakkai and Ikeda's background; all standard material in a biography.

But then come Ikeda's more than 50 dialogues published in book form with people from around the world (including the undersigned), and his annual peace proposals since 1983 – during the Cold War often focused on disarmament, after that more on a globalism far beyond the narrow economism of border-free trade. And in the final chapter an exploration of Ikeda's contribution to peace theory comparing his thought to that of others in the field (including this author).

I have no disagreement with Urbain's major conclusion where that comparison is concerned: Ikeda more spiritual, more focused on the unlimited potential of the human mind, heart and brain; I more down-to-earth, concerned with the nitty-gritty of peaceful transformation of hundreds of specific conflicts, and building positive peace with hundreds of specific projects. Which does not imply that I disagree with Ikeda's spirituality nor he with my peace politics, except for the attitude to the USA and the US Empire. Ikeda prefers by and large silence on Iraq, Afghanistan. I do not.

But here I want to celebrate not only Olivier Urbain but above all Daisaku Ikeda. I have seen Soka Gakkai producing miracles at the human level. People heading for criminality, drugs, or just plain emptiness, getting the strength to pull themselves out of that.

And not only that, but getting launched on a road of individual dignity and social usefulness. The secret? Togetherness, support groups, not letting go before the launch is reasonably stable. Then that person will join in the rescue of others in a cascading spiral, not unlike the circles originally supporting micro-credits. Very Buddhist: what matters is the net of relations in which that fragile thing, a human, is embedded. The stronger the net, the stronger the humans. Countless human revolutions have taken place where Soka Gakkai has worked. Ikeda has considerable basis for his optimism. And many societies have been spared much suffering, and expenses!

Of course this is controversial. That net spells sectarianism in more individualist cultures, like France; less so in more collectivist cultures, like Japan. But much more controversial in Japan was the rapid growth of a Soka Gakkai that became increasingly self-sufficient, accused of being a state within the state. I remember that when I was a member of an OECD delegation in 1970, examining the Japanese education system, the ministry warned me not to contact 'that man.' Needless to say, this stimulated my interest enormously.

But Ikeda reached beyond such borders in his dialogues. And we met. He has a big staff of specialists in many fields. But let me state unequivocally: face to face, leaning on nobody, he is both knowledgeable, creative and focused. Those three do not always come together, and certainly not in most academics – which Ikeda is not.

Topics and concrete questions for the first round were prepared by the staff. Then came round after round, and finally a very fine direct encounter after the groundwork had been done. Not all words in a dialogue have to be oral, face to face. But many must be.

As Urbain points out, very basic in Ikeda's work is the human revolution, creating the inner *and outer* conditions under which the best in us humans may flourish.

There is meditation in this, that powerful inner dialogue, so similar to the outer dialogue, that mutual search for understanding, solutions, for ways out. So different from a debate where the goal is verbal victory. In a dialogue the goal is to lift each other up to a We at a higher level. Thus, the TRANSCEND method is based on dialogue, starting with the mediator one on one with the parties to a conflict, moving on to the parties with each other.

To these two pillars on which his peace work is resting Ikeda adds an increasingly complex and sophisticated globalism, exploring humanism, a global ethic, culture of peace, global civilization. A wealth of good and concrete ideas. Nothing for the conservatively inclined to be afraid of: modest, but very important steps forward. And they are very well described and analyzed in this book as a very useful guide to Ikeda's writings. They are projects in the best sense of that word, roads we can walk together. Toward realities with more fulfillment, *sukha*, and less suffering, *dukkha*, trauma.

My problem is with the bumps and bombs on the road, the bombing from above, the ditches, the uncharted nature of the territory. In short, conflicts, meaning contradictions (C) between goals, values and interests, and means + behavior (B) that may range from fusion into oneness, via apathy, to genocide + attitudes (A) that may range from the deep love of suffering the suffering of others and feeling fulfilled by their fulfillment, via the tepid, to glowing hatred. The ABC-triangles at the individual, social, inter-state/nation or inter-region/civilization levels must be taken seriously. We need reconciliation to heal the traumas of the past, mediation to transform the conflicts of the present, and projects for the future.

Thanks Daisaku Ikeda for your gift to humanity. And thanks Olivier Urbain for making that gift more available.

Johan Galtung, Founder
TRANSCEND International

Acknowledgements

It is a great privilege to have had this opportunity to explore and attempt to systematize the philosophy of peace of Daisaku Ikeda. I am deeply grateful for his warm encouragement over the last 24 years, and for his work for peace for over six decades. Daisaku Ikeda's accomplishments have provided most of the inspiration, motivation and material for this book.

I wish to thank Peter van den Dungen, who was my supervisor at the University of Bradford. Without his support and guidance I could not have obtained a second PhD in peace studies. I also wish to thank Carol Rank and Oliver Ramsbotham, the examiners during the PhD final examination, for their very valuable feedback. The responsibility for the content of this book lies entirely with me, and the University of Bradford only approved the PhD thesis as it was on 6 March 2009. There have been substantial changes to the manuscript since then, and the University of Bradford has not approved this new version.

My profound gratitude goes to Tomosaburo Hirano and Tadashige Takamura in addition to Peter van den Dungen for supporting the main idea behind this work when it was proposed by this author for the first time in the fall of 2006.

I would like to thank the staff of the Toda Institute for Global Peace and Policy Research for their support, as well as the staff of several affiliates of the Soka Gakkai and Soka Gakkai International (SGI) for providing precise information and source material. Again the responsibility for the content is entirely mine as it was not approved by the Toda Institute or by the Soka Gakkai, the SGI, or their affiliates.

Numerous people have read the manuscript and provided very helpful criticism, advice and feedback at various stages of its development. I apologize in advance to anybody I may have forgotten in the following list but their support is deeply appreciated, and I wish to acknowledge at least the following friends, colleagues, teachers and mentors in alphabetical order of last name:

Karen Abi-Ezzi, Fady Abusidu, Virginia Benson, Elizabeth Bowen, Joseph Camilleri, Dietrich Fischer, Johan Galtung, Andrew Gebert, Alexandra Goossens, John M. Heffron, Prince Paa-kwesi Heto, Hiroshi Kanno, Yoichi Kawada, George Kent, Masahiro Kobayashi, Tomohiro Matsuda, Mikio Matsuoka, Toru Nishimoto, Jan Øberg, Glenn Paige, Terrence E. Paupp, Franklin Rausky, Masayuki Shiohara, Itir Toksöz, Richard Walker, Paul Wallace, Neil Walsh, Susan Zipp and Michael Yap.

My gratitude also goes to Masako Tanimura and Yoshiharu Suwa for allowing me to interview them and publish a summary of our exchanges in this book.

I am very grateful to all those who have supported the writing of this volume in some way, especially if their efforts went unnoticed.

Finally, I wish to thank my wife Yoko for her unstinting support during the three years of the planning, research, writing and rewriting of this book.

Introduction

This book represents an attempt to explore and systematize the peace philosophy of Daisaku Ikeda, the leader of one of the most dynamic lay Buddhist movements today, the Soka Gakkai[1] International (SGI), which has more than 12 million members worldwide. His voluminous writings span a wide range of themes and voices, including essays, poetry and fiction; those that are explicitly dedicated to advancing the cause of peace include more than 50 volumes of published dialogues and annual peace proposals since 1983. He is credited with the improvement of Sino–Japanese relations, and has received more than 250 academic honors from institutions throughout the world. Despite these achievements, Daisaku Ikeda's philosophy of peace has never been analyzed nor systematized before.

One of the reasons for this may be that Ikeda's principal concern has been to build a popular, international movement, rather than to develop a carefully elaborated philosophical system. In this sense, the work of systematizing his thought has been left to others. This book takes up that task, identifying three consistent themes or threads that can be seen running through all his writings on peace: *inner transformation*, *dialogue* and *global citizenship*. But it must be repeated that for Ikeda, these themes are not abstract concepts, but components of a way of life.

My position and stance

As a practicing SGI Buddhist and disciple of Daisaku Ikeda, I am a deeply engaged and committed participant in the process which I am attempting to study and analyze. My personal experience, including encounters with Ikeda and a sense of profound appreciation for the role his encouragement and guidance have played in my life, are inextricably woven through this book. At the same time, if I were not confident that Ikeda's philosophy of peace can be of significant value to people of all backgrounds, including of course those who do not embrace the Buddhist faith, I could not justify this research to myself or to the world.

As a member of the lay Buddhist organization headed by Ikeda, I have experienced the positive results of the practice of his Buddhist humanist philosophy. I joined the SGI in 1985. At the time I was a 24-year-old graduate student in Los Angeles, California, freshly arrived from Belgium with great hopes of becoming a successful immigrant. However, I was facing serious obstacles, one of them being my incapacity to study for long hours due to psychosomatic headaches. With meager resources and on a student visa, failure in my studies would have meant going back to Belgium a loser, a prospect that substantially increased the stressfulness of the situation. Another problem was that my underdeveloped social skills did not allow me to quickly build the support network I needed in order to succeed in a huge and dynamic city where I had arrived alone.

After a few months of desperate struggles, I began practicing Buddhism with the SGI, and for the first time I tasted what were considered as forbidden fruits for the proponents of the secular and materialist humanism on which I was raised. Indeed, the power of prayer and chanting and the effectiveness of a coherent philosophical system were all unfamiliar to me. The first results were convincing and, for instance, I was able to use my mind freely and study as much as I wanted without suffering from headaches and other ailments. To me, this was a spectacular change that opened up new horizons. Since I was now able to study hard, the sky was the limit. Moreover, my relational skills improved quickly, and I was able to recreate an enjoyable social life from scratch in my new environment. As a result of this personal transformation, among other achievements and events that were crucial for my well-being and further development, I received a PhD in French Literature in 1990, moved to Japan the year after and married Yoko Nagai in 1994.

After the events of 11 September 2001, I wanted to go back to school to try to understand an increasingly confusing world. With the intellectual confidence I had developed through the practice of Buddhism, I found myself starting a second PhD at the University of Bradford in the UK in 2002. My original research topic was the power of music for peace, but in 2006 I decided to devote myself to a study of a sample of 10,000 pages of Ikeda's writings instead.

Since I understood that I was being considered for the post of director of the Toda Institute for Global Peace and Policy Research,[2] established by Ikeda, I wanted to better understand the philosophy of peace of its founder. I was honored to have an opportunity to follow in the footsteps of Majid Tehranian, the first director of the Toda Institute, a well-known scholar of international communication, accomplished writer and noted Sufi Muslim.

At the same time this prospect was intimidating and I was not sure what my personal stance should be. In order to find out, I decided to study the thoughts of the founder of the institute and to systematize them. The result was a PhD in peace studies which I completed in July 2009, and which serves as the basis for this book.

As a peace researcher deeply confident of both the personal and more generalized value of Ikeda's philosophy, it was a source of personal frustration that I rarely if ever heard the ideas of my mentor discussed or mentioned in this academic field. It became increasingly clear to me that one reason for this is that his ideas have not been systematized in a coherent framework.

This is one of the goals of this book: to offer a comprehensive and systematic exposition of Daisaku Ikeda's philosophy of peace, so that his main ideas can be held up for scrutiny and discussed in the field of peace research. In doing this, I draw on my basic training as a Western European secular and rational humanist. In this sense, I am responding to another subjectively felt imperative, rooted in my cultural background: the need to know why it works, and how Ikeda's philosophy can be systematized in a coherent way for the benefit of a wider audience.

Through the work of systematizing it, I hope to make the values and principles of Ikeda's peace philosophy available to a wide range of people, because I believe their application can be highly beneficial at the personal, local and global levels. In other words, I am convinced that the values and principles at the core of Buddhism can be shared in a secular way, whether one is a Buddhist or not.

For whom

I have attempted to systematize the ideas of Daisaku Ikeda into a format that can be explained, compared, discussed, tested and be relevant for the peace research community and all those interested in a more peaceful world. Just as the ideas of Johan Galtung, Elise and Kenneth Boulding, Glenn Paige, Adam Curle, John-Paul Lederach, Gene Sharp and others are mentioned in the peace studies literature and discussed in conferences and papers, I believe the ideas of Ikeda also need to be included in the debates. The analysis offered in this book is not the only one possible, but it does show that systematization is possible. Daisaku Ikeda has held dialogues with thousands of people, founded dozens of institutions, published more than 100,000 pages of novels, poetry, religious writings, children's books, peace proposals and more; and trying to present a map that can serve as a guide through all these thoughts, words and actions is no small task. That is the challenge of this book.

Besides peace researchers, I hope to be able to reach anybody who is seriously interested in peace. Indeed, I am convinced that inner transformation, dialogue and global citizenship, as well as all the other ideas at the core of Ikeda's philosophy such as the Bodhisattva[3] spirit and the interconnectedness of all things, can be understood and practiced by people of all faiths and convictions. To understand and reap the benefits of this way of looking at life, it is not necessary to change one's religion or philosophy; the values and principles at the core of Buddhism are universal and applicable by anyone. It is for this reason that they need to be shared with as many people as possible around the world.

This book is therefore written for all who are interested in peace-generating values and principles, whether they are members of the SGI, believe in another religion or philosophy, or do not espouse any recognizable worldview. Anyone who chooses to explore this path can reap the rewards that come with making efforts at inner transformation, trying to have better dialogues and developing an identity based on global citizenship, for the sake of the peace and happiness of humanity.

A few definitions

After several years of research, I have come to the conclusion that the following definitions are most helpful when sharing these values and principles.

'Inner transformation' means cultivating the capacity to generate positive qualities such as courage, wisdom and compassion. When this is accomplished through the practice of Nichiren Buddhism by members of the SGI, it is called 'human revolution,' but there are many other ways to bring out these qualities. For instance in Islam inner transformation is called *Jihad al-Nafs*, the nonviolent spiritual struggle against one's weak self. Hindus, Christians, Jews and believers of other religions pray for self-improvement. Methods in humanistic psychology and other forms of psychotherapy enable many people to flourish. Self-scrutiny and introspection are some of the many other ways commonly used by people of diverse backgrounds in their attempts to perfect themselves.

In the context of the clarification of Ikeda's philosophy of peace presented in this book, 'dialogue' is defined as the communicative use of language, ideas and reason in order to bring out the best in oneself and others. The goal is not to win arguments, but to enhance the dialogue partners' feelings of shared humanity.

Finally 'global citizenship' means the capacity to care for all people, or in Ikeda's words, 'The compassion to maintain an imaginative empathy that reaches beyond one's immediate surroundings and extends to those suffering in distant places' (2001a, 101).

What is left out

Some elements which are not in this volume are the personal experiences of SGI members (except for a few examples), an analysis of the influence of the SGI movement on the world, and the religious aspects, especially what pertains to faith. In Ikeda's (and the SGI's) approach to Buddhism, the term 'faith' has a different meaning from the one usually assigned to it in mono-theistic religions. The assertions and faith claims of Buddhism are taken as being open and subject to testing; there is nothing that one must believe in advance or in the absence of any empirical proof. However, many of the writings and speeches of Ikeda refer to the specifics of Buddhist practice and faith, and an analysis of these writings is outside the scope of this work.

Ikeda himself addresses different audiences: sometimes members of the SGI, sometimes friends and acquaintances of various backgrounds, at other times dialogue partners, peace activists, scholars or political leaders. The language he uses is slightly different each time. The body of texts analyzed here is that which appears to have been written with a broader audience in mind, and not specifically for SGI members: the novels *The Human Revolution* and *The New Human Revolution*, the dialogues and the annual peace proposals published since 1983. This was the basic material for my PhD thesis, and in this book relevant passages from Ikeda's poetry, children's tales, university lectures and other writings have been added.

Layout and outline of the book

Part I introduces Daisaku Ikeda the philosopher. Chapter 1 is a short biography mostly for the benefit of the readers who are unfamiliar with his achievements, and contains an overview of the peace movement in postwar Japan.

In the next three chapters elements which are considered important in the formation of Ikeda's philosophy of peace are presented, namely his own experiences as described in his autobiographical novels (Chapter 2), his rela-tionship with his mentor Josei Toda (1900–58) (Chapter 3) and certain values and principles at the core of Nichiren Buddhism (Chapter 4).

Part II lays out the system I have designed to explain Ikeda's philosophy of peace, which can be seen as a concrete approach that starts with one individual asking the question: 'What can I do for peace?'

The way I see Ikeda's answer to this question is that the first step is inner transformation, in the direction of an increase in the strength of positive personal qualities (Chapter 5). Second comes dialogue, the capacity to discuss matters of mutual importance with other people, share insights about life and bring out the best in oneself and others (Chapter 6). Third is global citizenship (Chapter 7), a result of inner transformation and dialogue. This is a way of life that recognizes the common humanity of all human beings, regardless of gender or cultural, social and other backgrounds. An identity as a global citizen can be nurtured and developed. Then, as more and more people take action as global citizens, they can create elements of an emerging global civilization of coexistence and harmony. This system is compared to that of other peace thinkers in Chapter 8.

The main framework introduced in Part II can be represented as follows.

Individual Peace

****

Inner Transformation
Personal development along the lines of Humanistic Psychology, especially developing Courage, Wisdom and Compassion

Dialogue
The main goal is to bring out the best in oneself and others, along the lines of Communicative Rationality

Global Citizenship
Development of one's identity as a Global Citizen. As more people develop this type of identity, elements of a Global Civilization start appearing

****

World Peace

The interdependence of the main concepts

One way to envision the links between the three elements is one giving rise to the other in concentric circles. This representation favors the growth of the individual through inner transformation first, spilling over to a capacity for dialogue that leads to global citizenship. Elements of a global civilization also appear as a result of the activities of global citizens in the legal, political and administrative spheres.

Another way is to imagine each element as the corner of a triangle, with links back and forth between the three corners. Inner transformation allows for better dialogue and greater capacity for global citizenship, dialogue encourages inner transformation and polishes one's identity as a global citizen, and attempts to become a global citizen necessitate inner transformation and dialogue. As more global citizens contribute to a peaceful path, the elements of a global civilization will start to appear.

A third way is to visualize a loop with the directional flow always going back to the point of departure of inner transformation. When confronted with challenges blocking our attempts to develop dialogue, global citizenship or elements of a global civilization, we need to go back to making efforts in the realm of inner transformation, bringing out once again our capacity to work towards the development of a better world.

Theory and practice: an empowering praxis for peace

On the theoretical level, this work explores the similarities between these elements of Ikeda's philosophy of peace and principles and values found in humanistic psychology and virtue ethics, the dialogical theories of Jürgen Habermas and Martin Büber and ideas concerning global citizenship and cosmopolitan democracy developed by Daniele Archibugi, among many others. It also offers points of comparison with the thoughts of some of the main thinkers in the field of peace studies, especially Johan Galtung.

On the practical level, there are many advantages to Ikeda's philosophy of peace. One is that he is living proof that all these ideas can be implemented in the course of a very active, coherent and contributive life. Another is that all of us can find reasons to be engaged and empowered to change our world. No matter how alienated one may feel from the negotiations taking place at summit meetings or in the various national parliaments, there is always something that can be done here and now. We can always take positive action where we are, within the context of our daily life and immediate surroundings. As Ikeda writes:

> [R]ather than making the great leap to the vast and complex phenomena of life, we should start from the concrete realities of the tiny patch of land where we are now. It is only by paying relentless attention to those realities that we can freely direct our thoughts and associations to the larger dimension. If we develop such fresh and

vital imagination, a keen sensitivity to daily life and to life itself, we will be able to experience not only close friends but even the inhabitants of distant lands whom we have never met – and even the cultures and products of those lands – as neighbors (2009–PP, 11).

To set out from immediate and concrete realities, creating with every step new neighbors in an expanding network of human solidarity – this is the true path to peace. Without the steady accumulation of such efforts, the ideal of a perpetual peace will remain forever out of reach (2009–PP, 12).

Part I

A PHILOSOPHER OF PEACE

CHAPTER 1

Daisaku Ikeda and his Circumstances: Recollections of War and Peace

> I am myself plus my circumstance, and if I do not save it, I cannot save myself.
>
> José Ortega y Gasset (1961, 45)

> The burning commitment to peace that remained unshaken throughout his imprisonment was something he carried with him his entire life. It was from this, and from the profound compassion that characterized each of his interactions, that I most learned. Ninety-eight percent of what I am today I learned from him.
>
> Daisaku Ikeda about his mentor Josei Toda, in a lecture at Columbia University in 1996. (Ikeda 2001, 106–7)

The first time I met Daisaku Ikeda in person was in Los Angeles, USA, in 1987. The occasion was the official opening of the first campus of Soka University of America (SUA), and I was playing the vibraphone in the local SGI band. At some point I found myself looking straight into Ikeda's deep brown eyes, and even though he did not say anything and was only smiling and raising his arms in a welcoming gesture, I was overwhelmed with the very distinct feeling of hearing someone telling me: 'Please study hard and never give up!' I had just started my first PhD at the time and I was indeed in need of this type of encouragement, preoccupied as I was with my new endeavors. Why I gained the impression that Ikeda was responding to this need is still a mystery to me, but the fact remains that I was able to make a renewed and more profound commitment to my studies at that moment. The memory of this episode is still much alive today.

Ikeda's 80th birthday, on 2 January 2008, was celebrated by millions of SGI members around the world. Further, congratulatory messages were sent by prominent cultural and political figures, such as Ambassador Anwarul Chowdhury, former United Nations Under-Secretary-General.[1] Others included futurist and sustainable development expert Hazel Henderson; Elise Boulding, peace activist and professor emerita of sociology at Dartmouth College; and former Indian Prime Minister Dr. Inder Kumar Gujral. On 5 December 2007, Rep. Hank Johnson, D-Georgia, introduced a resolution in congress (H.Res. 844) 'recognizing the service and dedication of Dr. Daisaku Ikeda and celebrating his 80th birthday.'[2] On 27 February 2008, Peking University in Beijing, China, hosted an academic symposium in honor of Ikeda's birthday. It was attended by around 350 participants, including representatives of 20 Chinese universities.[3]

These events, as well as his achievements for peace mentioned below, present a contrast with Ikeda's humble origins. Hailing from a long line of fisher folk and seaweed farmers, he grew up poor and sickly amidst the miseries and devastation brought about by the Pacific War (1937–45). I believe that the turning point in his life was his meeting with Josei Toda in 1947.

Ikeda became the third president of the Soka Gakkai[4] in 1960, succeeding his mentor Toda. In 1975 he established the Soka Gakkai International (SGI), devoted to the 'promotion of peace, culture and education.' The SGI has spread to more than 190 countries and territories with more than two million members outside Japan. Under his leadership, the Soka Gakkai membership that stood at one million Japanese households[5] in 1960 has soared to about ten million members.

Besides academic honors, Ikeda has received a large number of honorary citizenships from cities throughout the world. More than 15 research centers devoted to a study of his philosophy have sprung up in China in the last few years. For instance, Shanghai Sanda University established a research center dedicated to the study of his educational philosophy in 2004. There is a travelling exhibition featuring his work for peace alongside that of two giants of nonviolence, Mohandas (Mahatma) Gandhi and Martin Luther King, Jr.[6]

Ikeda has established a complete educational system from kindergarten to university level, with a growing number of schools operating outside Japan. He has founded a concert association, a fine arts museum, two research institutes in Japan and one in the US, a newspaper and several magazines in Japan and the Komeito political party. He has championed friendly ties between China and Japan from as early as 1968, as well as proposed reforms of the United Nations (UN) and other original ideas for global peace in yearly peace proposals and other publications, a number of which have been implemented over the years. These achievements have not failed to trigger controversy, as Richard Seager reports after a meeting with Ikeda:

> From our brief encounter, I can see that Ikeda likes to connect with people, which is probably one reason he is so intense – that and the fact that he's a political-spiritual celebrity beloved by disciples and hated by enemies, a favorite target of the tabloid press, which pulls out his cult-leader reputation whenever Komeito faces a crucial election (Seager 2006, 49).

Having lived in Japan since 1991, I can confirm from first-hand experience that all kinds of rumors and scandals concerning Ikeda appear in the tabloid press around the time of important elections. The timing would make anybody suspicious, and moreover all attempts to trace the source of these slanders reveal that they are empty fabrications concocted for commercial purposes, and most often refuted and condemned in court. During my meetings with Ikeda, I have also noticed that he was intense. I interpret this as partly due to his capacity to give his interlocutors his full attention, as explained in Chapter 6.

I believe that the source of Ikeda's motivation for these endeavors can be traced to his relationship with his mentor, Josei Toda. Indeed, Ikeda as a boy and adolescent was swept away by the militaristic propaganda that dominated Japan at the time, and a brief overview of the country's imperialistic and colonial adventures will show why almost nobody could escape from that tidal wave. It was his meeting with Toda in 1947 that set Ikeda on the path to global peacebuilding. After his mentor's passing in 1958, Ikeda continued to forge a path based on Toda's teachings, showing remarkable consistency and tenacity through the domestic and international upheavals that have affected most pacifist movements in postwar Japan.

Growing up in militarized and wartime Japan (1928–40)

Ikeda grew up at a time when Japan was marching towards war, and his adolescence was spent in the middle of the second global conflagration of the twentieth century. This environment was to decisively shape his life trajectory. Another important event was the 1923 Great Kanto Earthquake, which drastically changed the Ikeda family's social and financial status five years before Ikeda's birth. The information concerning Ikeda's life until 1975 is taken from his autobiographical work entitled *My Recollections* (Ikeda 1980).

Part of Tokyo Bay, the Omori area where Ikeda grew up once led Japan in the production of *nori*, a form of edible seaweed. The Ikeda family had been fisher folk and seaweed farmers growing *nori* for a long time, and by the turn of the twentieth century, they had become so successful that they were the largest producers in Tokyo Bay. For instance, they had pioneered the setting up of large drying areas for the *nori*, as well as the technique of 'farming out' the seaweed in different areas. The 1923 Kanto earthquake dealt a lethal blow to the family *nori* enterprise, and by the time Ikeda was born the family was destitute. Moreover Ikeda's father became bedridden with rheumatism and could barely move for about two years, during which the family had to severely reduce its activities. Ikeda's mother became the pillar of the family, his elder brother Kiichi had to quit middle school in order to bring some money home, and Ikeda himself had to try his young hands at various jobs.

The year when full-scale war broke out between China and Japan (1937), Kiichi had to enter military service, followed by the next three brothers one after another, with Ikeda himself barely escaping the same fate. Within a few years the whole country was mobilized around the war effort, from elementary pupils marching around the schoolyard with oak staves to major industries converted to produce military materiel. In the collection of poems entitled *Fighting for Peace* (2004b), Ikeda wrote:

> Our family saw
> my four elder brothers,
> all in the prime of life, called away to war.
> All four were made tools
> of Japan's invasion of China (29).

Around the same time, Nazi Germany was preparing the 1939 invasion of Poland, and the whole world would soon be plunged into World War II. It is said that Japan was at peace during the Edo Era (1603–1867), so what happened during and after the Meiji Restoration of 1868, and how did Japan become part of the Axis during World War II, ending up with being the first country (and hopefully the last) to be hit by atomic bombs in August 1945? Ikeda wrote:

> None of us had wanted
> this war.
> We had never
> accepted or supported it.
> Yet over time
> almost without noticing,
> we were all influenced,
> maneuvered and brainwashed

> to extol the glories of war.
> The human heart holds
> terrible possibilities.
> More terrible still
> are those who use their power
> to mold and manipulate
> people's minds (2004b, 31).

In order to understand the context of Ikeda's upbringing and the indoctrination to which the Japanese population was subjected, it is necessary to review the rise of Japanese nationalism, militarism and imperialism leading up to the defeat of 1945.

The background of Japan's militarization and involvement in the Pacific War and World War II: Japanese imperialism (1879–1945)

Japan followed a policy of isolation for about 250 years from the seventeenth century, which can be said to have ended on the symbolic date of 8 July 1853, when four 'Black Ships' of the US Navy under the command of Commodore Matthew Perry entered Edo (Tokyo) Bay. Japan could no longer ignore the rest of the world and had to become actively involved in it for the first time in more than two centuries (Naval Historical Center 2008). The following year the Shogun reluctantly signed a treaty establishing formal diplomatic relations with the US, and within five years Japan had signed several similar treaties with other Western countries. This situation was experienced as threatening by most Japanese intellectuals, who felt Japan was brought into the Western sphere of influence against its will through 'gunboat diplomacy.' The treaties were considered as humiliating and unequal:

> Japan, like China, suffered under the unequal treaties it had signed with the West. Japan was particularly humiliated by the extraterritoriality provisions in the treaties, provisions that allowed Westerners in Japan to be subject to their own nation's laws, not Japan's. The Japanese were also unhappy about the privileges that foreigners living in the treaty ports enjoyed as a result of the unequal treaties (Menton 2003).

This pressure from the Western powers is one of the reasons behind the 1868 Meiji Restoration, when the Shogun resigned, the emperor was symbolically restored to power, the feudal system was abolished and Japan started to adopt numerous Western institutions and legal frameworks (Japan Society 2008). In 1875 Japan had to yield the Sakhalin Islands to Russia, but on condition that they received the Kuril Islands instead. Tensions with Russia were already mounting as early as the eighteenth century (Bukh 2009). This incident, among many other vexations, contributed to the mood of humiliation and defeat, and the conviction among the intellectual and political leadership that Japan was faced with a stark choice mostly due to the Western steamroller advance to conquer the world: Japan would be either among the colonized or the colonizers.

A first response came in the 1870s with military incursions into the Ryukyu Islands, culminating in 1879 with their formal annexation and renaming as Okinawa Prefecture. A second followed in 1895 with the annexation of Taiwan, ceded from China following its defeat by Japan. By 1898 the last of the 'unequal treaties' with the West had been cancelled and Japan was on its way to becoming a world power.

With its victories in the first Sino–Japanese War (1894–95) and the Russo–Japanese War (1904–05), Japan became the first non-Western modern imperial power, and showed that it could defeat a Western state (OnWar.com 2008). In 1908 the government 'reaffirmed its foreign policy of expanding Japan's colonial position on the Asian continent within a framework of continued division of spoils with the European powers and the United States' (Bix 2001, 31). The last decade of the nineteenth century and the first years of the twentieth century were a period of intense internal turmoil in Japan, as its leaders were trying to find the best way to react to Western imperialism. A photograph dating back to 1902 symbolizes the complexity and ambiguity of the situation. A one-year-old baby clutches a flag and joyfully waves it above his head. The baby is Hirohito, the future emperor of Japan, and he is holding the military flag of the Rising Sun (Bix 2001, 244).

Korea was annexed as part of the Japanese empire in 1910, and a long period of colonial occupation started for the Korean people, only to end in 1945. There were mass deportations to Japanese labor camps, the kidnapping of thousands of young Korean (and other Asian) girls turned into Imperial Army prostitutes through the 'comfort women system' (a euphemism for sexual slavery),[7] an attempt to wipe out the Korean language and other atrocities. Among a number of complex factors, this weakening of the Korean Peninsula can be considered as one of the reasons for the 1950–53 Korean War and the subsequent division of the Korean people into two states (Stueck 2002).

Japan joined the Western powers in quelling the Chinese Boxer Rebellion (1899–1901) and then entered World War I on the side of the Entente against the Central Powers. Several victories allowed Japan to secure territories previously held by Germany. After the war Japan was recognized by the Treaty of

Versailles (1919) as one of the 'Big Five' of the new international order, and it joined the League of Nations.

On the domestic political front, during the 1920s there was a failed attempt to develop a lasting democratic system of government, similar to the German experiment with the Weimar Republic (1918–33). The first two decades of the twentieth century saw a blossoming of Japan's political system, which came to fruition during the Taisho Era (1912–26) and particularly in the form of the Taisho Democracy (1918–26). This was again a period of intense internal turmoil for Japan, and the situation cannot be understood simply as an attempt to import Western democracy. Bix gives us a glimpse of the complexity of Japan's struggles at the time:

> Recent evidence suggests a slow, gradual decline, starting around the end of World War I, in the common reference point of the Japanese national identity: the myths that constituted 'the fundamental principles of the founding of the country.' Many military officers blamed the growing lack of belief in the founding principles on the Taisho democracy movement, just as they blamed 'democracy' for the decline of discipline in the ranks, and for the estrangement that had developed between the military and the people (Bix 2001, 165).

Partly due to the economic hardships brought about by the Great Depression, Japan just like Western Europe saw a sharp increase in the power of the militarists in the early 1930s. In 1938 a national mobilization law gave the government sweeping economic and political powers, and two years later major parties voted to dissolve themselves to become one single party, called the Imperial Rule Assistance Association (*Taisei Yokusankai*), which was established on 12 October 1940. Within a few years, the military would take over virtually all aspects of Japanese life (Tipton 2002).

After annexing Korea in 1910 and making several economic and political advances in the region, Japan invaded inner Manchuria in 1931 and created the puppet state of Manchukuo, and then resigned from the League of Nations in 1933. The second Sino–Japanese War started in 1937, and this is the year when the first of the Ikeda brothers, Kiichi, had to join the military service, as mentioned above.

Japan formed the Axis Pact with Germany and Italy on 27 September 1940, partly as a result of having joined the anti-Comintern pact in 1936. The concept of *hakko ichiu*, the divine mission of the emperor to unite and rule the world, was created to justify Japanese imperialism. After the 1937 Nanking Massacre and the invasion of French Indochina, the US decided to put a stop to Japan's advance through an embargo of oil and other essential products, freezing all Japanese assets in the US on 26 July 1941. The Japanese military leaders felt that there were only two ways to react to the US pressure: acknowledge defeat and let Japan lose its status as a great power, or go to war against the US, even though ultimate victory was far from assured. They chose the second option. Bix (2001) describes the beginning of the tortuous process that led to that decision, in his work describing the life of Japanese emperor Hirohito (1901–89):

> The American economic sanctions threw near panic into the Konoe Government and had the effect of further dividing opinion within the navy as well as between the navy and the army. Shocked, like everyone else, by this rapid escalation of Anglo-American economic pressure, Hirohito looked on as his navy and army leaders struggled to reach a consensus on how to respond to the crisis (401).

Japan attacked Pearl Harbor on 7 December 1941 (Honolulu time) and, until the battle of Midway (June 1942), was unstoppable. Hong Kong fell the same month, followed by the Philippines and Singapore at the beginning of 1942, and within a few months Japan had established an empire stretching over much of the Pacific, even threatening Australia. The defeat in the Battle of Midway in June 1942 put a final stop to the Japanese imperial headways. In *War without Mercy* (1986) John Dower captures the mood of racially tinged national pride that was rampant in Japan during the short period of successive victories following Pearl Harbor:

> In the January 1942 issue of *Bungei Shunju*, one of Japan's most popular middle-class monthlies, war with the Allied powers was greeted in racial terms (. . .). The outbreak of the war, it was stated in an article entitled 'Establishing a Japanese Racial Worldview,' had clarified the Japanese character, whose basic traits were brightness, strength, and uprighteousness. These qualities made the Japanese 'the most superior race in the world,' and it followed that all the other countries and peoples of Asia should be assimilated into the Greater East Asia Co-Prosperity Sphere in accordance with their particular abilities (211).

After the loss of three million Japanese lives and millions more in the rest of Asia, the US conquest of Okinawa, the atomic bombings of Hiroshima and Nagasaki, and the destruction of Tokyo, Osaka, Nagoya, Yokohama and more than 50 other cities, the Japanese government acknowledged defeat on

15 August 1945. The unconditional surrender of Japan officially took place aboard the battleship *USS Missouri* on 2 September of the same year.

In his journal-diary *Kudakareta Kami* (Shattered God) published in 1983, Kiyoshi Watanabe expresses the despair felt by most Japanese in a short poem written on 15 December 1945, the day the directive disestablishing Shinto was issued (Dower 2000, 342). The wording might not be very elegant, but I think it expresses well the spiritual mood of the time:

> What is the emperor?
> What is Japan?
> What is love of country?
> What is democracy?
> What is 'country of culture'?
> All this, all of this eats shit.
> I spit on it! (Watanabe in Dower 2000, 342)

On 12 November 1948 the International Military Tribunal for the Far East sentenced seven Japanese military and government officials to death for their roles in the war. In order to stabilize the country, the US decided to spare the emperor and most war criminals of all ranks, some guilty of atrocities such as the chemical experiments on thousands of Chinese civilians by Unit 731 in Harbin and elsewhere. In *The Tokyo War Crimes Trial* (2008), Yuma Totani asserts that '[t]he task of assimilating the records of the Tokyo trial and other still larger bodies of evidence will be a major challenge for future researchers' (Totani 2008, 262). My assertion that the US decided to spare the emperor for the reason given above needs to be complexified in light of recent scholarship:

> [T]he common belief that MacArthur granted immunity to Hirohito does not stand up to the test of primary documents. As will be shown in this [Totani's] book, MacArthur had no formal or informal power to make decisions regarding the trial of Hirohito. Those who decided the fate of the Japanese emperor were the leaders of the United States and its allies. The decision they made, moreover, was to keep the option of his trial open, *not* to grant him immunity; the Allied governments ruled out the latter possibility at the outset. How should one, then, explain the ultimate failure of the Allies to put him on trial? (Totani 2008, 4).

There has never been serious talk about condemning anybody for annihilating two cities with atomic weapons, showing that in military affairs, justice and history belong to the victors.

From indoctrination to confusion (1940–47)

Ikeda graduated from elementary school in 1940. He then took a two-year course called higher elementary school. When he was in his second year, he was still delivering newspapers, like the one in December 1941 announcing the attack on Pearl Harbor. The Pacific War had started in earnest with the full-scale battles in China in 1937, as Ikeda mentions in his dialogue with the futurologist Hazel Henderson:

> In Japan, with each passing day, the tramp of military boots grew louder. One by one, my older brothers were called up. Militarism was drilled into our young heads even in elementary school. First came the invasion of China, then the attack on Pearl Harbor in 1941, when we were plunged into total war. I was thirteen (Ikeda and Henderson 2004, 8).

Not long afterward, his next oldest brother joined the army and Ikeda became the family's main source of support. He took a job at the Niigata Iron Works in April 1942, when Japanese society was intoxicated with the dark joy of military triumph. The Japanese military invaded Hong Kong on 25 December 1941, barely two weeks after attacking Pearl Harbor. The Philippines followed in January 1942 and Singapore in February. As mentioned above, until the Battle of Midway in June, six months after Pearl Harbor, most Japanese leaders and ordinary citizens believed they were unstoppable and were certain of ultimate victory. The Niigata plant was required to set up a youth school, and all employees and workers had to participate in military education and close order drills, like most other enterprises at the time. The factory where Ikeda worked was essential for the war effort, and from about 3,000 workers in 1942 it had grown to about 10,000 in 1945. The whole country was obsessed with the war, and there were posters on the streets reminding the population to stay focused: 'In 1943 the slogan was "Keep at it! The enemy is desperate too!" By 1944, when war was the primary concern, the slogan had become: "Onward – like a single fireball!"' (Ikeda 1980, 30).

The Naval Ministry was directing the production of engine parts for warships, and gradually the Niigata Iron Works began producing miniature submarines, the 'human torpedoes.' The naval equivalent of the kamikaze planes, these weapons contributed to the reputation of fanaticism associated with the Japanese military: 'Young men imbued with the idea "Your life for an enemy ship – ram it!" sailed into the jaws of death' (Ikeda 1980, 30).

One can only imagine the shock millions of Japanese people must have felt when the emperor publicly announced the end of the war on 15 August 1945.

Ikeda and his compatriots had sincerely believed that all the sacrifices asked by the military government were going to lead them to victory and glory. Now there was only defeat, humiliation, poverty and the utter meaninglessness of it all. How were most people, including Ikeda, going to be persuaded that life still had some kind of meaning?

In the collection of poems *Fighting for Peace* (2004b) mentioned earlier, Ikeda wrote:

> Eventually
> the sad news came –
> my eldest brother
> was dead, killed in action in Burma.
> While many were discharged and returned quickly
> to their homes,
> one year passed,
> and then another,
> before each of my
> three surviving brothers
> managed to return home
> quietly alive.
> All three,
> unable to feel the new era's hope,
> returned dazed
> with forced smiles
> on their faces (36).

> August 15 –
> We must never forget
> the painful misery of that day.
> We must never forget
> the desolation of that day.
> And we must never forget
> that humiliating awakening
> to the folly of slavish obedience (41).

Meeting and studying under his mentor (1947–58)

On 2 April 2008, exactly 50 years after Josei Toda's passing, Ikeda received an honorary professorship from the Tolstoy State Pedagogical University (Tula, Russia), his 233rd academic distinction.[8] The conferment took place during the entrance ceremony of Soka University in Tokyo. Vladimir Tolstoy, a direct descendant of the great writer and director of the Museum-Estate of Leo Tolstoy, was also present for the occasion. I was invited to attend and was able to hear directly what Ikeda said.

During his acceptance speech, he shared how he felt at the end of World War II. He mentioned the fact that his four brothers were sent to the army, that his elder brother died in Burma, that he was in poor health, that war propaganda was pervasive in schools and elsewhere, and that it was in the middle of all this confusion that he met Josei Toda for the first time. He then added that the fact that this man had been imprisoned by the military, and had gone to jail for upholding his beliefs during these turbulent war years, made him decide to become his disciple almost on the spot. I have heard Ikeda make similar statements during other ceremonies, and I am personally convinced that his meeting with Josei Toda was the most important event in his life.

Ikeda was brought to a meeting of the Soka Gakkai one day in the summer of 1947. That is when he met Toda for the first time, and he was touched by the older man's warmth and sincerity. In particular, the fact that he had spent two years in jail for his humanistic ideals seems to have moved Ikeda, inspiring him to overcome the confusion of the postwar years. Accounts of this meeting by Ikeda himself are provided later in this book.

From 1947, Ikeda dedicated his life to learning from and supporting the work of Toda, and, after Toda's death, to the enhancement of his mentor's legacy, with outstanding enthusiasm and perseverance. I believe that Ikeda's main sources of inspiration were his war memories, his mentor and a desire to serve humanity. All three are inextricably linked, and if war memories gave him the impetus to struggle towards peace for the sake of humanity, Toda gave him the foundations of concrete plans to implement this ideal.

All of Ikeda's achievements, writings and activities are deeply linked with Toda's vision for peace, and he has declared on numerous occasions that all of the institutions and organizations he established are concretizations of Toda's dreams. I consider that Ikeda's own active contribution to peace started as early as 1947, when he began supporting Toda in the rebuilding of his business and private life as well as of the Soka Gakkai lay Buddhist society, which had been destroyed by the military government in 1943.

In 1948 Ikeda started working for Toda's publishing company, and was able to contribute as the editor of a magazine for boys while attending night classes. Toda had been a successful educator and businessman before the war, but lost everything on his imprisonment. He had started painstakingly rebuilding his businesses since his release from prison in 1945, but postwar hyperinflation in addition to strict economic policies such as the Dodge Line[9] of 7 March 1949 – which was meant to speed up Japan's economic independence – created an unfavorable climate and Toda was forced to declare bankruptcy. Undaunted by these difficulties, he envisioned building a university based on the philosophy of value-creation (*Soka*), an ambition that captured Ikeda's imagination. The disciple eventually realized his mentor's dream after Toda's passing with the establishment of the first Soka schools in the 1960s, followed by the founding of Soka University in Japan in 1971 and of Soka University of America in 1987.

During these hard times (1949–51), Ikeda continued to support his teacher single-mindedly, even working without pay, and devoting his energies to negotiating with creditors. Ikeda had to quit school to save Toda from ruin, and Toda offered to tutor Ikeda privately instead, taking care of his education until 1957. Ikeda often refers to these years as attending 'Toda University.'

In August 1950 Toda had resigned from his position as general director of the Soka Gakkai to protect the organization. Indeed, his businesses had failed and he did not want to damage the credibility of the Soka Gakkai. Within less than a year, on 3 May 1951, with his financial affairs in order, Toda became the second President of the Soka Gakkai. He vowed to turn a small group of 3,000 Buddhists into a vast organization of 750,000 households, and Ikeda took this goal seriously. Toda entrusted Ikeda with the leadership of many Soka Gakkai activities from that time.

Two notable achievements by Ikeda are the 1952 conversion of 201 new households in Kamata within one month, followed by the conversion of 11,111 households in Osaka in 1956. Concerning private matters, Toda was also instrumental in the marriage of Ikeda and Kaneko Shiraki in 1952. They had three sons (one of them passed away in 1984) and two grandchildren.

In 1955 Toda encouraged Soka Gakkai members to run for local elections, and 53 were elected. The political parties at the time represented either organized labor or big capital, and Toda thought it was time to do something for all the other citizens left behind, such as teachers, artisans, homemakers and owners of small businesses. In 1956 three candidates were elected to the House of Councilors during the national election.

There were several negative reactions to these developments, the two most famous of which were the persecution of Soka Gakkai members by the powerful Yubari Coal Miners' Union and the arrest of Ikeda in 1957 by the Osaka Prefectural Police on charges of being responsible for election fraud committed by some Soka Gakkai members. Both incidents were resolved to the advantage of the Soka Gakkai, and even though Ikeda spent about two weeks in an Osaka jail in 1957, he was exonerated of all charges in 1962 after a drawn out judicial procedure.

As mentioned above, Ikeda attributes his entire success to the education he received from Toda. The brief overview above has explored the origins of some of Ikeda's realizations, and they can indeed all be traced to the inspiration he received from Toda: his leadership as an international Buddhist leader (the 1952 and 1956 conversion campaigns supervised by Toda), his abundant writings (working for Toda's publishing company and becoming editor), his broad culture and intellectual curiosity (attending 'Toda University'), establishing educational institutions (Toda's dream of building a university), the founding of the Komeito political party in 1964 (the continuation of Toda's 1955 decision to encourage Soka Gakkai members to enter the political realm) and even Ikeda's family life (Toda persuaded Ikeda and Kaneko's parents to let them marry).

Ikeda was asked to become the next president of the Soka Gakkai after Toda's passing on 2 April 1958, but he waited two years before accepting this position.

From Japan to the world (1960–present)

Ikeda became the third president of the Soka Gakkai on 3 May 1960. A few months after his appointment he decided to expand the lay Buddhist association's activities abroad, and left for a trip to the US, Canada and Brazil in October 1960. This was the first of many travels overseas, including a trip to Guam to commemorate the establishment of the SGI on 26 January 1975. Since then the organization has grown into a vast network of about 2 million people in more than 190 countries outside Japan, in addition to the 10 million members of the Soka Gakkai in Japan.

During this first trip in 1960, Ikeda observed a session of the United Nations General Assembly (UNGA) in New York, and was impressed by the mission and potential roles of the world body. He also saw the enthusiasm of the leaders of several newly independent African nations and became convinced of Africa's future prosperity. In 1961 he took a second trip, this time to East and South Asia, fully aware of the atrocities the Japanese had committed there during the war, and eager to try to heal the wounds inflicted by the Japanese military, by building bridges of friendship and peace with Japan's neighbors. Ikeda very often offers his apologies for the past violence in speeches and writings. In 1962 he established the Institute of Oriental Philosophy (IOP), partly as a result of that trip.

In 1963 he established the Min-On Concert Association in order to promote friendship and cultural exchanges through musical activities, and in 1964 the Komeito political party. The contributions of the Komeito to peace, and the difficulty of applying a humanistic vision through Japanese politics, are being researched carefully from several angles, as by Anne Mette Fisker-Nielsen (2008), among others. She agrees with most observers today, who consider the relationship between the Soka Gakkai and the Komeito as that of an independent political party and its support base. Ikeda has made it very clear that there is no need for the SGI to be involved in politics outside of Japan.

The appearance of institutions sponsored by groups that espouse what seems to be a new philosophy rarely fails to arouse suspicion; the Soka Gakkai has been no exception, and has had to constantly clarify its intentions, in some countries more than others.[10] The situation in Japan in the 1960s is described as follows by Ikeda, illustrating this point:

> [M]any viewed Min-On as just another means of increasing Soka Gakkai membership, and regarded the Komei Political Federation as an attempt by the Gakkai to obtain political power. The tendency of Japanese society to always be looking for ulterior motives and to belittle noble ideals and deeds is a reflection of spiritual bankruptcy (Ikeda 2003–9, 44).

The sociologist of religion Karel Dobbelaere (2000) offers a positive evaluation of the activities of Soka Gakkai-affiliated organizations:

> The Soka Gakkai defines itself as a religious organization aiming at the promotion of education and culture, and it is indeed involved in the educational, cultural, mass media, and political fields. (. . .) In the case of religion, its societal functionality cannot be limited to the expressive socialization of individuals, nor even to the promotion of a 'human revolution.' It is expected to provide other subsystems with original resources that support and enhance them. This is what Soka Gakkai is doing in diverse fields – particularly in education, culture, politics, and the media (238–39).

Adapted from the short summary of Ikeda's activities provided by the website dedicated to his life and work (Ikeda Website 2009), the chronology of Ikeda's achievements can be broken down into five decades. In the 1960s he started writing the novel *The Human Revolution*, worked for Sino–Japanese relationships and established the Soka school system, ranging today from several kindergartens and elementary schools to a university in Japan and one in the US. In the 1970s he initiated a series of dialogues with prominent figures such as Arnold Toynbee, as well as citizen diplomacy and the establishment of the SGI mentioned above. He also started contributing to educational and academic exchanges, giving lectures at the University of California in Los Angeles in 1974 and Moscow State University in 1975.

On 24 April 1979 Ikeda was forced to resign from the presidency of the Japanese Soka Gakkai because of internal tensions in the organization. As the membership grew during the 1970s, Ikeda received more and more reports of Nichiren Shoshu priests abusing their authority, for instance by pressuring members to offer alms. In order to rectify the situation, Ikeda in his speeches and writings asserted that the equality between the priests and lay believers was one of the fundamental principles of Buddhism. At the same time, some individuals within the Soka Gakkai leadership started to exploit these tensions, hoping to gain more control of the organization. Ikeda decided to step down as president of the Soka Gakkai in order to defuse the situation.

It was a very difficult period for Ikeda, who could not even meet members of the Soka Gakkai in public. He devoted a lot of time to one-on-one meetings and continued upholding the beliefs of his mentor. Since then, it is in his capacity as SGI president that he has pursued his endeavors for peace. In the 1980s he redoubled his efforts, established the Tokyo Fuji Art Museum in 1983, and from the same year started publishing a lengthy and substantial peace proposal each year. In 1991 the Soka Gakkai became completely independent from the Nichiren Shoshu priesthood, and this allowed Ikeda to affirm even more his vision of a borderless Buddhist humanism that emphasizes free thinking and personal development on the basis of respect for life.

In 1993 he established the Boston Research Center for the 21st Century (BRC, which changed its name in 2009 to the Ikeda Center for Peace, Learning, and Dialogue) and the Toda Institute in 1996. Ikeda has devoted the first decade of the twenty-first century to the strengthening and improvement of the institutions he has established, including the promotion of younger people to most key leadership positions.

Ikeda's contributions to peace through his actions, writings and institutions

In the second part of this book, I show how the main elements of Ikeda's philosophy of peace – inner transformation, dialogue and global citizenship – are related to his activities as the leader of a Buddhist organization, the founder of various institutions and an active dialogue partner with countless individuals of all backgrounds. Here I would like to introduce three suggestions concerning the links between Ikeda's achievements and peacebuilding, and also contrast Ikeda's activities with those of the Japanese postwar peace movements.

The first suggestion is that the development of the Soka Gakkai and the SGI can be said to contribute to peace, transcending the realm of a specific religion. One study in the sociology of religion (Wilson and Dobbelaere

1994) which has addressed this issue has shown that many people are able to improve themselves by practicing Buddhism, and I consider that this constitutes an important contribution to world peace. A survey of 626 members of the SGI in the UK conducted in 1990 has shown that a large proportion[11] of the members identified the beneficial results of Buddhist practice as 'an increase in self-confidence, courage, strength, stability, or self-respect, adding to these terms self-control, self-determination, self-improvement, the capacity to take charge of one's life, and the ability to deal with its problems' (Wilson and Dobbelaere 1994, 205). The second suggestion is that the activities promoted by institutions established by Ikeda also contribute to peace-building. For instance, the IOP has been actively engaged in various forms of interfaith dialogue and Soka University (in Japan and in the US) aims at fostering individuals who will make positive contributions to society. The Min-On Concert Association seeks to 'deepen mutual understanding and friendship among all countries by promoting global music and cultural exchange that transcends differences of nationality, race and language'[12] and the Tokyo Fuji Art Museum's activities are based on the motto 'A museum creating bridges around the world.'[13]

The third suggestion is that the role of the Komeito in peacebuilding is complex, problematic and difficult to evaluate. In Japanese domestic politics, it has been successful in implementing several humanistic visions on the national level, for instance by ensuring that people who have suffered from discrimination because of leprosy are compensated, providing free transportation passes for elderly people and making cheaper housing available to the general public.

Still lacking experience on the international front, the Komeito has been criticized by several peace researchers and historians for not embodying its founder's humanistic ideals vigorously enough (Seager 2006, 23). For instance, Johan Galtung, one of the founders of peace studies, has expressed his disappointment with the Komeito's lack of outspoken opposition to the war policies of the US since 2001 (Galtung 2006). The party attributed many of its decisions, often criticized by members of the Soka Gakkai themselves, to the pragmatic imperatives of remaining in a coalition government with the conservative Liberal Democratic Party (LDP). The experiment in coalition participation which had started in 1999 ended in September 2009, when the LDP suffered a decisive electoral defeat at the hands of the Democratic Party of Japan (DPJ). The Komeito Party is currently undergoing a process of reassessment under new leadership.

As the leader of the lay Buddhist movement, Ikeda decided to focus on the growth of the Soka Gakkai organization, strengthening the achievements of his mentor. As a peace thinker, Ikeda chose not to be influenced by the ups and downs of pacifism in postwar Japan, concentrating on the promotion of peace based on Nichiren Buddhism and Toda's teachings.

Post-World War II pacifism in Japan has gone through many twists and turns in the more than 60 years of its development. In the aftermath of the war a number of substantial organized peace movements appeared in Japan, boosted by the enshrinement of pacifism in the new constitution which came into effect on 3 May 1947, and as a reaction against the absurdity and horror of war, the atomic bombings, ambiguous relationships with the US victors and other issues. After showing great potential for about 15 years (1945–60) these peace movements started to unravel, only to be brought back to life again by the Vietnam War. Since the end of that war in 1975, Japan has become more complacent about issues of peace and justice, partly because of its newly attained economic stability. Another reason might be the gradual disappearance of direct witnesses to the 1937–45 war. An overview of pacifism and peace movements in Japan is provided in Appendix 1.

In contrast, the Soka Gakkai, and Ikeda himself, have shown consistent and undiminished vigor in their pursuit of a better world during the same period. The main reason is that the Soka Gakkai is first and foremost a religious organization, and that its pacific goals are a result of the Buddhist philosophy of respect for life that it embraces. With hindsight, it can be said that Ikeda's focus on the steady sharing of the peace-enhancing principles of Buddhism has enabled him to bring consistency and coherence to his leadership and to his philosophy of peace. While addressing the same issues that drove the growth and decline of Japanese pacifist movements since World War II, Ikeda has not altered the basic principles of his philosophy of peace, but only strengthened and developed them. Ikeda's single-minded determination and sense of purpose, which characterizes his philosophy as well as his organizational skills, is one of the reasons for the success of the Soka Gakkai and the SGI. As Seager (2006) notes:

> Buddhism of all sorts is found almost everywhere today, but few groups equal the Gakkai in either its programmatic effort to adapt to new situations or its genius for organization (204).

Conclusion: a life of determined value-creation for peace

Throughout the twists and turns of his long life, Ikeda has been able to remain loyal to the commitment he made in 1947 when he met Toda for the first time. He has maintained his vision for a peaceful world and has shown that people can generate something positive, productive and useful for the peace and happiness of humankind by creating value and transforming reality.

The turbulence and misery of the war years, followed by the chaos caused by Japan's defeat, prepared the ground for the tremendous significance of Ikeda's first meeting with Toda. The difficulties experienced by his mentor, who had to cope with ill-health and financial ruin while rebuilding a grass-roots movement from scratch, provided strict and valuable training for Ikeda's continued growth as a peace worker and philosopher.

The ups and downs of Japanese society on the domestic and international fronts tested Ikeda's capacity to stay on course at the helm of a worldwide movement based on the philosophy of inner transformation, dialogue and global citizenship. His many achievements for peace through the development of a vigorous grassroots movement in Japan and in the world, the numerous dialogues he has held and the institutions he has established provide a model demonstrating that ordinary people do have tremendous potential for happiness, prosperity and the enhancement of peace.

CHAPTER 2

Autobiographical Sketches

> In order to live
> true to your sincere convictions
> create a world
> where many share
> your earnest view of life.
> Here you will find
> a world of peace.
>
> Daisaku Ikeda (2004b, 2)

A wealth of autobiographical data concerning Ikeda's life can be found in *My Recollections*, *A Youthful Diary*, *The Human Revolution* and *The New Human Revolution*, among other works. I believe that even though they substantially accord with the historical record, the overriding goal of the publication of these writings is to inspire, to encourage and to give hope, as Ikeda himself writes in the preface to *A Youthful Diary*:

> If, through this English version of the diary of a single individual, they [the young members of the SGI-USA] may respond to the spirit that was stirring in me at that time and gain some measure of encouragement in the business of living, I will count myself most fortunate. And if the diary can somehow hasten the progress of the movement for peace and cultural development in America, which constitutes a vital key to the happiness and prosperity of all humankind, I will be doubly gratified (2006a, ix).

In the preface to the 2004 English edition of *The Human Revolution*, in which Ikeda figures prominently as the character Shin'ichi Yamamoto, he explains why he included his own inauguration in the novel:

My original intention had been to end the narrative with the death of Mr. Toda on April 2, 1958. But in order to demonstrate the significance of Mr. Toda's spiritual legacy, which transformed the mission begun by this man and embraced by the Soka Gakkai in its peace-culture-education movement into a great river that would flow on for all time, I felt it was necessary to reveal how that movement had served as a gleam of hope to be realized in the future. So I added another chapter, 'New Dawn,' concluding the work with another inauguration on May 3, 1960, when Shin'ichi Yamamoto [Ikeda] became the third president (viii).

He adds: 'I was convinced that the life of my mentor constituted a model for the manner in which an individual could carry out a splendid human revolution within his or her own life' (viii). In the same preface, concerning *The New Human Revolution* which he started writing in 1993, he says: 'so long as I am able, I am determined to devote myself to depicting in all its brilliance and nobility the human revolution as it advances toward the ideal of a world in which life is treasured and the very word misery has been erased' (xi).

The last page of *My Recollections* contains these statements:

I feel certain that only a completely new way of thinking, a philosophy based on reverence for life, has the potential to alter man's destiny and actually it has switched on the light of hope in one corner of the world. I have by now discovered that life's meaning lies in dedicating my all to making the fire of that hope flare, to make sure that it never dies out. It is a task I must accomplish for the people in the next century as well as for my own children who will be numbered among them (Ikeda 1980, 145).

The passages above show a constant desire to inspire people to have hope and to work for peace, be they members of the SGI in the US, or more generally 'the people in the next century,' which means all of us in the twenty-first century. Ikeda believes that all human beings can improve their lives through a process of inner transformation, which takes the specific form of the human revolution for members of the SGI practicing Nichiren Buddhism.

Some differences between these works are worth noticing. *The Human Revolution* and *The New Human Revolution* can be considered as religious autobiographies, projecting the image of a successful spiritual leader at the helm of the SGI movement. The first one is focused on Toda, and can be considered as a biography of Ikeda's mentor. However, as mentioned above, Ikeda himself figures prominently in the novel and it therefore contains many autobiographical elements too. The second serialized novel shows how Ikeda has applied the teachings of his mentor. Mostly destined to encourage members of the SGI to progress in their human revolution, it is also addressed to the general public, written to inspire people of all backgrounds to improve themselves through inner transformation.

It is in *A Youthful Diary* that one can discover more intimate aspects of Ikeda's struggles and challenges, as some selected passages will show toward the end of this chapter. This work was not written to be published, and Ikeda states that it is 'an unadorned record of my life,' and that it was 'originally intended for my eyes alone' (Ikeda 2006a, viii–ix).

These four literary efforts contain a vast amount of autobiographical data, and they are widely read by SGI members throughout the world. I believe they are important for an understanding of Ikeda's philosophy of peace because they provide inspiration to contribute to the world, and because they illustrate the process of inner transformation. I have asked myself the following questions in order to evaluate their usefulness for this research: 'is there coherence throughout these works? Are there themes and issues running through all of them, forming a consistent series of motifs and preoccupations?' I have found coherence and consistency in at least five levels in these writings taken as a whole.

First there is internal consistency, as each of them describes a world of ideas and concepts that are logically organized around the main character's personality. Second there is consistency between each one of them, with for instance information and ideas in *My Recollections* being confirmed by passages from *A Youthful Diary* and corroborated by statements in the two *Human Revolution* novels.[1] Next the dates, facts and descriptions concerning places and events correspond to the broad historical framework around each of these works and this can be independently confirmed.

Fourth, based on the testimonies of the few people who have written about their meetings with Ikeda, I have noticed a coherence between the character painted in these works and the man they have met. For instance in the foreword to *Creating Waldens* (2009), the book of dialogues he published with Ikeda and Joel Myerson, Ronald A. Bosco, Professor of English and American Literature at the University of Albany, State University of New York, notes:

> Our visit to Tokyo provided us with an opportunity to meet with President Ikeda in both public and private settings; our meetings with him and Mrs. Kaneko Ikeda were warm and intellectually engaging. (. . .) A practicing poet, President Ikeda (. . .) shared with us his excitement as a young man in postwar Japan at first encountering the poetic sensibility and life-validating lessons of

Ralph Waldo Emerson, Henry David Thoreau, and Walt Whitman (Ikeda, Bosco and Myerson 2009).

In the foreword to the dialogue *On Being Human* (2002) former rector of the University of Montreal and authority on cancer research René Simard wrote:

> We discovered that we have a great deal in common, even though our cultural and scientific backgrounds are different. Mr. Ikeda impressed me both as a human being who cares about people suffering from illness, stress, and environmental degradation, and as an open-minded philosopher steeped in culture (Ikeda, Simard and Bourgeault 2002, 16).

Finally I can testify that what I have observed during my personal meetings with Ikeda, and the things I have directly heard him say, show remarkable coherence with the autobiographical information I have found in the works analyzed here.

In summary, I believe that because of the internal coherence of the works, as well as the consistency with which certain themes appear, they can be considered as an important source of information for an understanding of Ikeda's philosophy of peace. The systematization I am presenting in this book is mostly based on textual analysis of Ikeda's works, and as a result the autobiographical writings mentioned in this chapter constitute an integral part of the material I have used to draw a coherent picture of his philosophy.

In these works, Ikeda presents us with detailed accounts and narratives of many crucial episodes in his life. I consider four series of events as holding special importance, namely Ikeda's war memories, his recollections of his first meeting with Josei Toda, the way he narrates the birth of the idea of Soka University and how Ikeda celebrated his mentor's birthday from 1951 to 1960.

Childhood, adolescence and wartime memories

Ikeda presents himself as an average person, an ordinary human being just like anybody else. The opening line of *My Recollections* (1980) states: 'There is nothing at all unusual about my background' (1). Ikeda has consistently insisted on this point: 'My grades were around average. I was just a run-of-the-mill lad without a single characteristic to distinguish me from the others' (14). He also writes: 'I may well be from a most ordinary family, but I am loath to surrender my sense of pride in springing from such solid commoner stock' (4).

He also describes details about his poor health, attributing certain psychological strengths to his weak bodily constitution. He first remembers suffering from pneumonia just before entering elementary school: 'I vividly recall my feverish nightmares and the injections the doctor gave me' (Ikeda 1980, 13). Questions about the meaning of life, what happens after death and how to make the most of each day and each moment, which precociously filled young Ikeda's mind, are linked to the fact that he was constantly in poor health, suffering from a weak constitution for more than half of his youth. Several passages show that his sickness was made worse by the harshness of the overall situation in Japan at the time.

One summer day in 1944, at age 16, while marching together with 200 other workers carrying wooden rifles, Ikeda started to feel sick. There was no question of taking a break from work or of seeing a doctor at that time, however. For Ikeda, it is very important to clarify that his health was so poor that his life was in danger for most of his youth.

> The military training of the youth school gradually intensified. I remember one summer day in 1944. (. . .) I was marching in step with the squad (. . .) suddenly I felt weak and began to faint. (. . .) I had vomited blood. I quickly covered my mouth and wiped the phlegm away with paper. My tuberculosis had progressed considerably and I grew weaker by the day. The weaker I got, the more the work piled up. This vicious circle often caused me to burn with fever; sometimes I went to work despite running a fever of over 102 degrees. (. . .) I was forced to deal with my sickness on my own, depending entirely on the magazine *Health Advice*. But the truth is that my tuberculosis only got worse and I continued coughing and sweating at night and spitting up bloody phlegm. By the beginning of 1945 things had progressed to the state where a doctor advised me to go to a sanatorium in Kashima. Whether it was good or bad luck, the saturation air raid in Kamata on April 15, 1945 made it impossible for me to follow his advice (Ikeda 1980, 31–32).

As a child and adolescent, Ikeda had been thoroughly swept away by the state propaganda and had no doubt that the meaning of life lay in serving his country:

> It would be untrue to claim that in those days I felt we should have lost the war. I was interested mainly in having it end as soon as possible. Of course I was patriotic – patriotism had been thoroughly instilled, and I was quite aware that ultimate value lay

in the Emperor, in the State. The frightfulness of education is that it can paint whatever colors it pleases on the blank canvas of the tender mind. That much is clear to me now (Ikeda 1980, 23–24).

He even volunteered to join the Junior Division of the Naval Aviation Corps. However since the three oldest sons had already gone into the military service, and the fourth one would soon be going, his father opposed that decision and was able to convince the clerk in charge of naval volunteers to turn down Daisaku's application. His father gave him a thorough scolding, and young Ikeda was rather disappointed: 'Had I been able to volunteer and had the war continued . . . well by now I am grateful to my father, but at the time I was not very happy about his opposition' (Ikeda 1980, 25).

At the same time, he was horrified by the destruction and suffering he witnessed. In the spring of 1945 the saturation air raids over Tokyo were sure signs that defeat was imminent. The Ikeda house had to be torn down to prevent the spread of fires, and they had no choice but to take refuge in the home of an aunt. It took many hours to move all their belongings using a two-wheeled cart, and for Ikeda this was very difficult work, weakened as he was by tuberculosis. Despite his desperate efforts, the move was all in vain:

> Then, on the night before we were to move, a direct hit burned our aunt's house down. As incendiary bombs set the neighborhood aflame, my younger brother and I dashed about saving what little we could from our luggage. I still remember how frightened I was.

> We managed to drag out only one trunk, and it turned out to be the one filled with a set of dolls for the early spring's Girl's Day festival. Cheerfully, my optimistic mother said, 'We'll soon have a place to display them again' (Ikeda and Henderson 2004, 10).

He recounts how his oldest brother Kiichi, at home after being discharged in July 1941, and before going off to war again in December 1942, sharply criticized the atrocities committed by the Japanese army in China. These revelations left an indelible mark on Ikeda's young mind, especially since this brother was later killed on duty on 11 January 1945 in what was then Burma. Today, Ikeda attributes his passion for peace to these traumatic events:

> The war brought sorrow to my family. My beloved oldest brother died in battle in Burma. I was sitting behind my mother when she read the notification of his death. I can still visualize her trembling

body. These youthful experiences later motivated me to become a
devoted peace activist (Ikeda and Henderson 2004, 10).

Three of Ikeda's brothers came home one by one in 1946, but there was no
news of Kiichi until 30 May 1947. This is the day when they received the
announcement that he had died in Burma on 11 January 1945. This was a
blow for Ikeda's parents:

> I couldn't bear to look at Mother as she stood clasping to her breast
> the small white box, all that was left of Kiichi. She seems to have
> aged appreciably since then. Father too, took more and more to his
> bed as his asthma and heart condition worsened. I am certain that
> both of them, my diehard father and my stout-hearted mother who
> always tried to be so cheerful, plunged headlong into tears at the
> news of Kiichi's death – at least deep in their hearts (Ikeda 1980, 42).

After the war, like most Japanese who had survived the ordeal, Ikeda was
confused by the incompatibilities between his education, which had glorified
war and nationalism, and the state of devastation and chaos he was witnessing
in the ruins of the Tokyo firebombing, the ashes of Hiroshima and Nagasaki
and the overall destruction of Japan. As he later reflected, 'the human heart
caused wars and sent people to the battle field' (Ikeda 1980, 39).

Trying to overcome the confusion he felt after the war, Ikeda found a source
of inspiration in the study of various topics. He seems to have loved literature
from a young age, and to have started reading great works during the war:
'I was really sad about having lost all my books in the raid, but I "re-read"
some of them, like Tolstoy's *War and Peace*, in my mind' (Ikeda 1980, 39). He
describes his decision to study seriously as coming from his war experiences
and the sufferings imposed on him by his poor health during that time:

> My adolescent years happened to coincide with the war. Nothing
> of those years remained for me. My health also deteriorated to the
> point where I perspired profusely every night. But a conviction
> grew within me that the most important thing is learning. I looked
> forward to the dawn of another day with this vague notion in mind:
> When the war ends, I'd have to study (Ikeda 1980, 39).

After the war Ikeda continued reading voraciously. For a while he worked in
a factory, then for a printing shop, where he became responsible for proof-
reading, but with his health deteriorating steadily he had to stop after about
a year. He was still able to take a job as a clerk and keep that position. He also

joined a reading circle of about 20 young people in his neighborhood, and they supported one another's passion for reading, trying to find out what the meaning of life could be. They knew that they had been lied to, manipulated and swindled by the state, and that the nationalism combined with emperor worship they had been brought up with was worthless. However they had no idea how to fill the vacuum left in their minds by the destruction of this ideology.

One day in August 1947, a friend from grade school invited Ikeda to attend a meeting on 'life philosophy.' Hearing this, Ikeda expected to be able to discuss Bergson's ideas concerning the spontaneity of life, since he was acquainted with the French philosopher's concept of *élan vital*, but he was disappointed to learn that the main speaker would be a complete unknown, a businessman and educator called Josei Toda. He nevertheless chose to attend that meeting, a decision that was to determine the course of his entire life.

I consider this autobiographical account as an important element for an understanding of Ikeda's philosophy of peace. He describes himself as an ordinary person born poor and sickly, swept away by the war propaganda, deeply shocked at realizing the lies of the military and interested in literature and philosophy. This image, constructed through the literary vehicles of memoir, essay and novel, is consistent and matches well the documented actions of Ikeda over more than six decades. More than a literary creation, for me as a disciple, and for thousands of people who have interacted with him, the passages quoted above describe, as far as I have been able to observe, what he stands for and who he actually is.

Meeting his mentor, Josei Toda

In his search for an explanation for the sufferings brought on by the madness of war, and for a coherent philosophy of life, Ikeda found convincing answers during his first encounter with Josei Toda. He met Toda on 14 August 1947, as mentioned above, at a small gathering of the Soka Gakkai, the lay Buddhist movement that was established by Toda and his mentor Makiguchi in 1930. Ikeda shared his recollection of this event during his dialogue with Mikhail Gorbachev:

> It was at this stage that I met the man who was to exert an enormous influence on the rest of my life. One hot summer evening, a friend from my elementary school days invited me to a philosophical discussion held at a private house where some 20 people had gathered. There, a man of about 40 was lecturing on the Buddhist teachings

of the great Japanese priest Nichiren Daishonin. His simple, easy-
to-understand, relaxed style of talking generated an inspirational
atmosphere. That man was Josei Toda, who was to be my life teacher
(Ikeda and Gorbachev 2005, 6).

This is how the same event is described by Ikeda in *The Human Revolution*.
After finishing a lecture Toda asked him:

> 'How old are you now?' Instead of saying simply 'How old are you?'
> Toda asked, 'How old are you now?' Although it was their first
> meeting, he spoke as if he were talking to someone he already knew.

> 'Nineteen years old, sir.'

> 'I see. I was nineteen when I first came to Tokyo from Hokkaido.
> I was really a country boy. I had no friends and no money, and I
> was terribly lonely. I was overwhelmed, something unusual for me'
> (Ikeda 2004a, 227).

Immediately after this initial exchange, Ikeda asked Toda three or four questions. In *My Recollections* he recounts asking three, whereas in *The Human
Revolution* he describes four questions. This small difference can be explained
by the presence in Ikeda's writings and speeches of both a centripetal force
towards Buddhist religious conviction and a centrifugal movement towards
a spiritually boundless humanism. There are often semantic shifts back and
forth between these two tendencies.

The essays that were compiled into *My Recollections* were originally com-
missioned by several of Japan's leading periodicals and newspapers with
the goal of presenting the personal viewpoint of Ikeda as a human being,
not as a religious leader. Since out of the four questions, one was of a religious nature, Ikeda chose to focus on only three of them, presenting his
initial encounter with Toda in terms that do not require any knowledge
of Buddhism:

> I told him I'd like to have him answer some questions, I had three:
> 'What's the proper way to live? What is true patriotism? How
> should I regard the Emperor?' He responded succinctly and to the
> point with honest answers. He didn't seem in the least perplexed but
> was businesslike, and his responses had an ideological framework. I
> thought, *This is it* – what he's saying is true! I figured, here's a man
> I can put my faith in (Ikeda 1980, 54).

In *The Human Revolution*, Ikeda gives a much fuller account of the same encounter, developed over approximately ten pages of the 2004 English-language edition. Ikeda's first question was 'Sir, what is a correct way of life? The more I think about it, the more confused I become' (Ikeda 2004a, 227). Toda confidently answered that by trying to practice Nichiren's Buddhism himself, Ikeda would find out in a concrete way.

> Well now, that is the most difficult question of all. (. . .) There is no one else in this world who can confidently answer your question. I can, however, because I have been fortunate enough to live, to some extent, the Buddhism of Nichiren Daishonin. We encounter many problems in the long course of life – for example, the terrible difficulty of obtaining food and shelter at present. Nor can we predict what misfortunes may befall us (. . .). How can we solve the ultimate question of life and death? (. . .) You can of course ponder on what is the correct way of life if you have that much leisure time. However, you would do better to practice the Daishonin's teaching. You are still young, after all. Through your own practice, you will come to realize that you are paving the correct path of life. I can assure you this (Ikeda 2004a, 229).

Then Ikeda asked, 'What is a true patriot?' and Toda unhesitatingly answered:

> A true patriot is none other than one who believes in the Mystic Law. The reason is that a believer in Nichiren Buddhism can help people lead lives of happiness for eternity and be the driving force for reconstructing an unhappy nation; they can create the foundation for a happy, peaceful society. (. . .) A society based on the Buddhism of the Mystic Law must emerge in the future (. . .). The great power to bring this about exists (. . .) in Nam-myoho-renge-kyo. A hundred or two hundred years later, historians will come to recognize this (Ikeda 2004a, 230).

The third question was: 'What is Nam-myoho-renge-kyo, which you just mentioned?' and Toda's answer was:

> In brief, it is the fundamental Law of all phenomena. All phenomena in the universe, including people, trees, plants and the universe itself, are the manifestations of Nam-myoho-renge-kyo. Therefore, it holds the power to change even human destiny. In Buddhism, it is called the original power of the great universe. From another

standpoint, Nam-myoho-renge-kyo is the original Buddha, the name of the eternal Buddha's life. (. . .) If you ask me, I can explain this to you all night or for two nights, even. But before that, I hope you, Mr. Yamamoto [Ikeda's name for his character in the novel], will study a bit more about it (Ikeda 2004a, 230–31).

In the novel, Ikeda then adds the following comments concerning the exchange, which I believe are crucial for a correct understanding of Ikeda's Buddhist humanism:

> Toda spoke to this young man on an equal, one-to-one basis, treating him as an adult. Toda's attitude and language were indeed sincere. Shin'ichi Yamamoto knew nothing about Buddhism, but he was moved by Josei Toda's sincerity. He himself had the tendency of young people in those days to criticize for criticism's sake. (. . .) But though his feelings at the moment were complex, Shin'ichi was for some reason filled with a deep satisfaction. 'Yes, sir. If I said I understood, I would be telling you a lie. I want to study more. But please allow me to ask you one more question' (Ikeda 2004a, 231).

His fourth and last question was: 'Sir, what is your opinion of the emperor?' and again Toda gave a clear-cut answer:

> From the Buddha's eyes, even the emperor is a common mortal, like ourselves. (. . .) As you find in the new Constitution, sovereignty rests with the people and the emperor's position has become a symbolic one. I think this is satisfactory. The matter of prime importance is how we Japanese, including the emperor, can recover from the devastation of the war and construct a peaceful and highly cultural nation as soon as possible. (. . .) What do you think of this? (Ikeda 2004a, 231–32).

According to Ikeda himself, after the answer to the fourth question, he knew he had found his mentor. As mentioned earlier, I believe it is important to note that Ikeda presents his decision as resulting from the trust Toda was able to inspire in him, and not because of complex Buddhist theories:

> At this time, he [Yamamoto/Ikeda] came to his ultimate moment of decision. 'How succinctly he answers! There is no confusion in him. I think I can believe and follow this man. He answered my questions

politely and sincerely, without any superfluity. What will this man mean in my life?' (Ikeda 2004a, 232).

In *The Human Revolution*, Ikeda makes it clear that he became a Buddhist solely because he trusted Toda. He was not interested in religion and did not really understand the doctrinal part of Toda's explanations during their first encounter. However, he was very impressed with Toda's authenticity and humanism, his warmth and sense of humor, and especially the fact that he had been imprisoned for two years by the military authorities for resisting the war propaganda with which Ikeda had been thoroughly indoctrinated. In his dialogue with Mikhail Gorbachev, he writes:

> My encounter with Mr. Toda led me to accept the Buddhist faith. I became a Buddhist not because I immediately understood the essence of the teachings, but because this great humanist, so unlike ordinary religious leaders, evoked my profound trust and respect (Ikeda and Gorbachev 2005, 6).

Ikeda confirms this point in the preface to *A Youthful Diary*:

> Mr. Toda was forty-seven at the time; I was nineteen. I remember that I asked a number of rather bold questions. Though it was our first meeting, Mr. Toda, at times with an austere expression on his face, at other times in a more relaxed manner, explained his views, speaking like a kind father giving instructions to his son. His remarks seemed to glow with the light of profound conviction. I remember being deeply impressed by the fact that, though imprisoned during the war by government authorities because of his religious beliefs, he had adamantly refused to give in to the pressures brought to bear on him. Some ten days later, I expressed a desire to join the Soka Gakkai (Ikeda 2006b, vii).

Ikeda tells us that he decided to adopt a new belief system based on a single meeting with Toda, and I would like to use this idea to try to explain why Ikeda is at the same time a firm believer in Nichiren Buddhism and a genuine dialogue partner with people of all cultures, who has held heart-to-heart exchanges with more than 7,000 people (*Seikyo Shimbun* 2007) from virtually all backgrounds and convictions. The decisive factor for Ikeda in choosing a religion was Toda's behavior as a human being.

At the same time, if I had to explain Ikeda's enthusiastic and thoroughly serious attitude towards the practice of Nichiren Buddhism, I would say that this shows his conviction that once a choice has been made, one must be earnest in the pursuit of the chosen path, and make sure it leads one to a life of contribution to humanity. I believe that Ikeda chose Nichiren Buddhism because of Toda, and that he could have chosen another way to develop and express his spirituality. However, I also believe that Ikeda's Buddhist faith is thoroughly genuine and authentic.

A musical metaphor might help clarify this point. There is no music without instruments or human voice. Once a musician has chosen an instrument, the goal is still to play music. Seriously devoting oneself to one specific instrument, for instance the piano, and trying to reach musical excellence, makes it difficult and often impossible to practice several instruments at the same time. This corresponds to Ikeda having chosen Nichiren Buddhism. However the goal of becoming an excellent pianist is not to show the superiority of the piano over all other instruments, but to be able to produce music that will touch the hearts of many listeners, and also to perform in ensembles, bands and orchestras with other musicians playing other instruments. This corresponds to Ikeda's passion for dialogue and for the promotion of humanism regardless of its spiritual or intellectual sources. This is the best way for me to express the depth and richness of the phrase 'Buddhist Humanism' which characterizes Ikeda's philosophy, illustrated by the numerous accounts of his first meeting with Toda.

The founding of Soka University

Whereas I cannot personally testify to the veracity of all the events describing Ikeda's childhood and adolescence, or to that of his first meeting with Toda, I am compelled to comment on one passage from *The New Human Revolution* concerning Soka University, where I worked as a faculty member from 1991 to 2007, because it is related to the very existence of this book:

> Soka University is unsurpassed in its openness to the world. It is constantly receiving visitors from around the globe, ranging from the presidents and deans of other universities to world leaders and scholars from every country and in every field. Among those who have visited and applauded the school are such eminent figures as former Soviet President Mikhail Gorbachev, former US secretary of State Henry Kissinger, former Club of Rome President Ricardo Díez-Hochleitner and renowned Norwegian peace scholar Dr. Johan Galtung (Ikeda 2008–15, 242).

I started teaching modern languages at Soka University in 1991. It was when I met 'renowned Norwegian peace scholar Dr. Johan Galtung' on campus in

1996 that I became interested in peace studies. My wife Yoko was appointed to translate his lectures during the two months of his visit, and she made sure that I would be able to meet him and attend his lectures. After more than a decade learning directly about peace studies from Galtung, I decided in 2006 to use what I had learned to systematize and clarify the principles and concepts behind Ikeda's passion for peace.

I could write several volumes filled with personal comments inspired by my reading of the 160-page chapter 'Soka University' from *The New Human Revolution,* but to stay focused on the topic of this book, I will simply share one passage of moderate length which I find to have special significance for an understanding of Ikeda's philosophy of peace.

It shows how crucial the mentor and disciple relationship is in Ikeda's life and in his numerous endeavors for peace, culture and education. It illustrates the far-reaching effects the 1947 meeting between Ikeda and Toda had on their lives, but also on the world of education. I will now use this passage to show that the main concepts at the root of Ikeda's philosophy, namely inner transformation, dialogue and global citizenship, can also be found in the origins of Soka University.

On the afternoon of 2 April 1971, the anniversary of Toda's passing, Ikeda visited the grave of his mentor. He writes:

> Silently addressing President Toda, he [Shin'ichi Yamamoto/Ikeda] said: 'Sensei! Your long-cherished dream of Soka University has finally come true. The opening ceremony just finished, and the hope-filled voices of the university's new students are echoing across the campus.' Shin'ichi clearly saw Mr. Toda in his mind, smiling and nodding in satisfaction.
>
> Shin'ichi would never forget that late-autumn day when Mr. Toda had first talked to him about establishing a university. It was November 16, 1950, and Shin'ichi was twenty-two. Four days earlier, at the 5th Soka Gakkai General Meeting, Mr. Toda had officially resigned as the organization's general director because his company, the Toko Construction Credit Union, had been forced to suspend business operations due to financial trouble, and he wanted to avoid putting the Soka Gakkai at risk. It was a truly difficult time.
>
> On that day, Mr. Toda and Shin'ichi were eating lunch at a university cafeteria near the company's offices in Tokyo's Nishi-Kanda when Mr. Toda declared: 'Shin'ichi, let's build a university. A Soka University.' Mr. Toda recalled fondly that first Soka Gakkai

president Tsunesaburo Makiguchi had been determined to establish a school based on his theories of value-creating education. In his *Soka Kyoikugaku Taikei* (The System of Value-creating [Pedagogy]), the first volume of which was published on November 18, 1930, Mr. Makiguchi had already set forth ideas that would lead to the establishment of a Soka University and a Soka Schools system.

Mr. Toda's eyes lit up as he declared: 'For the sake of humanity's future, I must create a Soka University. But this may not be possible for me to achieve during my lifetime. If that's the case, I am counting on you, Shin'ichi. Let's make it the best university in the world!'

Amid the direst of personal circumstances, Mr. Toda spoke to his disciple Shin'ichi of his hope of creating a university and entrusted the fulfillment of that dream to him. Shin'ichi accepted these words as his mentor's cherished wish and engraved them deeply in his heart.

In the twenty-one years that followed, Shin'ichi had devoted himself wholeheartedly to actualizing President Toda's vision (Ikeda 2008–15, 87–89).

The first fact to note here is that Toda was in a very difficult situation when he mentioned the creation of Soka University for the first time. He had to resign from his position as leader of the Soka Gakkai due to financial trouble. In order to be able to joyfully introduce such a grand idea as establishing a Soka University, Toda had to go through a process of inner transformation, leading him from discouragement and despair, which are to be expected in such a situation, to the kind of hope and enthusiasm necessary to dream about a better future again.

Second, as long as this idea stayed within Toda, nothing would happen. It is through a process of dialogue with Ikeda that the idea of establishing Soka University started to stand a chance of being realized. Within the context of the mentor and disciple relationship, dialogue may be characterized more by respectful agreements than by heated deliberations and arguments, but Ikeda and Toda nevertheless communicated through logic and reason, *dia-logos*, enabling the idea of Soka University to leave the realm of imagination and become a concrete reality.

Third, Toda's goal as stated in the novel was to establish a university 'for the sake of humanity's future,' not to serve the interests of one religious group, or not even of one country, but to spread the humanistic ideals of Makiguchi throughout the world. I interpret this as showing a confidence that the educational philosophy of Toda's mentor is universal, and can contribute to the development of global citizenship.

The fact that Soka University was established in 1971, that Soka University of America was established in 1987 (with the current campus and under-graduate and graduate programs inaugurated in 2001), and that both are fully functioning universities today, shows that the power of ideas and dialogue cannot be overestimated.

For those who believe that peace also needs to happen from the bottom up, it is important to see examples of dreams generated through inner transform-ation being articulated through dialogue. I believe that anybody is able to do this. Following the model introduced in this book, these ideas can then enhance and encourage global citizenship, as well as the development of some elements of a peaceful and harmonious global civilization.

Celebrating Toda's birthday on 11 February in *A Youthful Diary*

A Youthful Diary is a compilation of entries in Ikeda's personal journal from May 1949 to May 1960. I have focused on the entries recorded on the birthday of Josei Toda, 11 February, and I have selected excerpts that show Ikeda's vulnerability and weaknesses, because I believe that even these are consistent with the themes explored in this book.

The years when 11 February was recorded in this published work are 1951, 1954, 1955, 1958, 1959 and 1960. This selection of excerpts, as with many other entries, shows that among other feelings and thoughts, on the day of his mentor's birthday throughout the years Ikeda experienced: being troubled, sad (for forgetting Toda's birthday), ashamed, determined not to lose, con-cerned, nostalgic, doubtful, having fearful thoughts. . .

(1951) Sunday, February 11. Clear.
Up at 10:00. Awakened by B. Pleasant weather continues. Went to a small restaurant for a leisurely brunch. A single person is a free spirit. (. . .) M. and U. broke our appointment to discuss Buddhism. Troubled. I am young, however. Must never become mean-spirited. Visited Mr. Toda's home at 6:00. (. . .) Today was Mr. Toda's birthday. Sadly reflected that I did not offer him my best wishes. Home just before 11:00.

(1954) Thursday, February 11. Fine weather.
Today is President Toda's fifty-fourth birthday. In the morning, I gave him a white shirt and a necktie as a gift. He seemed quite

fatigued. At 2:00, I helped administer the Study Department oral examination (. . .) Ashamed about my own lack of ability. Must study. Must not be defeated. Got home just before midnight.

(1955) Friday, February 11. Partly cloudy.
Today is President Toda's fifty-fifth birthday. I am twenty-seven. (. . .) I am satisfied being just a common person. I shall live my entire life, however, spreading the Mystic Law, the fundamental power of the universe itself. (. . .) Only a life lived strictly protecting the Law possesses the essence of reality, and herein lies the truth. Such people will definitely prosper. Twenty-seven years of life – I do not want to lose.

(1958) Tuesday, February 11. Cloudy.
Visited Sensei's home at 9:00 in the morning. Relieved to see his spirited face. Today is his fifty-eighth birthday. (. . .) Could not help being concerned about how emaciated his body is. But my heart leapt with joy to see him asking everyone to sing and giving resolute guidance. Everyone seemed to have refreshed their spirit. Wonderful. Happy.

(1959) Wednesday, February 11. Fair.
Today would have been my mentor's fifty-ninth birthday. Felt nostalgic. (. . .) On this great day, held a youth division leaders conference. (. . .) How many among them can dedicate their entire being to the human revolution called kosen-rufu[2] throughout their lives? Felt confident . . . then doubtful.

(1960) Thursday, February 11. Clear.
Today is President Toda's birthday. If he were alive, he would be celebrating his sixtieth birthday. My wife and I talked about this as if we were Sensei's son and daughter. (. . .) Fearful thoughts weigh heavily on my mind – thoughts about my responsibility, my seniors and my accomplishment.

These expressions of vulnerability found in *A Youthful Diary* seem to suggest that the successful leader depicted in the *Human Revolution* novels was actually going through inner transformation almost every day, trying to bring out such qualities as courage, wisdom and compassion despite the ups and downs of everyday life. They provide an encouraging message about the power of common people to build peace from the ground up. They affirm that it is not necessary to be perfect in order to progress along the path of one's inner transformation and to contribute to peace.

Concluding comments

In the collection of poems *Fighting for Peace* (2004b), Ikeda expresses in lyrical terms what he thinks is most important in order to assess the 'value and significance' of one's life:

> For the value and significance
> of a person's life
> must be assessed in its entirety.
> We must ask:
> Has this been a life
> which brightly cast the light
> of *conviction and justice*
> over past, present and future –
> like a jewel whose facets mutually capture and reflect? (14–15)
> (Italics added).

> Never chaotic or flustered,
> let us strike out toward the future,
> manifesting unparalleled strength.
> Let us leave our *mark on history*,
> a worthy marshalling toward peace;
> and let this mark be precise,
> built and based
> on our robust solidarity (77) (Italics added).

> We must give *full*
> *and unrelenting voice*
> to the call for justice
> in order to realize peace,
> in order to achieve happiness.
> In such actions above all
> will be found
> a bright and happy future (110) (Italics added).

One of the themes pervading Ikeda's philosophy, and captured in the excerpts above, is that each human being can become a hero or heroine for peace, leading a life based on 'conviction and justice,' and that each person can leave a 'mark on history,' giving 'full and unrelenting voice' to calls for peace and justice.

In this context, the four autobiographical works analyzed in this chapter add a literary dimension to a life devoted to action for peacebuilding. Taken together as a whole, they constitute an important source of information concerning Ikeda as a human being, and also as a religious leader and a peace thinker. I have chosen to present these works here because I believe that the way Ikeda narrates his childhood memories, his first meeting with Toda, and the episodes describing how he has received his mentor's legacy and thoughts penned down in his personal diary all contribute to our understanding of his philosophy of peace.

CHAPTER 3

Josei Toda: Ikeda's Mentor in Life

> It is not my purpose to debate matters of victory or defeat in war or the pros and cons of policies and ideologies; rather, I grieve at the thought that war causes countless people to lose their husbands or wives, and leaves countless people seeking for lost children or parents.[1]
>
> Josei Toda, 10 May 1951

> I want to rid the world of misery.[2]
>
> Josei Toda, 1 January 1957

After meeting Toda in 1947, Ikeda worked closely with him until his passing in 1958, and has continued implementing his mentor's vision for more than six decades. I consider Toda as the most influential person for Ikeda's formation as a peacebuilder, and his life, thoughts, words and actions as an integral part of Ikeda's philosophy of peace. In this chapter, which contains many elements of Toda's biography that can be verified independently, I will highlight the way Ikeda has shared his memories of his mentor's life. The main source of information is Ikeda's novel *The Human Revolution*, which relates the reconstruction and revitalization of the Soka Gakkai from Toda's release from prison in 1945 until his passing in 1958.

Six major aspects of Toda's life are introduced, mostly based on *The Human Revolution* and sometimes on other sources. First, his formative years from his birth in 1900 to his departure for Tokyo in 1920. Second, the relationship with his mentor Tsunesaburo Makiguchi (1871–1944),[3] which was to define his whole life. Together they established the *Soka Kyoiku Gakkai* (Value-creating Educational Society) in 1930. Next, his imprisonment by the Japanese military government. While in jail, through intense study of the Lotus Sutra,[4] daily spiritual practice and an unshakeable commitment to his beliefs, Toda was able to feel that his life was one with the 'life of the entire universe' (Ikeda 2004a, 409), and that he had a mission to awaken humanity to the universality of the Buddha nature as one of the 'Bodhisattvas of the Earth'[5] (Ikeda 2004a, 412). After surviving two years in a prison cell, Toda was transformed into a mature leader for peace.

Fourth, his meeting with Ikeda, which was explored in detail in Chapter 2. Next, Toda's singlehanded rebuilding of the Soka Gakkai, the organization he had started with Makiguchi in 1930, which was destroyed in 1943 due to oppression by the military government that led to Makiguchi's death and Toda's imprisonment. Starting with a few people in 1945, Toda was able to rebuild the Soka Gakkai into an organization that reached 750,000 Japanese households in late 1957, three months before his death.

Finally, his 1957 'Declaration Calling for the Abolition of Nuclear Weapons,' which is still relevant today as a source of inspiration in the struggle for a nuclear free world (Krieger in Ikeda and Krieger 2002, 131).

The first 20 years:
the shaping of a peace leader (1900–20)

Josei Toda was born as Jin'ichi[6] in Shioya Village (now Kaga City), Ishikawa Prefecture, on 11 February 1900, the seventh child of a family struggling with financial hardships. Hoping to improve their situation, the Todas moved to Atsuta, Hokkaido, on the coast of the Sea of Japan, when Jin'ichi was two years old. Despite their best efforts, the family was never well off and even though Toda graduated from elementary school with high marks, he had to abandon full-time formal education in order to support his family financially and he worked his way through school. One of his greatest joys was admiring the waves crashing off the coast of Atsuta, standing tall in the wind, and dreaming about the wide world beyond the sea (Ushio 2000, 6).

Ikeda attempted to recreate the atmosphere of Toda's family home in a poem entitled 'Atsuta Village':

> Atsuta Village by the cold northern sea
> amid endless snowstorms
> that silver house by the seaside, poor as it was,
> that was your ancient castle of glory
>
> Atsuta River with the poetry of spring and summer,
> herring-filled waves of the Japan Sea,
> this region opened up by the lords of Matsumae,
> sheer cliffs, fishing-village gardens

The boy unmoving, beneath the bright full moon,
reading works of biography and history,
on the ruddy cheek sadly a tear,
music of a heart that beats with uprightness (. . .) (Ikeda 1997a, 30).

One of Toda's fondest memories was listening to his father telling stories with all his children around the fire in the humble family living room. Toda and his siblings would learn about heroes from ancient and recent times, and these happy moments left a deep impression on Toda's mind (Ushio 2000, 4, 14). For the rest of his life, Toda would love holding discussions with small groups of ordinary people. Toda was also inspired by his older brother Sotokichi's passion for studying, and decided to follow in his footsteps after the latter's premature passing as an adolescent. At Atsuta elementary school, Toda was fortunate enough to have two teachers, Raseki Kawai and Chinmoku Hasebe, who were also novelists and shared with the young boy their passion for literature and writing (Shiohara 2008a).

Toda had to work as an apprentice for a wholesale dealer in Sapporo at age 15, pulling a heavy cart, packaging and distributing goods. At the time when Toda was raised in Atsuta, the atmosphere of the city was staunchly traditional, most of the inhabitants being survivors of the 1868 Meiji Restoration who had resisted the winds of change, preferring to hold on to the old ways of the Edo Era. In contrast, the city of Sapporo was bustling with influences from the US and the West, following Japan's opening to the outside world in the latter part of the nineteenth century (Shiohara 2008a).

Toda's diary[7] around that time reveals a young man burning with ambition despite his unfavorable circumstances (Ushio 2000, 9), and he continued studying while working, receiving a license as a substitute elementary school teacher at the age of 17. One day he fell exhausted in the snow and had to be hospitalized for several months. In order to repay the debt he had accumulated due to medical and hospital bills, he started working as a store clerk in the coalmining city of Yubari. It is there that he was offered his first position as a substitute teacher at age 18, deep inside the mountains near Yubari, in the 400-pupil elementary school of the village of Mayachi.

This is a town where fathers worked in tunnels, their faces blackened with coal, and mothers sift[ed] and sort[ed] the coals. He [Toda] said: 'At an agricultural college in Iwamizawa, I saw a coal miner's lungs preserved in alcohol. They were completely blackened by coal dust. It was frightening' (Shiohara 2008b, 149).

Toda was appointed associate teacher of the school in June 1918, and continued studying until he obtained his license as full-time elementary school teacher in the fall of 1918. He started developing an original method of instruction tailored to his pupils, and it is around that time that he began to use the name Jogai (Shiohara 2008b, 149). At the end of 1919 he also obtained a license to teach several scientific subjects (Ikeda 2004, 235). He was loved by the pupils and would spend a lot of time entertaining them at his home. The young coalminers in the area also started gathering at Toda's house to discuss politics and history. At the same time he had to continue paying off his debts and saving on everything, but this difficult situation did not deter him from writing a proposal for reform addressed to the Ministry of Education. It contained concrete ideas on how to improve the condition of teachers, and a system of examinations in order to foster more capable school principals.

In early 1920 Toda decided to leave Mayachi and Hokkaido for good and to move to Tokyo in order to make his way in the world, discover what his mission in life was, and how he could contribute to society (Ikeda 2004a, 1726). He knew that he would need to learn from a mentor, and despite the hardships of surviving in a new city he was able to find Makiguchi and to become his disciple. Around that time, in one of his diary entries (1 April 1920), he mentioned his dream of becoming a 'world citizen' (Ushio 2000, 25).

Learning from his mentor (1920–43)

When Toda arrived in Tokyo in early 1920, he soon met Tsunesaburo Makiguchi, who was well known for his original ideas in the educational circles of the capital. During this initial meeting, they discovered a common passion for a type of education that enables individuals to flourish. Makiguchi helped the young educator to secure employment as a temporary teacher, and Toda remained loyal to him for the rest of his life.

Makiguchi was often transferred from one school to another because of his refusal to cater to the needs of authority figures. His non-conformist attitude would become increasingly unpopular with the authorities, culminating in his arrest and imprisonment in 1943. At the time of his initial meeting with Toda, Makiguchi had been transferred to Nishimachi Elementary School, but he was transferred again after six months to Mikasa Elementary School, where Toda followed him and became a full-time teacher.

Makiguchi organized a system of cheap lunches at the school, first for pupils who could not afford a meal, and ultimately for all the pupils. He was inspired by the example of the 'Penny Lunch System' practiced in the suburbs of Chicago (Shiohara 2008b, 149). Toda would later show the same attention to the needs of the youth in his care, providing pork soup for 6,000 youngsters during his last public appearance on 16 March 1958. In 1922 Makiguchi was again forced to resign from Mikasa Elementary School, and began working at Shirokane Elementary School.

It is around that time that Toda started studying to enter university, and in 1923 he opened an elementary tutorial school which he named Jishu Gakkan, where he could apply Makiguchi's educational theories. In 1928 he was accepted in the Department of Economics of Chuo University, but during the same period disaster struck in his personal life. He had married Tsuta Urata in 1922 (or 1923) and they had a daughter, Yasuyo, but the infant died of tuberculosis in 1924, with her mother suffering the same fate in 1926. Toda himself was affected with the disease for about eight years (Shiohara 2008a). He was able to overcome those hardships and continued focusing on his educational projects. Sometime between 1928 and 1930, he joined the Nichiren Shoshu school of Buddhism, following his mentor Makiguchi who had joined in 1928.

Both were impressed with the similarities between Makiguchi's theories of education, resting on the belief in the potential of each individual, and the teachings of Nichiren based on the Lotus Sutra, which affirms that each human being possesses inexhaustible treasures of the heart. Rather than a conversion, their taking faith can be interpreted as adding a spiritual dimension to a life-enhancing philosophy they were already practicing. At the same time, I would like to suggest that it is quite possible that adopting a new spiritual practice helped Toda overcome the loss of his wife and daughter. He eventually married a second time in February 1935, with Ikuko Matsuo, and their son Takahisa was born in November 1936.

In December 1929, Toda published his first book, *Katei Kyoikugaku Soron* (*An Anatomy of Home Education*),[8] for parents with children in the sixth grade of elementary school, and his second, *Suirishiki Shido Sanjutsu* (*A Deductive Guide to Arithmetic*), in June 1930. This book on arithmetic eventually sold one million copies over about 11 years, going through at least 126 editions until 1941.

Toda's next big project was the publication of Makiguchi's magnum opus, *Soka Kyoikugaku Taikei* (*The System of Value-creating Pedagogy*), which started in late 1930. He devoted himself wholeheartedly to this project for about ten months and abandoned his university studies the same year (Shiohara 2008a).

Makiguchi had begun jotting down his thoughts on education around 1893, at age 22, when he first began teaching. In the *Seikyo Shimbun* newspaper of 10 April 1952, Toda published an installment of his autobiographical novel *Ningen Kakumei* (*Human Revolution*)[9] in which he described the birth of the term *Soka* (value-creation).

An abbreviated form of the expression *kachi sozo* (the creation of value), it refers to the inner capacity of each human being to create something valuable in any circumstance. It was in the middle of one night in February 1930, during a discussion with Makiguchi, that Toda offered to devote himself entirely to the publication of the ideas his mentor had written down, talked about and practiced for decades.

Makiguchi's pedagogical system needed a name, and they decided to call it *Soka*, since at its core was the belief that each learner needed to be equipped with the skills necessary to create value, in order to be empowered to transform reality for the better. In *A Deductive Guide to Arithmetic* published a few months later, Toda states that the book is based on the principles of Soka pedagogy, a term that was born on that February night.

To support the publication of *The System of Value-creating Pedagogy,* friends of Makiguchi and Toda created a Value-creating Pedagogy Support Group. It included 28 prominent figures, including Tsuyoshi Inukai who was soon to become the 29th prime minister of Japan. Among the three individuals who wrote the foreword was the famous Christian educator and politician Inazo Nitobe, who was an Under-secretary general of the League of Nations and who had published the famous essay *Bushido: the Soul of Japan* in 1900.

The date of the publication of the first volume of Makiguchi's work, 18 November 1930, is also the date of the foundation of the Soka Kyoiku Gakkai. It is described as follows on a website dedicated to his life and philosophy:

> The organization Makiguchi founded, the Soka Kyoiku Gakkai, sought to promote his views on value-creating education, which Makiguchi saw as fundamentally compatible with the interpretation of Nichiren Buddhism passed down through the Nichiren Shoshu school with its head temple at Taiseki-ji. Originally made up of teachers and educators, the organization expanded over the course of the 1930s to embrace people from all walks of life, and its purpose evolved from the promotion of educational reform to promoting reform of society based on reform of religion. Its activities centered on small gatherings in members' homes, as well as periodical large-scale meetings in public venues (Makiguchi Website).

While fully supporting his mentor's activities for the development of the Soka Kyoiku Gakkai, Toda continued his own intellectual work. For more than six years starting in 1930, Toda published an educational magazine in order to promote the value-creating pedagogy. Besides *A Deductive Guide to Arithmetic*, Toda published more than 20 other educational reference books (Shiohara 2008b, 154). In the preface to his first book, *An Anatomy of Home Education*, Toda 'encourages parents to raise their children into people of intellect who can reason and make decisions, rather than turning their brains into memorizing machines' (Shiohara 2008b, 155). At the same time, there is some irony in the fact that Toda was a pioneer in the field of large-scale coaching of young people to take the standardized entrance examinations and that this is how he made his fortune.

Already in his first book, Toda shows his belief in what would later become a major element of the concept of inner transformation, the fact that each individual has tremendous potential that needs to be brought out through appropriate methods. This conviction is probably related to his experiences in Hokkaido and his struggles in Tokyo together with Makiguchi. Toda's adoption of Nichiren Buddhism sometime between 1928 and 1930 only reinforced his belief in people's potential. In *A Deductive Guide to Arithmetic* Toda emphasized the importance of thinking for oneself, and this would remain a component of his philosophy of peace. I would like to propose that Toda and Ikeda's use of rationality as a tool for communication is very similar to Habermas's concept of 'communicative rationality,' an idea that will be explored in Chapter 6 of this book. It is important to note the absence of a clear distinction between rationality and spirituality running through both Toda and Ikeda's ideas. I believe that for them, they are just two of the potential aspects of a very complex entity, the human heart.

In May 1939, Makiguchi shared his dream of establishing a school based on value-creating pedagogy, and entrusted that vision to Toda. In an interview, Sadako Kaneko, Makiguchi's daughter-in-law, recalls him saying: 'In the future, either I, or if I am unable, Toda, will definitely establish a school implementing the value-creating education I have been researching. We will have schools from elementary to university level' (Makiguchi Website). It is eventually Ikeda who made this project a reality starting with the creation of Soka High School in the 1960s, followed by a complete Soka educational system in the ensuing years. Up until 1943, Toda was running a number of successful businesses, such as the publishing companies Daidoshobo (novels) and Nihon Shogakkan (educational materials) as well as the trading company Nihon Shote. He was also a member of the board of directors of, and otherwise involved in, different business ventures, about ten in all. He lost everything when he was arrested and jailed by the government in 1943 on charges of blasphemy and violating the Peace Preservation Law of 1925.

Imprisonment and awakening (1943–45)

To unify the entire nation towards the war effort, the military government was promoting and imposing the worship of the Sun Goddess Amaterasu, the core symbol of State Shinto (a term retroactively coined by the Occupation authorities to describe the belief system promoted by the state and since widely – but not uncontroversially – used by scholars both inside and outside Japan). Legend has it that it was Amaterasu who sent the famous 'divine winds' (*kamikaze*) to destroy the invading Mongol fleets in the thirteenth century.[10] In 1281 the Mongol armada, dispatched by Kublai Khan, was almost assured to conquer the Japanese islands. It was only due to a powerful typhoon off the shore of Kyushu that the expedition failed. Seven centuries later, the Japanese government was trying to mobilize the country around that legend:

> Bewitched by the capricious doctrines of Shintoism, they forced the entire nation to worship the Sun Goddess by forcing people to enshrine Shinto talismans and vainly hoped for the miracle to repeat itself. Makiguchi and his followers denied all doctrines of Shinto, resisting the military thought control (Ikeda 2004a, 86).

National law demanded that Shinto talismans be enshrined in each Japanese home. This allowed the government to target those who refused to comply and treat them as traitors, effectively allowing the military powers to control the entire Japanese population.

Moreover, the Ministry of Education was trying to forcibly unite different Buddhist groups. This was a way to simplify control of the believers and to make sure they accepted the Shinto talisman. Indeed, it was possible to keep one's religion while still showing support for the war effort by adding the talisman to the family collection of religious objects. The head temple Taiseki-ji, headquarters of Nichiren Shoshu, had decided to accept the Shinto tablets as a temporary expedient. Nichiren Shoshu summoned Makiguchi and Toda to the temple to urge them to do likewise, but Makiguchi, in his capacity as head of the Soka Kyoiku Gakkai, categorically refused. Toda wholeheartedly supported his mentor's decision to oppose the solution offered by the priests, and less than a month after the meeting at the temple they were both detained on 6 July 1943 on charges of violating the 1925 Peace Preservation Law. This law was used to suppress 'thought crimes,' and was first enacted to target leftist groups. It was amended in 1941 to include religious organizations, and a total of 21 leaders of the Soka Kyoiku Gakkai were arrested around the same time as Makiguchi and Toda. It is estimated that about 80,000 people were arrested for violating the Peace Preservation Law between 1925 and 1945 (Hosei University 2000).

Makiguchi passed away in prison on 18 November 1944. Despite malnutrition, interrogation and physical abuse, he never compromised his beliefs. Toda was in a separate cell, and did not know that his mentor had died. He was only informed on 8 January 1945 and was deeply shocked. Toda pledged that if he came out of prison alive, he would stand up by himself and continue his mentor's work – a promise he kept.

At the beginning of 1944, Toda began a fierce struggle to survive physically and mentally in prison. He started meditating and chanting more earnestly than ever and studied the Lotus Sutra thoroughly. This allowed him to experience two awakenings that were to influence the course of his remaining years. First he realized that the Buddha is life itself, the essence of cosmic life. According to Ikeda, this first awakening concerning the nature of the Buddha was formulated as: 'It is the life of the entire universe' (Ikeda 2004a, 409).

From that moment in his solitary cell in March 1944, Toda seemed to be free of fear for the rest of his life. This first revelation gave him tremendous courage to overcome all obstacles. It also made him aware of how precious life is, and of the importance of the dignity of each individual. It confirmed his attitude and conviction as an educator, which he had forged as a disciple of Makiguchi, that each human being is precious and worthy of respect.

In November of the same year, Toda had a second awakening when he experienced a powerful sense of self-identification as a 'Bodhisattva of the Earth' (Ikeda 2004a, 412). This is the name of legendary figures found in the Lotus Sutra, which symbolize the benevolent functions latent in all people. When brought to full bloom, this capacity is expressed as active compassion for all living beings. This is the spirit of the Bodhisattva at the core of Toda and Ikeda's philosophy of peace.

To recapitulate, Toda's two revelations were: first, that each person deserves complete respect since they have the ultimate source of spirituality within them, and second, that each person has a mission to share this respect for life with others. Here I would like to establish a parallel between these elements of Toda's life, as related by Ikeda, and the three essential qualities of courage, compassion and wisdom that are at the heart of the process of inner transformation. The first revelation gave Toda boundless *courage* to overcome all hardships, and the second gave him the *compassion* to devote his life to helping others come to the same realization. Since he was able to share these two revelations with 750,000 households in a mere 13 years before his death in 1958, it can be inferred that Toda was able to tap the necessary *wisdom* to find the best way to share this courage and compassion with countless people.

The numerical expansion of the Soka Gakkai under Toda's leadership can be explained by a combination of factors, but according to many testimonies Toda's personality and conviction was one of the most crucial elements for this successful growth. What follows is the account of an interview that took place on 11 November 2009 in Hashimoto, Kanagawa Prefecture (Suwa 2009).[11]

Yoshiharu Suwa was born in Machida, Tokyo, on 28 March 1936 and grew up in Yokohama. He moved back near Machida during the war when his family's house was burned down. After graduating from junior high school in 1953 he started working for the fruit shop owned by his uncle, who was a member of the Soka Gakkai. After a year, Yoshiharu decided to join, on 10 October 1954, and he attended a lecture by Josei Toda for the first time in Tokyo in 1955. He still remembers his first impression of Toda, which I asked him to describe in detail:

> Suwa: During the lecture, Mr Toda said: 'Without compassion, you cannot propagate this Buddhism.' Even though his words were strict, I could feel that he really cared. At that time everybody was poor, and I wanted to try my best through my Buddhist practice in order to become a person of sufficient material wealth. Inspired by President Toda's own compassion, I wanted to try my best, and I felt like I had the strength to do anything. I worked very hard and participated in Soka Gakkai activities enthusiastically.

> Urbain: Could you tell me a bit more concretely what you mean by President Toda's compassion?

> Suwa: At that time, we all had to watch out for each other, we had to take care of each other. I was living in my uncle's house, and my aunt prepared good food, and I felt grateful for their support. I tried my best to take care of the Soka Gakkai members in my group, and I felt it was very important to let as many members as possible attend the meetings and to have a good attendance.

> Urbain: Is it because you felt that if people would come to Soka Gakkai meetings they would learn how to overcome their problems, and in this way that would be an act of compassion on your part?

> Suwa: Yes, but not only that. I felt that what I had learned from President Toda was that in order to be happy, one must be compassionate. In other words, compassion is a way of life, and being

compassionate means being happy. When President Toda said, 'Without compassion, you cannot propagate this Buddhism,' I understood how important compassion, consideration and care are, and I have been living my life based on that ever since. I have come to own my own fruit shop and to open up a space for Soka Gakkai members to come and have discussion meetings, which is this place here where we are sitting now.

Urbain: Well, it looks as though the encouragement from President Toda worked for you.

Suwa: Today I am 73 years old, and I have devoted my life to work and activities since I was young. I am happy with my wife, and we have four children and six grandchildren. I am still active as owner of my fruit shop, and even though business has become difficult since six years ago because of supermarkets, I am trying my best.

Yoshiharu explains that a few months ago he had decided to take responsibility for a 200-meter stretch of road between his house and a fellow Soka Gakkai member's house, in order to help his community. 'Especially now that autumn has come, leaves clog the drain along the street and it is not good for the sewage system. I would like to contribute something to the neighborhood, and I have decided to be in charge of cleaning that part of the street.' With a beaming face, shining eyes and rosy cheeks, he adds: 'I do this with a great sense of responsibility.'

The interview lasted about one and a half hours, and as I left, Yoshiharu offered me a large paper bag filled with apples, pears and persimmons.

I also remember hearing the following anecdote at a discussion meeting. A Soka Gakkai member who had just graduated from high school met President Toda in the early 1950s and felt that he was a very warm person with whom he felt immediately comfortable. Among all the factors that contributed to the growth of the Soka Gakkai in those days, this person believes that 80–90 percent was due to President Toda's attractive personality.

One day Toda encouraged him by imparting profound philosophical principles in a way he could grasp easily. At that time, the young man was deeply worried because of his family's financial difficulties. They were so poor that they could not even afford to buy salt. His brothers and sisters knew that he was going to a Soka Gakkai meeting and were expecting him to bring home some candy from a nearby store. However he could not afford to buy anything and was vaguely hoping that someone would help him out. Toda sensed the young boy's agony and gave him encouragement. This is the way I remember their exchange being reported during the meeting:

> **Toda:** Stop complaining and saying things like these. Do you know the taste of water?
>
> **Member:** No, I don't know.
>
> **Toda:** Those who don't know the taste of water don't know the power of this Buddhism. You know, people just need water and salt in order to survive!
>
> **Member:** I have water, but I don't have any salt.
>
> **Toda:** Oh, I am so sorry about that. [They both laughed heartily and Toda continued:] Persevere for ten years in your Buddhist practice and everything will turn out to be all right.

He felt deeply encouraged and went straight home. He asked his brothers and sisters to prepare water in cups and then shared the encouragement Toda had given him. Then they took a sip of water together, and it tasted like the most delicious drink they had ever had. It was better than any candy. He still vividly remembers the marvelous taste of that water.

The encouragement he received from Toda was a turning point for him, and he went on to overcome all his financial difficulties within ten years and became a prominent leader in his field. One of the reasons behind the growth of the Soka Gakkai between 1945 and 1958 is the quality of such person-to-person exchanges, initiated by Toda upon his release from prison.

Like any religious experience, Toda's awakenings in prison are not verifiable by objective, scientific means. However, these subjective experiences gave Toda a clarity of purpose which had real effects on people. Like many others, Ikeda was able to feel that clarity during their first meeting in 1947, and during the chaos of postwar Japan thousands of desperate Japanese felt energized by Toda's authenticity. Whereas the personal belief and commitment of each member must be taken into account to explain why one would join the Soka Gakkai, the enthusiasm that never left Toda after his two revelations played a large part in the development of a very large grassroots movement.

At the deepest level, this must have confirmed to him that he had made the right decision when he refused to compromise his beliefs and followed his mentor to prison. In the context of this book, I would like to describe

Toda's awakenings as powerful experiences of inner transformation which enhanced his courage, wisdom and compassion, and also his capacity for dialogue.

Rebuilding the Soka Gakkai (1945–58)

After his release from prison on 3 July 1945 Toda started to rebuild his life, slowly regaining his health which had been damaged by two years of malnutrition and harsh conditions. The reasons why he was released on that day are based on a complicated system of investigation, pre-trial, bail, parole and potential release that was unique to Japan.[12]

Toda first had to find the strength to encourage himself. The two revelations he had experienced in 1944 as well as his pledge to continue the work of his deceased mentor enabled him to take on the formidable task of rebuilding the Soka Gakkai from scratch. He decided to change the name of the organization from Soka Kyoiku Gakkai (Value-creating Educational Society) to the shorter Soka Gakkai (Value-creation Society) since he believed that its philosophy would benefit all members of society, and not just educators. He also decided to change his own name from 'Jogai' (meaning 'outside the castle') to 'Josei,' which means 'castle sage,' to symbolize his awakening to his responsibility as the leader of the movement to rebuild the Soka Gakkai (Ikeda 2004a, 55).

His first challenge was to find an audience willing to listen to him. He started with four businessmen who had been Soka Kyoiku Gakkai members. The humble beginnings of this grassroots movement are humorously described by Ikeda:

> He then thought of the four businessmen who called on him so often. Whatever else one might say about them, they did come, at least, and they had four perfectly good pairs of ears. One evening he broached the subject. 'It's a waste of time, just drinking here like this. Why don't we study the Lotus Sutra?'
>
> 'Lotus what?' Yoichiro Honda [not his real name] stared at him with a dazed expression, eyes blurred by sake (Ikeda 2004a, 99).

The lecture does not go very well, and Toda is disappointed, but then catches himself:

> Didn't they have even the faintest glimmer of a seeking spirit? He felt depressed. Hold on, he thought. Do not think of them as four old friends. Think of them as four pairs of ears, he reminded himself.

> They were all he had right now, and he'd have to protect them.
> Perseverance, he knew, must underlie any great endeavor (Ikeda
> 2004a, 101).

Then on 1 January 1946 Toda gave a lecture on the Lotus Sutra to the four of them at the Nichiren Shoshu head temple, Taiseki-ji. That first official lecture can be considered as the starting point of the Soka Gakkai's reconstruction after the war.

To summarize what I consider to be the essential message of the novel *The Human Revolution*: by teaching wholeheartedly, and taking care of each individual with great respect, Toda was able to encourage several more people to join him, then hundreds, thousands, and by 1958 the Soka Gakkai had reached 750,000 households. *The New Human Revolution* narrates how Ikeda followed the same recipe of genuine and sincere teaching combined with great care for each individual, with the result that the SGI today has members in almost all countries. It is hard to imagine that it actually started with that small meeting with one mouth and 'four pairs of ears,' but this is what gives the members of the SGI the conviction that one individual can change the world.

I believe that the fast numerical expansion of the Soka Gakkai between 1945 and the 1970s is a unique phenomenon,[13] and that now that the rapid growth has subsided it is important to share the values and principles at the core of Ikeda's philosophy of peace without necessarily using the vehicle of religion. One of the main principles at the core of that historic expansion, the idea that the inner transformation of one person can positively affect countless others, is explored more fully in Chapter 5.

On 14 August 1947 a frail young man of 19 suffering from tuberculosis, named Daisaku Ikeda, attended one of the small meetings Toda was leading. As mentioned previously, Toda's simplicity, human warmth, authenticity and clarity were able to convince Ikeda that he would gain a lot by changing some of his convictions, altering his belief system voluntarily. The exchange that took place on 14 August 1947 was an example of human interaction causing someone to review their construction of reality; this is how the human revolution spreads from one person to another, through a process of inner transformation. Ikeda felt he had been lied to by the war propaganda, and since Toda had spent two years in prison because of his convictions, his passion and sincerity were especially appealing to young Ikeda.

I believe that Ikeda found in Toda a convincing example of the power of inner transformation and of dialogue. I would like to suggest that during their first meeting, as well as in subsequent ones, Ikeda felt Toda's capacity to use language and logic to bring out the best in others. I also think that Toda inspired Ikeda to develop his capacity for global citizenship.

One important concept proposed by Toda was that of *chikyu minzoku shugi*. The translation of this term is problematic. In the postwar period, perhaps reflecting the global decolonization process, the term *minzoku* (nation/people) became more prominent in Japanese discourse. *Nihon minzoku*, the Japanese people, replaced the wartime terminology of imperial subjects. A literal translation of *chikyu minzoku shugi* would be 'global nationalism,' but in the English version of the novel *The Human Revolution* it is translated as 'one-worldism.' In a similar vein, Theodore F. Lentz, the founder of the Peace Research Laboratory in 1945 in the US, used the term 'humatriotism' to describe 'a value which would emerge from rigorous research into human attitudes and personality' (Ramsbotham et al. 2008, 40). I believe that this attempt to coin a term to describe a sense of belonging to the whole of humanity is similar to Toda's declaration that he believed in 'one-worldism.'

It was during a panel discussion before several hundred Japanese young people on 17 February 1952 that Toda mentioned for the first time his belief in 'one-worldism.' He did not explain what he meant at the time, but simply mentioned the term at the end of his speech congratulating the young participants in the panel discussion.

In the novel *The Human Revolution*, Ikeda gives his own interpretation of Toda's use of the term, based on numerous conversations with Toda over the years. Toda's 'one-worldism' can be considered as a call for people to place priority on humanity instead of the state (Ikeda 2004a, 641). In other words, it can be seen as a normative statement emphasizing that people should dedicate themselves to humankind and not only to their own country (Ikeda 2004a, 641). I would like to suggest that in modern terms, Toda's idea of 'one-worldism' as defined by Ikeda corresponds to 'global citizenship.'

Declaration Calling for the Abolition of Nuclear Weapons (1957)

On 8 September 1957 Toda made a declaration[14] calling for the abolition of nuclear weapons, addressing an audience of 50,000 people. The occasion was the 'Eastern Japan Youth Division Sports Meet' (Ikeda 2004a, 1774) also called the 'Festival of Youth' held at Mitsuzawa Stadium in Yokohama. I believe that the sense of urgency pervading the declaration was due to the seriousness of the world situation, but also to the degradation of Toda's personal health. He knew he did not have much longer to live and wanted to share his greatest concerns with young people. Toda poured his entire life into a very short text of about one page, which contained just a few ideas, but has had a lasting impact as it continues to be referred to as the point of departure of the Soka Gakkai and the SGI's activities for peace, including nuclear disarmament. The content of the declaration can be summarized in the following way.

Toda expresses his joy at being able to admire the young participants' enthusiasm, and he now wants to share the foremost of his 'final instructions for the future.' Toda reaffirms that the religious mission of the Soka Gakkai is *kosen-rufu* (world peace through individual happiness), but on this occasion he shares his ideas concerning the testing of nuclear weapons.

He attacks the problem at its root, 'to rip out the claws that are hidden in the very depths of this issue.' To send a clear message that there can be no real victors in a nuclear confrontation, he advocates the death penalty for anybody using nuclear weapons, regardless of their nationality or whether their country wins or loses the war. Toda was consistently opposed to the death penalty, as will be clarified later in this section. In my opinion, by mentioning the death penalty, Toda was establishing a difference between temporary military victory and the fundamental victory of human beings in a philosophical and ethical sense. Toda often spoke of the difference between relative and absolute happiness. Relative happiness comes with the fulfillment of a wish or the accomplishment of a goal. It comes and goes based on the events in our lives. On the contrary, absolute happiness is completely self-motivated, and depends only on the quality of one's character – the amount of courage, wisdom and compassion one is able to generate. If winning the war is followed immediately by a death sentence, it cannot be called a meaningful victory.

In the declaration, when Toda uses words such as 'victorious,' 'winning side' or 'conquer the world,' he is talking about military victory, which is to be placed in the same category as relative happiness, a transient phenomenon that can be called relative victory, which depends on defeating an enemy. In contrast, absolute victory as a human being would mean the capacity to live one's life fully and enable others to do the same. To understand Toda's meaning better, one can use the image of a supreme judge, an allegory of justice, handing out death sentences to the leaders of countries that would use nuclear weapons, symbolizing the utter defeat of the human spirit.

He explains that 'we, the citizens of the world, have an inviolable right to live' and that anyone who threatens other people's lives is 'a devil incarnate, a fiend, a monster.' Toda concludes his declaration by encouraging the members of the Soka Gakkai youth division 'to spread this foremost appeal of mine to the entire world.'

Ikeda recently commented:

> While we may find such expressions as 'devil incarnate,' 'fiend' or 'monster' disconcerting, Toda's main intent in the use of such language was to expose the aberrant nature of nuclear deterrence. For at

the heart of deterrence theory lies a cold and inhuman readiness to sacrifice vast numbers of people in order to realize one's own security or dominance. He was, at the same time, pressing political leaders to reflect on their assumptions and attitudes (Ikeda 2009a, 4).

This declaration contains many important concepts that are useful for a systematization of Ikeda's philosophy of peace, showing that elements such as trust in ordinary people and the dignity of human life were already part of Toda's own thinking.

First, there is a *belief in civil society* and the power of ordinary people. This takes the form of both religious activities and non-religious awareness-raising. Toda admires the 'Soka Gakkai spirit' of the youth and reasserts that their religious mission is the achievement of *kosen-rufu*. However, in this declaration Toda wishes to transcend the religious context to speak of an issue that concerns all human beings. I believe that the fact that he wants the youth to spread the spirit of his declaration throughout the world originates in his belief in civil society, or 'common mortals,' one of his favorite expressions, meaning ordinary, real people. Toda is not waiting for governments to act; he is encouraging ordinary people to take the initiative in raising awareness concerning nuclear weapons.

Second, Toda *transcends the dichotomy of the Cold War* and sides with the whole of humanity. He condemns the use of nuclear weapons by anybody, regardless of the camp they might defend. His recommendation that the death penalty be used is problematic for a peace leader who advocates the 'right to live.' Toda had consistently shown his opposition to the death penalty based on his respect for the dignity of life, but this text presents an exception to the rule. In 1948 when seven 'Class A' Japanese war criminals were sentenced to death, Toda clearly stated his opposition to the death penalty (Ikeda 2004a, 1782). Against this background, it is reasonable to assume that Toda was using the extreme language of capital punishment for its rhetorical impact on his listeners, and to uproot a certain type of logic. Ikeda recently commented:

> As a Buddhist for whom respect for life was a core principle, Toda was adamantly opposed to the death penalty. His invocation here of capital punishment should therefore be understood as *an effort to undermine and uproot the logic that would justify the use of nuclear weapons.* For Toda, nuclear weapons, which fundamentally threaten humanity's right to survival, represented an 'absolute evil.' He was determined to counteract any attempt to justify them as a 'necessary evil' whose use might be viewed as an extension of conventional warfare (Ikeda 2009a, 5) (Italics added).

In the 1957 declaration, Toda wanted to attract attention to the seriousness of the situation and to the horror of the potential crime of using nuclear weapons. In the context of the Cold War, each camp was condemned in the strongest terms by the other, but each reserved the right to deploy nuclear weapons for deterrence. Toda wanted to overturn this logic. During the Toda Institute conference entitled 'The Challenge of Abolishing Nuclear Weapons' held in San Francisco on 8–9 September 2007 to commemorate the 50th anniversary of Toda's declaration, David Krieger, President of the Nuclear Age Peace Foundation (NAPF), affirmed his support for Toda's wording in the declaration. He stated that starting a nuclear war meant potentially annihilating entire civilizations, and perhaps human life on Earth itself. He mentioned that if Toda had recommended 'life imprisonment' for the perpe-trators of such a crime against humanity, his declaration would have sounded hollow (Krieger, 2007).

Third, Toda defines the root of the problem in terms of *the dignity of human life.* Based on Buddhist principles, Toda asserts that the desire to control others and use their lives for one's purpose lies at the origin of the nuclear arms race. The theory of deterrence is based on fear and mistrust, and on the human impulse to dominate others. For Toda this is the real problem, and based on his belief that 'we, the citizens of the world, have an inviolable right to live,' Toda severely condemns the human tendency to deny this right to others in order to protect one's own interests. This is why he describes people who have succumbed to this tendency as 'evil incarnate.'

The declaration can thus be framed in the overall context of this book, namely the hypothesis that the main concepts at the root of Ikeda's philosophy of peace, consistent with his mentor Toda's, can be identified as inner transformation, dialogue and global citizenship.

Toda's emphasis on the need to challenge the inner tendency to dominate others that threatens the dignity of human life is a major component of efforts towards inner transformation, and his greatest wish is 'to rip out the claws that are hidden in the very depths of this issue.' His belief in civil society and awareness-raising shows his trust in dialogue, and he expects the 50,000 participants in the Festival of Youth 'to spread this foremost appeal of mine to the entire world.' His ability to transcend the Cold War dichotomy is rooted in his belief in the need for global citizenship, as when he says, 'we, the citizens of the world, have an inviolable right to live.'

Since Toda's declaration was delivered 12 years after the Hiroshima and Nagasaki bombings, it is worth exploring briefly what Toda's reactions had been at the time, in that fateful summer of 1945. The Japanese population had been told that a 'new type of weapon' had been used by the enemy, but were not informed of the details. Because people a certain distance from the epicenter had not been burned where they were covered by white clothes, people were encouraged to wear white as protection against a possible attack. It is quite probable that Toda had not heard about the nuclear holocaust by 15 August, when the emperor publicly announced Japan's defeat. According to Ikeda, the same evening he immediately focused on organizing a correspondence education course in order to restart his business (Ikeda 2004a, 47).

In November 1948, after hearing the news that the International Military Tribunal of the Far East had sentenced seven war criminals to death, Toda had already formulated the essence of his 1957 declaration. Interestingly, his reactions about the atomic bombings are mixed with his opposition to the death penalty. The context of the 1948 Tokyo Tribunal sheds further light on the 1957 declaration. Ikeda (2004a) records Toda's words as follows:

> The judgment contains two inherent mistakes. First, the death penalty is absolutely futile. Life imprisonment is more proper. Killing another, even through the death penalty, goes against Buddhism.

> Second, those who dropped the atomic bombs should equally be found guilty. Whatever their reason may have been, the employment of atomic bombs was an act of evil, wasn't it? Whether one wins or loses the war, the claws of evil must be eradicated from the face of the world. These people should face the same penalty as the other war criminals (371).

To understand the reasons behind Toda's concern, it is necessary to take a brief look at the historical context. The first successful nuclear test, codenamed 'Trinity,' took place on 16 July 1945 in Alamogordo, New Mexico, US. Then on 6 and 9 August, the civilian populations of Hiroshima and Nagasaki were subjected to the first two (and hopefully the last) nuclear attacks in the history of humankind. After the end of World War II the US military carried on developing and testing more and more powerful nuclear weapons, hoping to keep a military edge through this new technology. At the same time there were several attempts to reach agreements on the international control of nuclear materials. For instance on 14 June 1946 the US presented the Baruch Plan before the United Nations Atomic Energy Commission. Six months later, the plan appeared dead (Arms Control Association 2006). On 29 August 1949 the Soviet Union successfully tested its first nuclear device and the two superpowers then became entangled in an accelerating nuclear arms race. Britain's first test was conducted on 3 October 1952. All other countries that joined the 'nuclear club' did so after Toda's declaration, for instance France (1960), China (1964) and India (1974).

A new type of device, the hydrogen bomb, was tested by the US on 1 November 1952 at Eniwetok Atoll in the Pacific, inaugurating the 'thermonuclear age.' This new weapon was 500 times more powerful than the 'Trinity' device. The contamination of a Japanese tuna fishing vessel, the *Daigo Fukuryu Maru* (Lucky Dragon No. 5) on 1 March 1954 struck the Japanese psyche much more than any of the initial tests performed by different countries before that. This accident was caused by nuclear fallout from the US Castle Bravo thermonuclear device test on Bikini Atoll, and it was later found out that about 100 other boats had been contaminated, as well as many inhabitants of the Marshall Islands. The Soviet Union tested its first thermonuclear bomb on 22 November 1955. On 21 August 1957 they succeeded in testing an intercontinental ballistic missile (ICBM) several years ahead of schedule. The missile, called R-7, carried a dummy warhead more than 5,600 kilometers. This meant they could launch a nuclear strike on virtually any city in the world. A second successful test took place on 7 September, the day before Toda's declaration. Was this just a coincidence? To what extent was Toda aware of the situation?

In an appendix to *The Challenge of Abolishing Nuclear Weapons* (Krieger 2009), Tatsushi Arai mentions a declaration delivered in Tokyo and points to a potential link with Toda's own:

> One of the most highly-publicized declarations that caught attention in Japan was the Tokyo Appeal on August 16, 1957, at the conclusion of the third international conference against nuclear and hydrogen bombs. The ten-day event attracted 9,000 participants from 22 countries who had gathered in Tokyo. The Appeal called for an immediate and unconditional cessation of nuclear and hydrogen bomb tests to be agreed upon by the three nuclear weapons countries. In preparation for his September 8 declaration, Toda must have studied public appeals of this nature, at least as a way of gauging the level of public interest in this subject (Arai in Krieger 2009, 246–47).

The United Nations Disarmament Subcommittee had convened on 18 March 1957 hoping to place a moratorium on the testing, manufacture and use of nuclear weapons, but it ended with no agreement on 6 September. It is also possible that Toda was aware of this failure on 7 September, the day before he delivered his declaration. Adding the fact that the Soviet Union's second successful ICBM test took place on 7 September, I would advance the hypothesis that Toda was very much aware of the situation when he wrote his declaration, and had grown impatient with the bickering between the superpowers concerning an issue that could determine the survival of the human species, regardless of national boundaries.

Voices against nuclear tests around the time of the Toda Declaration

Numerous voices opposing nuclear weapons appeared around the time of Toda's declaration, many in the spring and summer preceding it, and several others in the few months following it. Looking at the frequency and importance of those movements and declarations at the time, compared with any other period of two years, one can talk of a small 'axial age' of protests against nuclear weapons around 1957–58. Of course the first reactions date back to 6 August 1945.

On the day of the Hiroshima bombing, Norman Cousins wrote an editorial for the *Saturday Review* entitled 'Modern Man is Obsolete.' This immediate reaction against the inhumanity of nuclear weapons is considered by some as the starting point of the 'nuclear pacifism' movement in the US and the world (Katz 1987, 1–2).

Following World War II, as the Cold War developed, Japan chose to be completely dependent upon the US 'nuclear umbrella,' and this was formalized in the 1952 Security Treaty between the two countries. In the years after the occupation, the Japanese public was strongly against the use or presence of nuclear weapons on Japanese soil as a result of the Hiroshima and Nagasaki bombings. The irradiation of the Japanese fishing vessel Lucky Dragon No. 5 turned into a public outcry against atomic and nuclear weapons testing. On 28 July 1955 the US announced its intention to equip military bases in Japan with conventional missiles which could also be fitted with atomic warheads, but this sparked such public outrage that the Japanese government had to make assurances to the Diet that the missiles would not be equipped with nuclear warheads on Japanese territory. The Atomic Energy Basic Law adopted in December 1955 reflects the public sentiment, restricting the use of atomic energy to peaceful purposes. In 1957, Prime Minister Nobusuke Kishi stated that nuclear weapons were not technically prohibited by Article 9 of the Peace Constitution, but that both their use and introduction should be prohibited as a matter of national policy in accordance with the feelings of the Japanese public and for humanitarian reasons.

The history of UN efforts to oppose nuclear testing started in 1946 with the first resolution of the General Assembly of the United Nations to set up an Atomic Energy Commission. Its purpose was to make proposals for the peaceful uses of atomic energy and for the elimination of nuclear weapons. The Baruch Plan called for an international agency to control atomic power and weapons, but it was vetoed by the USSR in the Security Council, and the commission reached a major impasse in 1948. Then in 1952 a UN Disarmament Commission was formed under the Security Council.

In April 1954 India's Prime Minister Jawaharlal Nehru led the nonaligned nations in criticizing the US H-bomb tests in the Pacific, and on 15 July the Mainau Declaration drafted by two German scientists was circulated at a conference of Nobel Prize laureates in Lindau, Germany, and was signed by 52 Nobel laureates within a year.

From 7 to 11 July 1957, the first Pugwash Conference was organized by Bertrand Russell and Josef Rotblat in Canada, as a concrete response to the Russell-Einstein Manifesto released on 9 July 1955 in London. This initial conference was so successful that 'Pugwash Conferences on Science and World Affairs' and related meetings have been held at least once a year since then.

On 24 April 1957 Albert Schweitzer's 'A Declaration of Conscience' was broadcast worldwide from Oslo, Norway. He had been encouraged by Norman Cousins to speak out against nuclear weapons. Radio Oslo also broadcast Schweitzer's 'A Declaration of Conscience' on 28, 29 and 30 April 1958, and it was transmitted by 140 radio stations around the world. Many more wanted to do so but were forbidden by their governments to broadcast it, both in the East and West. From 1952 until his death in 1965 Schweitzer worked against nuclear tests and nuclear weapons with Albert Einstein and Bertrand Russell (ICAN 2008).

In June 1957 Linus Pauling wrote a petition that garnered signatures from 2,000 scientists when it was released to the press and sent to the White House. In 1958 Pauling wrote the book *No More War*, which warned against the harmful effects of radioactive fallout from nuclear weapons testing. On 15 January 1958 he handed UN Secretary General Dag Hammarskjöld a petition signed by 9,235 scientists, including 37 Nobel laureates, urging an international agreement to stop nuclear testing.

On 21 June 1957, 27 prominent US citizens met in New York City, responding to an invitation by Norman Cousins and Clarence Pickett, former secretary of the American Friends Service Committee. They launched a movement to focus US public opinion on the dangers of nuclear weapons testing. This was the origin of the group which made its debut on 15 November 1957 with an advertisement in the *New York Times*, called the National Committee for a Sane Nuclear Policy (SANE). The one-page ad, which called for the immediate suspension of nuclear testing by all nations, had a huge impact, and by the summer of 1958 SANE had some 25,000 members, becoming the largest peace group in the US. It was renamed Peace Action in 1993 and is still a prominent US peace movement today (Wittner 2007).

Toda thus joins the ranks of the numerous scholars and activists who made a public declaration against those weapons which he considered a product of the darkest side of human nature and of humankind. Other well-known compatriots were Hideki Yukawa, the Japanese Nobel laureate who signed the Russell-Einstein manifesto in 1955 and participated in the first Pugwash Conference in 1957. Also since 1947, the Mayor of Hiroshima has delivered a Peace Declaration on 6 August every year during the Peace Festival, except in 1950 when the festival was cancelled because of the outbreak of the Korean War in June.

It is worth mentioning the failure of a large-scale Japanese movement against nuclear weapons, the *Gensuikyo*, in order to understand Toda's sense of frustration and urgency even better. Horrified by the March 1954 Lucky Dragon No. 5 tragedy, a women's group in Suginami Ward, Tokyo, began a petition drive toward abolishing nuclear weapons. Their efforts led to the founding of the Japan Council for the Petition to Abolish Atomic and Hydrogen Bombs (Japan Council) in August 1954 (Ikeda 2001–7, 26). In September 1955 this group merged with the Japan Preparatory Committee for the World Congress against Atomic and Hydrogen Bombs (Japan Committee) to form the Japan Council against Atomic and Hydrogen Bombs (Gensuikyo), the largest Japanese organization in the nuclear abolition movement.

However, gradually the Japan Communist Party (JCP) and other groups started to dominate the Gensuikyo. Their goal was to orient the antinuclear weapons movement against the US, arguing that Soviet nuclear weapons possession and testing was only a peaceful defensive measure. This lack of neutrality in the struggle against nuclear weapons caused bitter infighting, mostly between the JCP, the Democratic Socialist Party and the Japan Socialist Party, eventually forcing the Gensuikyo to split into three groups within ten years, completely losing its momentum. In this context, I believe that by using terms such as 'evil incarnate' in his 1957 declaration, Toda wanted to focus on the fundamental issue, insisting that the horror of nuclear weapons was absolute and did not depend on who was willing to use them.

Toda's declaration is mentioned in such works as *The Challenge of Nuclear Weapons* (Krieger 2009) and Lawrence S. Wittner's *Resisting the Bomb* (Wittner 1997, 40). In the second work, it is grouped together with declarations made also in 1957 by the Central Committee of the World Council of Churches, a major Protestant federation, on 5 August, and the statement issued by Pope Pius XII on 22 December of the same year. I believe that because of its depth, clarity and enduring relevance, it deserves more recognition outside of the Soka Gakkai and the SGI, where it serves as the basis for activities for nuclear abolition and is a symbol of Toda's legacy for peace:

> In 1975, Soka Gakkai youth members collected 10 million signatures for nuclear abolition which were presented to the UN secretary-general. In 1978, SGI President Ikeda submitted a proposal on nuclear disarmament to the First Special Session of the UN General Assembly on Disarmament, and in 1982 the exhibition 'Nuclear Arms: Threat to Our World' opened at the UN head-quarters and began to tour different countries. Continuing Toda's legacy, in 1998, Japanese youth members collected over 13 million signatures in support of the Abolition 2000 campaign calling for the abolition of nuclear weapons (*SGI Quarterly* 2000).

There have been numerous other exhibitions since then, and in September 2007, to commemorate the 50th anniversary of Toda's declaration, the Toda Institute co-organized a conference entitled 'The Challenge of Abolishing Nuclear Weapons,' already mentioned above. The Soka Gakkai, the SGI and the Toda Institute continue to promote nuclear disarmament based on the original spirit of Toda's 1957 declaration. On 8 September 2009 Ikeda published a new and detailed proposal for nuclear abolition in the *Seikyo Shimbun* newspaper, entitled *Building Global Solidarity Toward Nuclear Abolition* (Ikeda 2009a).

Conclusion: Josei Toda and peace theory

I would like to suggest that in Toda's speeches and actions we see clearly the pattern that I believe underpins Ikeda's own philosophy of peace: first inner transformation, then dialogue and finally global citizenship, leading to the appearance of elements of a global civilization.

From a religious viewpoint, Toda showed that it is possible for one indi-vidual to come out of prison with nothing but faith in Nichiren Buddhism and in humanity, and to establish an organization of 750,000 households within 13 years. This is the foremost example of what Toda and Ikeda call the human revolution.

From a secular point of view, transcending the context of a single religious movement, Toda also showed that it was possible to advance towards peace by focusing on the inner transformation of each individual, starting with oneself.

Toda's favorite technique to promote the Soka Gakkai movement was dialogue. He spent an inordinate amount of time talking to individuals, and this was at the heart of his activities as the leader of a burgeoning grassroots movement. It is through dialogue that Toda educated Ikeda as his successor, and it is he who further developed the unique system of propagation and sharing of Buddhist philosophy in small discussion groups (*zadankai*) which had been initiated by his mentor Makiguchi. Toda believed that to be consistent with the principle of human revolution, the only way to propagate Buddhism was through dialogue.

Finally, as early as his twenties Toda showed strong interest in the concept of global citizenship, as mentioned at the beginning of this chapter. According to Ikeda, at the end of his life, sometime during the week following 16 March 1958, Toda dreamed he went to Mexico:

> It became increasingly rare for Toda [to] get up from his futon, even just to sit up. But he continued to call Shin'ichi [Ikeda] to his side each day to talk with him. One morning when Shin'ichi went to Toda's room, Toda called out cheerfully from his bed, 'Shin'ichi, yesterday I dreamt I went to Mexico.' (. . .) 'They were all waiting. Everyone was waiting. They were all seeking Nichiren Daishonin's Buddhism. I want to go – to travel the world on a journey for kosen-rufu.' (. . .) 'Shin'ichi, you must live! You must live as long as you can and travel the globe!' (Ikeda 2004a, 1901).

This appeal at the end of his life was consistent with Toda's passion for the peace of all humanity. As mentioned above, his use of the word 'one-worldism' was the expression of a compassionate love embracing all of humanity, in contrast to the narrow interest for a single country that characterizes nationalism.

Toda's initial meeting with Ikeda was crucial for the latter, but of course it was also of utmost importance for the former. I would like to assert that Ikeda's philosophy of peace revolves around the mentor-disciple relationship, which I consider as a specific form of dialogue, deeply linked to inner transformation and global citizenship.

CHAPTER 4

Nichiren Buddhism: Principles and Values for the Twenty-first Century

There can be no doubt that all people, from the ruler on down to the general populace, rejoice in and desire the stability of the nation and the peace of the world (Nichiren 1999, 107).

Though I may sound presumptuous, my most fervent wish is to realize the security and peace of the entire land (Ibid., 200).

There can be no doubt about the sutra passages that say, 'This sutra can fulfill their desires, as a clear cool pond can satisfy all those who are thirsty,' and 'They will enjoy peace and security in their present existence and good circumstances in future existences' (Ibid., 412).

How reassuring it is to know that not only the people here, but those of India, China, and the entire land of Jambudvipa will be able to attain Buddhahood! (Ibid., 482).

More valuable than treasures in a storehouse are the treasures of the body, and the treasures of the heart are the most valuable of all (Ibid., 851).

In the systematization of Ikeda's philosophy of peace presented here, the principle of inner transformation is the starting point, and I believe that this is consistent with the emphasis on self-mastery found in Buddhism.

The principles of the Four Noble Truths (Sanskrit *chatur-arya-satya*)[1] and the Eightfold Path (Skt *arya-astanga-marga*)[2] are fundamental to Buddhist philosophy, and they emphasize the importance of the inner world, of perspectives and attitudes. As a result, Buddhism encourages the cultivation of qualities and virtues. In *Peace is Every Step: The Path to Mindfulness in Everyday Life* (1992), the Vietnamese Zen Buddhist monk and peace activist Thich Nhat Hanh wrote that we 'only need to be awake' in order to experience 'peace, joy and serenity,' emphasizing the crucial importance of the inner world:

> We can smile, breathe, walk, and eat our meals in a way that allows us to be in touch with the abundance of happiness that is available. We are very good at preparing to live, but not very good at living. We know how to sacrifice ten years for a diploma, and we are willing to work very hard to get a job, a car, a house, and so on. But we have difficulty remembering that we are alive in the present moment, the only moment there is for us to be alive. Every breath we take, every step we make, can be filled with peace, joy and serenity. We need only to be awake, alive in the present moment (5).

In *The Art of Happiness* (1998), the Dalai Lama also emphasizes the importance of our attitude and outlook, and adds that the quality of 'inner discipline' is one way of achieving personal transformation:

> I believe that happiness can be achieved through training the mind. (. . .) I am not referring to 'mind' merely as one's cognitive ability or intellect. Rather, I'm using the term in the sense of the Tibetan word *Sem*, which has a much broader meaning, closer to 'psyche' or 'spirit'; it includes intellect and feeling, heart and mind. By bringing about a certain inner discipline, we can undergo a transformation of our attitude, our entire outlook and approach to living (14–15).

Along the same lines, Ikeda suggests that 'if we discipline ourselves well, we will obtain a master like no other,' in a lecture delivered in 1994 at Moscow State University entitled 'The Magnificent Cosmos,' in which he highlighted the connection between the teachings of Shakyamuni Buddha[3] and the concept of human revolution:

> After Japan's defeat, the established values seemed to have been wiped out or turned upside down. In that time of spiritual desolation, Toda preached that the people must return to the very

beginning and recreate their own inner human revolution. His teaching brought alive Shakyamuni's observation that we are our own masters, as no one else can ever be; if we discipline ourselves well, we will obtain a master like no other, which in our time can be called human revolution (Ikeda 1996a, 47).

I consider the concept of human revolution at the core of Toda and Ikeda's philosophy of peace as a specific type of inner transformation. The term 'revolution' implies that it is not limited to one individual, but that it spreads from person to person throughout society. Also, whereas inner transformation can be carried out through a number of different means, the term 'human revolution' as used by Toda and Ikeda refers specifically to personal development based on Buddhist practice. I believe this statement by the thirteenth-century priest Nichiren, whose school of Buddhism the Soka Gakkai considers the basis of its practice, sums up a fundamental aspect of the human revolution:

> More valuable than treasures in a storehouse are the treasures of the body, and the treasures of the heart are the most valuable of all. From the time you read this letter on, strive to accumulate the treasures of the heart! (Nichiren 1999, 851).

This passage emphasizes that in Buddhism the cultivation of human qualities is more important than the attainment of material goods or the possession of natural talents, but it does not specify what kind of 'treasures of the heart' one needs to develop. I would like to suggest that the virtues of courage, wisdom and compassion are highly appropriate based on the following passage from Ikeda's 1996 lecture at Columbia University entitled 'Education for Global Citizenship':

> I think I can state with confidence that the following are essential elements of global citizenship[:]
>
> — The wisdom to perceive the interconnectedness of all life and living.
>
> — The courage not to fear or deny difference; but to respect and strive to understand people of different cultures, and to grow from encounters with them.
>
> — The compassion to maintain an imaginative empathy that reaches beyond one's immediate surroundings and extends to those suffering in distant places.

The all-encompassing interrelatedness that forms the core of the Buddhist worldview can provide a basis, I feel, for the concrete realization of these qualities of wisdom, courage and compassion (Ikeda 2001a, 100–101).

I interpret this passage to mean that for Ikeda, by becoming aware of the principle of interrelatedness, also called interdependence, interconnectedness or dependent origination[4] (Skt *pratitya-samutpada*), people can enhance their courage, wisdom and compassion. These human qualities are recognized as essential by many religions and philosophies and provide the basis for my understanding of the concept of inner transformation.

In the same speech, Ikeda further develops his argument in a passage where he clarifies the links between courage, wisdom and compassion. This has become the starting point of my understanding of Buddhism and of Ikeda's philosophy of peace:

In the Buddhist view, wisdom and compassion are intimately linked and mutually reinforcing. Compassion in Buddhism does not involve the forcible suppression of our natural emotions, our likes and dislikes. Rather, it is to realize that even those whom we dislike have qualities that can contribute to our lives and can afford us opportunities to grow in our own humanity. Further, it is the compassionate desire to find ways of contributing to the well-being of others that gives rise to limitless wisdom.

Buddhism teaches that both good and evil are potentialities that exist in all people. Compassion consists in the sustained and courageous effort to seek out the good in all people, whoever they may be, however they may behave. It means striving, through sustained engagement, to cultivate the positive qualities in oneself and in others. Engagement, however, requires courage. There are all too many cases in which compassion, owing to a lack of courage, remains mere sentiment.

Buddhism calls a person who embodies these qualities of wisdom, courage and compassion, who strives without cease for the happi-ness of others, a bodhisattva. In this sense, it could be said that the bodhisattva provides an ancient precedent and modern exemplar for the global citizen (Ikeda 2001a, 101–2).

In his dialogue with Lokesh Chandra, a well-known scholar of Buddhism and Indian arts, Ikeda shows the direct links between the Buddhist concept of the 'Three Virtues'[5] (Skt *tri-guna, traigunya, guna*) and the three qualities:

> What kind of practice will help actualise a world in which the diversity and solidarity of humankind can blossom? Nichiren expounded on the three virtues of sovereign, teacher and parent as criteria for humanity to follow. (. . .) In my speech at Columbia University, I spoke about the Bodhisattva Way as one criterion for being a global citizen in the 21st century. I identified three qualities that make up a global citizen.
>
> First is the courage to embrace diversity with respect and understanding, treating all people equally without regard to race, ethnicity, or cultural difference. The virtue of the sovereign, which is to protect the people, can be explained in this way.
>
> The second quality of a global citizen is the wisdom to become deeply aware of the interrelationship of all living beings. This corresponds to the virtue of the teacher, who interacts with individuals to help develop their character and bring forth the potential in each one.
>
> The third quality is the parental virtue of compassion in which all people are nurtured and raised with the same affection that one would have towards one's own child. This ability to empathize with the suffering of others is felt with the same sense of solidarity with those in close proximity as well as those who are distant (Ikeda and Chandra 2009, 214–15).

In Ikeda's literature for children, there is a special emphasis on courage, persistence and hope, as well as friendship and kindness. In *The Snow Country Prince* (1990): 'Whatever happens, don't give up' (8); in *The Cherry Tree* (1991): 'But I never gave up hope – and you see I was right!' (14). In these passages from *Kanta and the Deer* (1997b), the first praises the courage and hope displayed by the deer, and the second the power of friendship, compassion and kindness:

> The deer fought hard to escape the hunters' bullets and to survive the cold northern winters. They may not have been big and strong like the bears and wolves, but they had hope. They never gave up. Kanta admired the deer's courage (20).

If he had been struggling only for himself, Kanta might have given up right then and there. But because he knew that Poyu [the deer] needed his help, he kept trying and trying. Friendship has the power to give you strength. It also makes you want to be kind. And it can give you the will to carry on (42).

I find these stories quite effective in that they convey deep philosophical values. They assert the importance of hope, friendship and kindness; simple feelings that can facilitate the daily process of transforming our inner world which is at the core of the Buddhist teachings. What follows is my attempt, as someone trained in the Western rationalist tradition, to offer a contemporary, secular and psychological interpretation of some principles found in Nichiren Buddhism and referenced by Ikeda in his writings.

The first is the Three Virtues mentioned above. The second, 'Respect for all life,'[6] is found in the Lotus Sutra,[7] one of the most important canons of Mahayana[8] Buddhism which serves as the textual foundation of Nichiren's philosophy. The third, the 'Oneness of Life and its Environment,'[9] offers interesting links between inner transformation and world peace.

Confidence in the human potential: the Three Virtues

The Japanese priest Nichiren (1222–82) devoted his life to a revitalization of Buddhist philosophy during the Kamakura[10] period (1185–1333). At that time, the country was governed by a military dictatorship, and natural disasters were frequent. There were numerous floods, earthquakes, droughts, epidemics and famines. Moreover, the Mongols under Kublai Khan attempted to invade the country twice, in 1274 and 1281, but failed both times due to heavy storms that sank most of their warships.[11]

How can Nichiren's emphasis on the 'treasures of the heart' in such harsh circumstances be explained in modern terms? My understanding is that Nichiren wanted to reassess the purpose of Buddhism in these troubled times in order to help people come to terms and effectively deal with challenging conditions. His main goal was to explain how human life could have meaning in such circumstances, and how people could positively affect society and the environment by initiating an inner change. Emphasizing the primacy of the inner world, he wrote:

> You must never think that any of the eighty thousand sacred teach-ings of Shakyamuni Buddha's lifetime or any of the Buddhas and bodhisattvas of the ten directions and three existences are outside yourself. Your practice of the Buddhist teachings will not relieve

you of the sufferings of birth and death in the least unless you perceive the true nature of your life. If you seek enlightenment outside
yourself, then your performing even ten thousand practices and ten
thousand good deeds will be in vain. It is like the case of a poor man
who spends night and day counting his neighbor's wealth but gains
not even half a coin (3).

I believe that for Nichiren, the validity of Buddhism was to be shown through
the thoughts, words and actions of those practicing it. In a famous passage, he
wrote: 'The purpose of the appearance in this world of Shakyamuni Buddha,
the lord of teachings, lies in his behavior as a human being' (852). He further defined this ideal attitude in the following passage, referring to himself
specifically in terms of the Three Virtues: 'I, Nichiren, am sovereign, teacher,
and father and mother to all the people of Japan' (287).

I believe that this concept is fundamental to an understanding and practice
of inner transformation and has universal implications beyond the confines of
a specific religion. Nichiren's injunction to 'accumulate the treasures of the
heart' suggests the effort to become ever more courageous, compassionate and
wise while facing all kinds of circumstances, trying to emulate the qualities
of an ideal sovereign, parent and teacher.

Respect for all life: the main message of the Lotus Sutra

A number of scholars have recognized the importance of the central message
of the Lotus Sutra, such as John R. Mayer:

> When in the *Lotus Sutra* we learn that Buddha nature is recognized
> in all, be they disciples such as Shariputra, great bodhisattvas,
> relatives of Buddha Shakyamuni, such as Rahula, or indeed, villains
> such as Devadatta, we can see the universality of compassion and
> generosity (Mayer 1998).

There are many canonical texts in Buddhism, and a wide range of interpretations concerning what the historical Buddha, Shakyamuni, actually taught and
said. There was no writing system in India at the time, and most of his teachings were transmitted orally by his disciples for centuries before they were put
down in writing. This is also the case for the Lotus Sutra. There is no certainty
concerning its origins, as renowned translator Burton Watson (2002) writes:

> We do not know where or when the Lotus Sutra was composed, or
> in what language. Probably it was initially formulated in some local

dialect of India or Central Asia and then later put into Sanskrit to lend it greater respectability. All we can say for certain about the date of its composition is that it was already in existence by 255 CE, when the first Chinese translation of it was made. It was translated into Chinese several times subsequently, but it is through the version done in 406 by the Central Asian scholar-monk Kumarajiva that it has become widely known and read in China and the other countries within the Chinese cultural sphere of influence. This version has been universally acknowledged as the most authoritative and felicitous in language (xvi).

The version of the Lotus Sutra used by Nichiren was the above-mentioned translation from Sanskrit to Chinese made by Kumarajiva (344–413) in 406. Nichiren asserts that it was the most accurate: 'With the exception of one man, the Tripitaka Master Kumarajiva, all of these translators have made errors of some kind' (554). Thus, among all translations, Kumarajiva's work was the concrete basis for Nichiren's teachings, and the textual foundation of the Buddhist lineage extending to Makiguchi, Toda and Ikeda.

There is a rich tradition of interpreting the meaning of the Lotus Sutra, which I will not attempt to review here. Rather, the interpretation presented here focuses on its description of the inner aspects of human life and its significance for peace research. It is based on the translation Burton Watson made of Kumarajiva's Chinese version (Watson 1993) and is focused on three important symbolic events in this work: the appearance of the Treasure Tower, the enlightenment of the Dragon King's Daughter and the emergence of the Bodhisattvas of the Earth.

Regarding the first, while Shakyamuni Buddha is preaching to countless living beings who have come from throughout the universe, a huge treasure tower adorned with seven kinds of jewels appears from beneath the earth, and the whole assembly is lifted up in the air.

Several extraordinary scenes then take place: the eight-year-old daughter of the Dragon King Sagara, for instance, becomes a Buddha instantly, showing that women can attain Buddhahood just as men can, contradicting the prevalent notion that women first had to become men in another lifetime in order to reach enlightenment. She actually does become a man, but only for an instant.

Shakyamuni then entrusts the task of sharing the message of universal Buddhahood to the 'Bodhisattvas of the Earth.' After the teachings have been transferred to each participant, the Treasure Tower recedes back underneath the earth, and all present return to their respective lands and galaxies, bringing home the wonderful revelation they just heard.

Nichiren gave this advice concerning the best way to interpret Shakyamuni's teachings in a passage mentioned above:

> You must never think that any of the eighty thousand sacred teachings of Shakyamuni Buddha's lifetime or any of the Buddhas and bodhisattvas of the ten directions and three existences are outside yourself (3).

Working from this kind of interior, psychologized reading of the Lotus Sutra, one way to understand its narrative is to start from the point of view that the millions of living beings gathering around Shakyamuni represent the myriads of thoughts that occur in an unfocussed mind. Once a person starts meditating,[12] it is possible to reach full concentration, and I believe that the appearance of the Treasure Tower may be a symbol for this.

In this state one feels at one with life itself, full of joy and confidence, and a natural urge to share this awakening with other living beings arises, symbolized by the appearance of the Bodhisattvas of the Earth. Once all the psychological functions, thoughts and desires have been united in the compassionate goal of helping others, one is ready to start sharing this awakening with people in the real world and contribute to their happiness. This is represented by the Treasure Tower going back beneath the earth.

My interpretation of the complex story told in the 28 chapters of the Lotus Sutra focuses on inner peace as a point of departure for implementing concrete actions towards world peace. Ikeda describes this state of intense concentration, called *samadhi* in Sanskrit, as follows:

> A *samadhi* is a state of life that is abundant in wisdom, a state of inner peace. It indicates a rock-solid condition that nothing can perturb. From this inner peace, the great song of the spirit capable of moving people's hearts surges forth. Inner peace is not born of indolence. It is exactly the opposite (Ikeda et al. 2003–VI, 45).

The transformation of the female character named the 'Dragon Girl' symbolizes the fact that all women can attain Buddhahood. In India at the time when Shakyamuni was sharing his teachings, women were heavily discriminated against, and it was believed that they had first to be reincarnated as men before they could attain Buddhahood. I find it interesting that the text of the Lotus Sutra seems to be offering a way to declare the equality of people of different genders while trying to avoid a direct confrontation with the customs and traditions of the time. In the following excerpts, the first passage has Shariputra justify why women cannot attain Buddhahood:

At that time Shariputra said to the dragon girl, 'You suppose that
in this short time you have been able to attain the unsurpassed way.
But this is difficult to believe. Why? Because a woman's body is
soiled and defiled, not a vessel for the Law. How could you attain
the unsurpassed bodhi? The road to Buddhahood is long and far-
stretching. Only after one has spent immeasurable kalpas pursuing
austerities, accumulating deeds, practicing all kinds of paramitas,
can one finally achieve success. Moreover, a woman is subject to the
five obstacles. First, she cannot become a Brahma heavenly king.
Second, she cannot become the king Shakra. Third, she cannot
become a devil king. Fourth, she cannot become a wheel-turning
sage king. Fifth, she cannot become a Buddha. How then could a
woman like you be able to attain Buddhahood so quickly?' (Watson
1993, 188).

Second, the dragon girl contradicts Shariputra's statement and affirms that she
can actually attain Buddhahood quickly:

At that time the dragon girl had a precious jewel worth as much
as the thousand-million-fold world which she presented to the
Buddha. The Buddha immediately accepted it. The dragon girl
said to Bodhisattva Wisdom Accumulated and to the venerable one,
Shariputra, 'I presented the precious jewel and the World-Honored
One accepted it – was that not quickly done?' They replied,
'Very quickly!' The girl said, 'Employ your supernatural powers
and watch me attain Buddhahood. It will be even quicker than
that!' (188).

Finally, the dragon girl does attain Buddhahood almost instantly, but she still
has to become a man first, albeit briefly:

At that time the members of the assembly all saw the dragon girl
in the space of an instant change into a man and carry out all the
practices of a bodhisattva, immediately proceeding to the Spotless
World of the south, taking a seat on a jeweled lotus, and attaining
impartial and correct enlightenment. With the thirty-two features
and the eighty characteristics, he expounded the wonderful Law for
all living beings everywhere in the ten directions (188).

In this way there was no frontal attack on tradition (she had to become a
man first) but at the same time the Lotus Sutra asserts that women can attain

Buddhahood in this lifetime without having to be reincarnated, and can do so quickly, 'in the space of an instant.'

Nichiren confirmed that this passage was a metaphor for the enlightenment of all women: 'When she [the dragon girl] attained Buddhahood, this does not mean simply that one person did so. It reveals the fact that all women will attain Buddhahood' (269).

In the same chapter, it is also said that the evil Devadatta, who had committed serious crimes including an attempt on the Buddha's life, will attain Buddhahood without fail. I interpret this as meaning that no human being is forever good or bad, but that each person is capable of self-improvement and inner transformation. This is a crucial message affirming the equality and dignity of all human beings, opposing any form of discrimination.

Hiroshi Kanno asserts that the three human qualities of courage, wisdom and compassion were already highlighted in the Lotus Sutra. His starting point is the concept of 'eighteen unshared properties' found in the third chapter of the Lotus Sutra:

> The two main qualities of a Buddha are basically wisdom and compassion, as described in these eighteen unshared properties. Unshakeable confidence and imperturbability may be added to the basic qualities of wisdom and compassion. Since the importance of compassion might give an impression of gentleness, perhaps we should add courage to this list of basic qualities. 'Exerting oneself bravely and vigorously,' as given in the Expedient Means Chapter [of the Lotus Sutra], represents in effect the practice of showing courage (Kanno 2004, 107).

By emphasizing the inherent potential of each human being for self-improvement, the Lotus Sutra and Nichiren Buddhism affirm the preciousness of each individual as well as the principle of the dignity of all life. This is essential if one is to trust that inner transformation, dialogue and global citizenship are possible, and that ordinary people can be empowered to contribute to world peace by practicing them.

The oneness of life and its environment: pathways from inner to global peace

Buddhist doctrine affirms that life and its environment are one. This contradicts the body-mind and subject-object dualisms that have been prevalent in the West at least since René Descartes. I also find that this principle has important implications for the possibilities of world peace through inner transformation. From the Buddhist assumption that life and its environment are one, it follows that a key reason we do not have world peace is because we lack inner peace.

More specifically, since we are often the victims of negative tendencies such as greed, anger and foolishness or ignorance, these negative impulses must find collective expressions as catastrophes at the local and global levels. One way to reduce the frequency and magnitude of these calamities is to reduce the power of the negative tendencies, and this can be done by letting positive human qualities flourish. It follows that inner transformation can directly influence a positive change in the lives of the people around us, then in our communities and eventually in the whole of humanity. While couched in rational language, the above explanation is steeped in Buddhist principles. Let us examine them in turn.

Based on the principle of the Oneness of Life and its Environment, the fact that there are catastrophes in the world must come from the impurities in people's hearts. In Buddhism, the most negative tendencies of people are known as greed, anger and foolishness, collectively known as the Three Poisons (Skt *akusala-mula*).[13] If this is the case, people need to find an antidote for the Three Poisons.

According to Yoichi Kawada, one way to overcome them is to generate the courage, wisdom and compassion symbolized by the Three Virtues (Kawada 2008) and this point was confirmed by Tomohiro Matsuda (Matsuda 2009). I would like to suggest that an approach that starts from inner transformation enables one to enjoy a broader and more inclusive perspective transcending the smaller self, the ego preoccupied with selfish needs. This in turn can make dialogue with people of different backgrounds much easier and rewarding.

In a lecture on Nichiren's letter entitled 'On Attaining Buddhahood in this Lifetime,' Ikeda confirmed the importance of overcoming the Three Poisons for the sake of peace:

> Without surmounting the fundamental human delusions of greed, anger, and foolishness, we will not be able to solve the many problems that the world faces today, including the preoccupation with economic growth, politics that are devoid of humanism, international conflicts, warfare, growing disparity between rich and poor, and rampant discrimination. One conclusion from my dialogues with leading thinkers is that the only real solution is for human beings themselves to change, that the sole key lies in 'human revolution' (Ikeda 2006b, 77).

I believe that the three qualities of wisdom, courage and compassion mentioned throughout this chapter are an excellent antidote against the three poisons.

Praising the awakening of the famous Indian King Ashoka[14] in an article entitled 'Sustainable Development: Transform Self to Heal the Earth,' Ikeda wrote:

> As a political leader, Ashoka demonstrated the power of enlightened
> policy choices. But even more moving is the depth and intensity of
> his inner, personal transformation. The bloodstained tyrant became
> a monarch of humanity and peace. What Buddhism refers to as the
> 'three poisons' – greed, anger and ignorance – were transmuted into
> the virtues of wisdom and compassion (Ikeda 2009c).

Some additional links between Nichiren Buddhism and Ikeda's Philosophy of Peace

Concerning inner transformation, in the treatise 'On Establishing the Correct
Teaching for the Peace of the Land,' Nichiren wrote: 'you must quickly
reform the tenets that you hold in your heart' (25). I interpret this passage as
meaning that Nichiren asserted the power of each individual to change their
own destiny and that of the society around them, in virtue of their capacity to
strengthen and manifest the inner potential called Buddhahood, characterized
by boundless courage, wisdom and compassion.

While Nichiren's treatise was directed at the person wielding the highest
actual political authority in Japanese society at the time, this statement can
also be read as placing the responsibility for peace and prosperity firmly into
the hands of ordinary people willing to 'reform the tenets' that they hold in
their hearts. He had no doubt that his contemporaries could overcome the
hardships of the Kamakura era, and could even create a new history through
their own efforts. All these ideas are at the root of Toda and Ikeda's concept
of human revolution and inner transformation. The principles of the Three
Virtues, respect for all life and the oneness of life and its environment all point
to an affirmation of the potential of human beings for inner transformation.

Nichiren also showed his belief that dialogue was the best way to share
this empowering philosophy with others, never refusing to engage others
in debate[15] or conversations, while refusing to yield 'so long as persons of
wisdom do not prove my teachings to be false' (280).

Concerning the concept of dialogue, in order to spread his teachings
throughout Japan, harsh as the times were, Nichiren never bore arms nor used
physical violence. In a lecture delivered at Harvard University in 1993 entitled
'Mahayana Buddhism and Twenty-first-Century Civilization,' Ikeda said:

> Always unarmed in the chronically violent Japan of his time, he
> relied exclusively and unflinchingly on the power of persuasion

and nonviolence. (. . .) The following passage, written upon his exile to a distant island from which none was expected to return, typifies his lionesque tone: 'Whatever obstacles I might encounter, so long as men [persons] of wisdom do not prove my teachings to be false, I will never yield!' Nichiren's faith in the power of language was absolute. If more people were to pursue dialogue in an equally unrelenting manner, the inevitable conflicts of human life would surely find easier resolution. Prejudice would yield to empathy and war would give way to peace (Ikeda 1996b, 156).

Many of Nichiren's treatises take the form of a dialogue. For instance the major treatise 'On Establishing the Correct Teaching for the Peace of the Land' mentioned above is written as a conversation between two people. One is a traveler, probably representing Hojo Tokiyori, the retired regent of the Kamakura shogunate, and the other is the host, Nichiren himself. Masahiro Kobayashi comments:

Even if the social standing (. . .) [of] the most powerful leader of the nation and a nameless priest (. . .) [are] different, or even if two people hold differing views concerning religion, if their wish for peace remains intact then a basis for dialogue can be established. The fact that Nichiren uses the format of a dialogue between a Buddhist and a political leader to present his case shows his understanding of the power of dialogue as a means to effect change, and the starting point for this treatise is a discussion about peace and how to achieve it (Kobayashi 2007, 29).

It must be noted that Nichiren was also strict concerning the teachings of other Buddhist schools which he considered erroneous. I believe that since he was convinced that only the Lotus Sutra, with its message of the dignity of each human being, was the correct teaching, he was concerned about the potentially negative impact of other teachings. He therefore did not mince his words in his debates and refutations. He was ready to discuss Buddhist doctrine with anybody and was not dogmatic about imposing his teachings on others.

Here I would like to note parenthetically that Nichiren has not always been used as a model for inner transformation, dialogue and global citizenship. I believe that Makiguchi, Toda and Ikeda's emphasis on the humanism inherent in Nichiren Buddhism has a lot to do with their own compassion, cosmopolitanism and desire for world peace. Nichiren's works include more than 400 letters and treatises, and they deal with many varied topics. Among conflicting interpretations, his teachings have sometimes been used for just the reverse of peace and understanding, to serve narrow nationalistic and militarist interests.

In *Hirohito and the Making of Modern Japan* (2001), Herbert Bix explains the development of the Japanese national polity, or *kokutai*, in the 1920s:

> Centered on the imperial house, *kokutai* meant the best possible principles of Japanese state and society. As dissatisfaction with society deepened, the belief spread that reform could be achieved by utilizing the emperor's authority (Bix 2001, 10).

Bix then states the role of some Nichiren believers in the strengthening of *kokutai*:

> One particularly influential form of millenarian *kokutai* thought that flourished during the 1920s was expounded for urban, middle-class audiences by nationalist groups within Nichiren Buddhism. Tanaka Chigaku, the spiritual leader of one of these groups, was deeply hostile to Taisho democracy. Tanaka linked Nichiren to the expansion of the Japanese empire and made 'clarification of the *kokutai*' his lifelong theme. (. . .) The nationalistic Nichiren movement thus figures as an important catalyst in generating the phenomenon of Japanese ultranationalism (168–69).

It is noteworthy that two decades after Tanaka advocated his imperial interpretation promoting the 'nationalistic Nichiren movement,' Makiguchi and Toda were imprisoned, and Makiguchi lost his life, for opposing the very Japanese ultranationalism which Tanaka helped to bring about.

Before closing the parenthesis, I would like to show one of the many reasons why I believe there is a complete incompatibility between the 'nationalistic Nichiren movement' and the SGI's interpretation of Nichiren Buddhism. Bix writes: 'Like many other conservatives who took democracy as the enemy during the 1920s and 1930s, Tanaka added hatred of Jews to his agenda (. . .)' (168). In contrast, it is the Soka Gakkai under the leadership of Ikeda that organized the very first exhibition revealing the reality of the Holocaust to the Japanese public. Organized in collaboration with the Simon Wiesenthal Center, it has been viewed by more than two million Japanese since it first opened in May 1994.[16]

From the point of view of Ikeda's philosophy of peace, Nichiren's teachings are first and foremost considered as a source of encouragement to 'strive to accumulate the treasures of the heart,' which I interpret as the struggle to bring out inner qualities through self-improvement. The SGI's interpretation of Nichiren's writings is not the only one possible, and this is why the mentor and disciple relationship, linking Makiguchi, Toda and Ikeda over a span of almost one century, is crucial for an understanding of Ikeda's philosophy of peace and of the SGI's activities, no matter how familiar one may be with the writings of Nichiren. Another aspect of the thirteenth-century priest's teachings which is often emphasized by Ikeda is the importance of dialogue.

Concerning global citizenship, there was no equivalent to this modern concept in thirteenth-century Japan, but here I would like to emphasize what I consider to be the universality of Nichiren's teachings. My understanding is that Nichiren believed one should be loyal to the values and principles of the Lotus Sutra rather than simply to one's country's narrow interests. The mandala[17] established by Nichiren (*Gohonzon*), combines aspects of three languages. The word 'Nam' comes from Sanskrit, and the other script is made of Chinese characters, while everything inscribed on the Gohonzon is pronounced the Japanese way. The teachings are meant to spread throughout Jambudvipa,[18] which was a legendary continent. Transposed to our twenty-first century, Jambudvipa can be interpreted as meaning the entire world, and this idea was confirmed by Matsuda (Matsuda 2009). It is quite possible to have a more Japan-centered reading of this term, as Tanaka did, but I favor the SGI's interpretation, which is consistent with the Lotus Sutra's teachings that beings from the entire universe gathered to listen to Shakyamuni Buddha's sermon.

Finally I believe that Nichiren's philosophy reflects the spirit of universal equality found in the Lotus Sutra, and for instance he showed gratitude to the people of what are now the countries of India, Korea and China for having brought Buddhism to Japan. His teachings were clearly intended for human beings in the entire world, whom he thought all had an equal potential for enlightenment, as when he stated: 'How reassuring it is to know that not only the people here, but those of India, China, and the entire land of Jambudvipa will be able to attain Buddhahood!' (482).

Seen from my vantage point at the beginning of the twenty-first century, and based on my understanding of Daisaku Ikeda's philosophy of peace, it seems to me that the teachings of the human potential for self-improvement, the inherent dignity of human life and the oneness of life and its environment found in Nichiren Buddhism are an effective basis for the promotion of inner transformation, dialogue and global citizenship, which I believe provide an excellent roadmap towards world peace.

PART II

A PHILOSOPHY OF PEACE

Inner Transformation and Human Revolution: Enhancing Courage, Wisdom and Compassion for the Creation of a Better World

> We but mirror the world. All the tendencies present in the outer world are to be found in the world of our body. If we could change ourselves, the tendencies in the world would also change.
>
> Mahatma Gandhi ([1913] 1994, 241)

> People want only special revolutions, in externals, in politics, and so on. But that's just tinkering. What really is called for is a revolution of the human mind.
>
> Henrik Ibsen ([1871] 1992, ix)

> A great inner revolution in just a single individual will help achieve a change in the destiny of a nation and, further, will cause a change in the destiny of humankind.
>
> Daisaku Ikeda (2004a, viii)

Inner transformation as an empowering point of departure towards world peace

I believe that the concept of inner transformation is crucial for peace work because it provides an empowering point of departure in the face of most circumstances. By focusing on self-improvement, people can find the necessary energy to conduct better and more productive dialogues and to contribute to society and the world as global citizens. Apparently without awareness of Buddhist concepts, the Austrian psychiatrist and holocaust survivor Victor Frankl expressed the essence of his own philosophy in a 1984 postscript to his work *Man's Search for Meaning*. I consider the following passage as an excellent formulation of the essence of inner transformation:

> 'Saying yes to life in spite of everything,' (. . .) presupposes that life is potentially meaningful under any conditions, even those which are most miserable. And this in turn presupposes the human capacity to creatively turn life's negative aspects into something positive or constructive. In other words, what matters is to make the best of any given situation (Frankl [1959] 2006, 137).

For me then, the question at the heart of a practice of inner transformation becomes what type of human qualities are necessary to 'creatively turn life's negative aspects into something positive or constructive.' As mentioned in the previous chapter, I believe that in the context of Ikeda's philosophy of peace, courage, wisdom and compassion are the human virtues at the core of our capacity to actualize inner transformation effectively.

Human beings have a virtually limitless potential for many different types of qualities, such as hope, perseverance, a sense of justice, creativity and imagination, but I think that the terms courage, wisdom and compassion taken together cover most of these positive characteristics. For me, courage is a general label covering qualities such as hope, will, positive energy and enthusiasm. Wisdom is associated with intelligence, imagination, creativity and the effective use of knowledge. Compassion includes such feelings as generosity, kindness and empathy. I therefore define inner transformation as an effort to increase one's own courage, wisdom and compassion, and all the other virtues associated with them, in order to deal with the circumstances at hand in the best way possible.

Ikeda has emphasized the importance of these three qualities in numerous writings besides those mentioned in the previous chapter, for instance in his peace proposal of 2002 and in his dialogue with Mikhail Gorbachev.

Among Ikeda's yearly peace proposals, the one released on 26 January 2002 contains a response to the tragedy of 11 September 2001. After condemning not only the attacks but also the ensuing US retaliatory aerial bombardments of Afghanistan, Ikeda pinpoints 'dehumanization' as the main source of this destructive cycle of violence. He then adds: 'Since the ultimate enemy is dehumanization, the ultimate solution must be a revitalization and restoration

of humanity. The wellspring for this must be a philosophy of humanism'
(2002–PP, 10). He then describes the ideal way of life in terms of Buddhist
humanism: 'The world of enlightenment, or Buddhahood, is regarded as the
ideal way of life, one characterized by great compassion, courage and wisdom'
(ibid.).

In the following passage from his dialogue with Mikhail Gorbachev, Ikeda
also emphasizes a similar set of qualities, if one considers 'the will to overcome
difficulties' as cognate with the idea of courage.

> In Buddhist philosophy, the highest being is a Buddha, who has
> attained inexhaustible wisdom, compassion, perspicacity, and the
> will to overcome difficulties. This being is, however, no deification
> capable of miracles and mystical actions. A Buddha is a human
> being filled with energy, the joy of life, and love for all living things
> (Ikeda and Gorbachev 2005, 4).

Whereas the English translations of Ikeda's texts do not always mention these
three qualities as such, one can often find near-equivalents. For instance, in
the 2008 peace proposal, Ikeda mentions 'goodness, strength and wisdom'
(2008–PP, 10). I consider that the first two qualities are very similar to
compassion and courage. In his lecture entitled 'Mahayana Buddhism and
Twenty-First Century Civilization' delivered at Harvard University in 1993,
he wrote: 'The function of the Buddha nature is always to urge us to be strong,
good, and wise' (Ikeda 1996b, 159).

Many other people have mentioned this triad as indispensable in endeavors
towards self-fulfillment and world peace. Martin Seligman, one of the
founders of positive psychology, confirms their importance in his book
Authentic Happiness (2002), after researching various religious and philosophical traditions:

> [W]e read Aristotle and Plato, Aquinas and Augustine, the Old
> Testament and the Talmud, Confucius, Buddha, Lao-Tze, Bushido
> (the samurai code), the Koran, Benjamin Franklin, and the
> Upanishads – some two hundred virtue catalogues in all. To our
> surprise, almost every single one of these traditions flung across
> three thousand years and the entire face of the earth endorsed six
> virtues (. . .) (132–33).

Among the six, the first three are remarkably close to the triad of courage,
wisdom and compassion, namely wisdom/knowledge, courage, and love/
humanity.[1]

One of the most celebrated peace figures of South Africa, Archbishop Desmond Tutu, also mentions these three qualities in his foreword to Stuart Rees's book *Passion for Peace*:

> A passion for peace means being in touch with our humanness which in turn requires that universal quality of *compassion* for the vulnerable (. . .). Such passion is influenced by a philosophy and language and an accompanying street wisdom and skills. This *wisdom* and these skills can be seen in the values and practice of great leaders, Mahatma Gandhi, Martin Luther King and my inimitable colleague the former President of South Africa Nelson Mandela. (. . .) He [Stuart Rees] also identifies *courage* as an indispensable quality in struggles for peace and in public life generally. Such courage may be displayed alone or shown in solidarity with others (Desmond Tutu in Rees 2003, 9–10) (Italics added).

In *Songs from My Heart* (1997a), Ikeda confirms that no external type of transformation will be able to 'fulfill the hopes of the people':

> In the past there have been different kinds of revolution
> political, economic, educational
> But when one type of revolution is carried out in isolation
> it lacks solidity, gives rise to strain and onesidedness
> A political revolution alone calls forth bloodshed, insures no safety
>   for the populace
> and once again those in authority lord it over the masses
> Likewise economic revolution
> fails to fulfill the hopes of the people,
> the penniless commoners are trampled underfoot in a process
>   of meaningless change
> A revolution in education only
> again is no blessing to the people –
> it cannot bear up before the turmoil of the world's shifts and movements
> What the people long for
> to carry them through the twenty-first century
> is not reorganization of external forms alone
> They desire a sound revolution
> carried out within themselves
> gradually and in an atmosphere of peace
> founded upon the philosophy and beliefs of each individual
> This calls for farsighted judgments
> and a profound system of principles (21)

To conclude this section, I would like to assert that an empowering way to begin answering the question 'what can I do for peace?' is to start with inner transformation, challenging oneself to generate as much courage, wisdom and compassion as necessary in order to overcome even the most severe obstacles and create something positive in any situation. This is how I understand inner transformation in the context of Ikeda's philosophy of peace.

Exploring various aspects of the idea of inner transformation in religions, philosophies and social science

The idea that a personal transformation can trigger a change in society and the world is not unique to Buddhism and can be found under various labels in different traditions. For instance in Islam, the highest form of *Jihad* (striving) is a nonviolent effort at self-improvement which entails an inner struggle against one's weak tendencies.

> The other dimension of jihad is striving against the ego and against the Devil – the inner jihad; which many refer to as *jihad al-akbar*; 'the greater jihad.' Far from being a baseless notion (as some falsely claim), the inner jihad being the 'greater' or 'most obligatory' form of jihad is something rooted in the texts of the Revelation, and in the normative reading of the scholars. (. . .) It refers to the personal struggle against one's *nafs*; the lower self or ego (Sharif 2006, 1).

I believe that many spiritual and religious traditions enable people to effect an inner change, since even a prayer to God, who is typically placed outside creation in the Abrahamic religions, implies a personal effort and a desire to improve oneself.

Emphasizing the importance of the inner world, the title of Tolstoy's famous work *The Kingdom of God is within You* comes from the New Testament,[2] Luke 17: 20–21:

> (20) And when he was demanded of the Pharisees, when the kingdom of God should come, he answered them and said, The kingdom of God cometh not with observation:

> (21) Neither shall they say, Lo here! or, lo there! for, behold, the kingdom of God is within you.

In 'The Torah Code of Honor,' Rabbi Ariel Bar Tzadok asserts that the change for good must start with self-scrutiny:

> We can transform our religious communities and remove from them all the problems from which they suffer, but the change for good starts with the individual. Look in the mirror, change yourself, and only when one is successful with this should one stand to address the change in others (Tzadok 2005).

The Baha'i faith also recommends placing the priority on inner transformation:

> Baha'is seek to solve social problems by attempting to address what they see as the spiritual root of the problem facing humanity – its failure to recognize and wholeheartedly embrace the oneness of the human race. This recognition that spiritual transformation needs to be the foundation of lasting material improvements is central to the Baha'i approach to social change (*One Country* 2004).

The individual change recommended by the Baha'i philosophy of peace is a shift from a conception of humanity divided into different groups towards a belief in the 'oneness of the human race.'

In his 2002 peace proposal, Ikeda defines the term 'human revolution' as 'inner renewal,' emphasizing the importance of each person's 'fundamental, inherent humanity':

> Altering the course of human history – throughout which 'peace' has been but an interlude between wars – will require of each individual a profound inner resolution, a truly existential determination to seek their fundamental, inherent humanity and to transform their entire being. *In the SGI we call this ceaseless struggle for inner renewal 'human revolution.'* It is the steadfast effort to construct 'the defenses of peace' within our own hearts and minds as proclaimed in the Constitution of the United Nations Educational, Scientific, and Cultural Organization (UNESCO) (2002–PP, 5) (Italics added).

The term *ningen kakumei* (human revolution) was first mentioned by Shigeru Nambara in a speech as president of Tokyo University in 1947 (Seager 2006, 54). Toda and Ikeda have used the term to define the 'ceaseless struggle for inner renewal' which is the essence of Buddhist practice. In his dialogue with French writer and art philosopher René Huyghe, Ikeda wrote:

> The term human revolution seems to have been coined by Professor Shigeru Nambara, president of the University of Tokyo, shortly after the end of World War II because, in those times, he realized that, more than changes in exterior political systems, the people of Japan required the adaptability and support that self-revolution could provide. At about the same time, my mentor Josei Toda, second president of Soka Gakkai, employed those words in his explanations of the practice of Buddhist teachings (Ikeda and Huyghe [1991] 2007, 144).

Although he originally borrowed it from an outside source, it was Toda who made the term 'human revolution' famous in Japan, and Ikeda who has promoted it globally. Today, it is firmly associated with the process of inner transformation pursued through the practice of Nichiren Buddhism within the Soka Gakkai and the SGI. This is the sense in which Ikeda almost always uses the term.

The famous exhortation 'Be the change you wish to see in the world,' attributed to Gandhi, also emphasizes personal responsibility in effecting change. Whereas there is no proof that Gandhi said these exact words, he did write the following statement: 'If we could change ourselves, the tendencies in the world would also change.' I believe that Gandhi meant that whatever transformation one wishes to see outside should be used as a source of inspiration to accomplish a change inside. In a 2006 interview Indian activist and author Arya Bhushan Bhardwaj, the founder of Gandhi-in-Action, an organization that promotes Gandhian nonviolence internationally, mentioned that Gandhi was first and foremost a 'spiritual revolutionary':

> To change minds is difficult. From time immemorial society has relied on violent ways which have dominated the human mind. Gandhi had full faith in the human heart's ability to change. He was optimistic and continued his ceaseless effort in this direction, throughout his life. Therefore, I say, Gandhi was a spiritual revolutionary (Bhardwaj 2006).

A prominent admirer of Gandhi was Bart de Ligt, a Dutch anarchist and pacifist who exchanged letters on nonviolence with him and wrote *The Conquest of Violence* (De Ligt 1937). At the beginning of Chapter 6, 'The Effectiveness of the Non-violent Struggle,' he quotes a passage by Gandhi that praises 'the strength of the spirit':

> Non-violence is the Law of our species as violence is the law of the brute. The spirit lies dormant in the brute and he knows no law but that of physical might. The dignity of man requires obedience to a higher law – to the strength of the spirit (Gandhi in De Ligt 1937, 86).

In his historic 1963 speech 'I have a dream,' Martin Luther King Jr., one of the most well-known followers of Gandhi's philosophy, emphasized the primacy of the inner qualities of 'dignity and discipline' in the struggle for social justice, and recommended the use of 'soul force,' or strength of the spirit:

> But there is something that I must say to my people, who stand on the warm threshold which leads into the palace of justice: In the process of gaining our rightful place, we must not be guilty of wrongful deeds. Let us not seek to satisfy our thirst for freedom by drinking from the cup of bitterness and hatred. We must forever conduct our struggle on the high plane of *dignity and discipline*. We must not allow our creative protest to degenerate into physical violence. Again and again, we must rise to the majestic heights of meeting physical force with *soul force* (King 1963) (Italics added).

Inner transformation, in the sense of the enhancement of inner qualities, is also emphasized in virtue ethics, one of the three main branches of moral philosophy (Timmons 2002). I am especially struck by the clarity of English Catholic philosopher Elizabeth Anscombe's appeal as described in this passage from *Virtue Ethics* (1997), edited by Roger Crisp and Michael Slote. They mention her 1958 article 'Modern Moral Philosophy,' which had a seminal influence on contemporary virtue ethics:

> Now that many of us no longer believe in God, our only route to providing a foundation for ethics is in the notion of virtue, understood independently from obligation as part of human flourishing. And to approach the notion of virtue, we must stop doing philosophy until we get our psychology straight (Crisp and Slote 1997, 2).

This can be interpreted to mean that a foundation for morality and ethics must be based on the fostering of human qualities. Furthermore, the notion of obligation (especially in the absence of an enforcing eternal power) will not be as effective as a self-motivated desire to improve one's inner world. I believe that an emphasis on human flourishing has the potential to encourage consensus among all people, those who 'no longer believe in God,' those who do and those who embrace various creeds and convictions, once an emphasis on inner transformation is recognized as conducive to peace and harmony.

Ikeda emphasizes the ideal of the absolute happiness of each individual: 'The Lotus Sutra teaches that all (. . .) have the ability to savor a state of absolute happiness' (Ikeda 2000–I, 47). I believe that this type of confidence in the human potential is a core element needed, to use Crisp and Slote's words, to 'get our psychology straight.'

According to the founder of virtue ethics, Aristotle, human qualities such as justice, charity and generosity are dispositions to act in ways that benefit both the person possessing them and that person's society (Timmons 2002). Virtue ethics considers character as the main driving force in attempts to lead the good life. This type of ethics recommends the development of human qualities such as *arete* (excellence), *phronesis* (wisdom) and *eudaimonia* (flourishing). I believe that there are strong links between Aristotle's virtue ethics and Ikeda's emphasis on inner transformation and human revolution.

In social science, the question of where change should start has been framed as the 'agency–structure debate.' Anthony Giddens's concept of 'structuration' highlights that agents and structure mutually influence each other:

> The concept of structuration involves that of the *duality of structure,* which relates to the *fundamentally recursive character of social life, and expresses the mutual dependence of structure and agency.* (. . .) Structure forms 'personality' and 'society' simultaneously – but in neither case exhaustively: because of the significance of unintended consequences of action, and because of unacknowledged conditions of action. (. . .) *Structure thus is not to be conceptualized as a barrier to action, but as essentially involved in its production:* even in the most radical processes of social change (. . .) (Giddens [1979] 2007, 237–38).

Giddens advocates an awakening to the interdependence of agency and structure, which is roughly equivalent to a notion of the interconnectedness between individuals and society. Considering the web of relations between individuals and their societal environments, it is possible to isolate two extreme positions in the agency–structure debate, Methodological Individualism[3] on the one hand, and Structural Functionalism[4] on the other.

Methodological Individualism is a sociological paradigm that asserts that all societal phenomena can be brought back to personal decisions by individual human beings. It is associated with Max Weber, as well as Thomas Carlyle, William James, Friedrich Hayek and Karl Popper (Stanford Encyclopedia of Philosophy 2009a). As Popper wrote:

> [A]ll social phenomena, and especially the functioning of all social institutions, should always be understood as resulting from the decisions, actions, attitudes, etc. of human individuals (. . .) we should never be satisfied by an explanation in terms of so-called 'collectives' (Popper quoted by Giddens [1979] 2007, 241).

I believe Ikeda's philosophy of peace can be placed on this side of the agency–structure debate. For instance, in the following passage he refers to US President John F. Kennedy's decision during the Cuban Missile Crisis (1962). He describes the moment when several advisers had insisted on direct military attack as the best option:

> In this state of crisis, almost sparking an all-out nuclear war, the final decision rested with one person and one person alone, President John F. Kennedy. On the afternoon of the fifth day of meetings, October 20, he decided on his response: a naval blockade of Cuba (Ikeda 2001–7, 56).

Ikeda then extrapolates and asserts that it is the character of each individual which is the decisive factor for changing the world:

> No matter how far civilization advances, no matter how times change, in the end everything depends on character. The decisions of human beings determine their fate and that of the world. The Cuban Missile Crisis was another reminder of this essential but oft-forgotten truth (56).

There is ongoing debate concerning the role of specific individuals in the decision-making process leading to the resolution of the Cuban Missile Crisis.[5] For Ikeda, there is no doubt that the personal decision of President Kennedy to opt for a blockade instead of a direct military attack opened the way for a peaceful outcome. This interpretation is consistent with Ikeda's systematic emphasis on inner transformation, which asserts the primacy of the human being as the agent of change even in complex situations.

On the other side of the agency–structure debate, Structural Functionalism is one of the outgrowths of Functionalism, which 'in the philosophy of mind is the doctrine that what makes something a mental state of a particular type does not depend on its internal constitution, but rather on the way it functions, or the role it plays, in the system of which it is a part' (Stanford Encyclopedia of Philosophy 2009b). Structural Functionalism, developed by Claude Levi-Strauss, Edmund Leach and Samuel P. Huntington, states that society consists of sub-groups such as hospitals, schools, farms, armies and governments, which have their own functions and ideally should work together to ensure social stability. The fundamental units of analysis are therefore groups and institutions. This worldview can be placed on the opposite side of the spectrum from Methodological Individualism which focuses on individual human beings.

In the agency–structure debate, Ikeda's emphasis on human revolution and inner transformation can therefore be located on the side of 'agency,' because he asserts that the capacity of each individual for personal transformation is what determines the quality of all other changes. Along the same lines, the nineteenth-century Norwegian playwright Henrik Ibsen wrote that 'People want only special revolutions, in externals, in politics, and so on. But that's just tinkering. What really is called for is a revolution of the human mind' (Ibsen [1871] 1992, ix).

To conclude this overview of the concept of inner transformation across disciplines, I would like to mention the strong links I see between Ikeda's philosophy of peace and humanistic psychology.

I believe that Carl Rogers's trust in the hidden talents of human beings and Abraham Maslow's acknowledgement of the universality of human needs and desire for fulfillment are very close to what I define as Ikeda's belief in the capacity of human beings for inner transformation in processes leading towards peace. In the following passage, Carl Rogers, one of the founders of humanistic psychology, asserts his belief in the potential of each human being:

> Individuals have within themselves vast resources for self-understanding and for altering their self-concepts, basic attitudes, and self-directed behavior; these resources can be tapped if a definable climate of facilitative psychological attitudes can be provided (Rogers [1980] 1995b, 115).

Rogers then defines these attitudes as genuineness, caring and empathic understanding (115–16). In *On Becoming a Person* ([1961] 1995a), in a chapter entitled 'A Therapist's View of the Good Life,' he wrote:

> This process of the good life is not, I am convinced, a life for the faint-hearted. It involves the stretching and growing of becoming

more and more of one's potentialities. It involves the courage to be. It means launching oneself fully into the stream of life. Yet the deeply exciting thing about human beings is that when the individual is inwardly free, he chooses as the good life this process of becoming (196).

In the same work, he sums up the trust in the positive potential of human beings asserted by Abraham Maslow: 'Maslow puts up a vigorous case for man's animal nature, pointing out that the anti-social emotions – hostility, jealousy, etc. – result from frustration of more basic impulses for love and security and belonging, which are in themselves desirable' (91).

Victor Frankl, already mentioned above, comes even closer with his conviction that people can always bring out their highest potential, even in the worst of circumstances. As he wrote in a passage of remarkable clarity:

> As a professor in two fields, neurology and psychiatry, I am fully aware of the extent to which man is subject to biological, psychological and sociological conditions. But in addition to being a professor in two fields I am a survivor of four camps – concentration camps, that is – and as such I also bear witness to the unexpected extent to which [human beings are] capable of defying and braving even the worst conditions conceivable (Frankl [1959] 2006, 130).

I believe that a similar confidence in the capacity of each person to create value and bring out positive qualities in a self-motivated way is at the root of Ikeda's philosophy of peace. What follows is one person's testimony showing that human beings 'are capable of defying and braving even the worst conditions conceivable.' Like Victor Frankl, she is also a survivor and her experience concretely illustrates the meaning of the term 'human revolution.'

A personal story of human revolution: interview with Mrs. Masako Tanimura in Hachioji, Tokyo, 17 October 2009

Masako settles down in the armchair in front of me at the coffee shop in Hachioji, the suburb of Tokyo where she has lived for decades. Her eyes are shining behind her pink glasses. Her flowery dress in hues of green, orange and grey goes well with her pink jacket and her black bag. She exudes dynamism and enthusiasm and looks many years younger than her actual age, 78. She eagerly awaits my first question, which I put to her through my wife Yoko, who is acting as our interpreter.

Masako was 14 years old when the bomb was dropped on Hiroshima. She was at school, 4.1 km from the epicenter. She was not crushed or burned, but she was irradiated. Her mother was a bit closer, around 3 km, working near a watermill. When the bomb detonated, she hid in a ditch in the paddy field, and contaminated water got into her mouth. Masako was living with her father's parents, her five brothers and sisters and her mother, and they were all affected by the black rain resulting from the atomic bombing. Her father was not home. He had been drafted to support the war in the Philippines and had been forced to leave his family.

Immediately after the bombing, Masako's mother started to feel sick, vomiting, running a fever and suffering from headaches most of the time. After two years of painful struggle, she died of radiation sickness in December 1947. In the meantime, the family had received notice that Masako's father had been killed in the Philippines. Masako herself became sick and weak, like her younger brother, and the death of both her parents was a hard blow for the adolescent. Her maternal grandmother also started suffering from fever, bleeding and diarrhea. Today, Masako can say with certainty that all her friends and relatives who were exposed to the atomic bombing and who are deceased died of radiation sickness after a few years, or of cancer later.

Masako had to endure thyroiditis, heart disease, colon polyp and recently paralyzing pain in her legs, but she overcame all of them without any operation. Her father died at 36 and her mother at 40, and as a result she was worried that she would die young herself. However, she asserts with a smile: 'President Ikeda encouraged me to live a long life, and I took his advice seriously. Here I am today, in great shape at 78! In retrospect, I can say that President Ikeda saved my life.'

Masako got married at 23, and five years later her sister-in-law invited her to join the Soka Gakkai. Masako was not really interested, but she became a member to please her. It was one year later that she discovered that practicing Buddhism was actually to her advantage. She was very impressed by the fact that Josei Toda had made a declaration against nuclear weapons in 1957, and by the opening sentence of the novel *The Human Revolution* by Ikeda: 'Nothing is more barbarous than war. Nothing is more cruel. And yet, the war dragged on' (Ikeda 2004a, 3).

She was also impressed with the warm atmosphere she witnessed during Soka Gakkai meetings, with people singing songs, sharing experiences and learning about Buddhism together. Asked to describe if there was a difference before and after she started practicing seriously, she said: 'I became such a happy person. Before practicing, I was sick and weak and complaining most of the time. With Buddhism, I learned to overcome all obstacles, and started to really enjoy my life. Whenever I met my old schoolmates, they could not recognize me because they thought I was a different person. That is how much I have changed thanks to the practice.'

Because she was rather weak, Masako was not sure whether she should get married, or if she could have healthy children. Later on, doctors told her that her children, grandchildren and all her descendants may suffer from cancer or other serious disease because she had been irradiated. This has been an additional source of suffering for Hiroshima and Nagasaki atomic bomb survivors as well as for their children and grandchildren.

However, today Masako is proud of her very successful son and two daughters, and of her four healthy grandchildren. She attributes all these victories to her Buddhist practice. Asked to describe one of the greatest results she experienced directly from chanting, she answered:

> Very early in my practice, whenever I chanted sincerely, I could feel that my mother was right next to me, happy, smiling and serene. Actually my mother died in great pain, coughing and vomiting blood. I was told by the believers of some other religion that it was all my fault and that I should repent. The image of my dying mother was a source of deep suffering for me, for many years. To be able to remember her smile and her warmth through chanting was one of the greatest results I have been able to enjoy from the practice of Nichiren Buddhism.

Masako kindly answered all my questions, sometimes seriously, sometimes humorously, always earnestly, for more than two hours, and at the end she explained the secret of a long and healthy life that she learned from Buddhism:

> I read an encouragement concerning good health in President Ikeda's novel *The Human Revolution,* and it surely worked for me. It goes something like this: first you have to base yourself on a great philosophy that you feel teaches you the correct way to live. Second, you have to feel gratitude for the founders of that philosophy, and for all those that have made it possible for you to learn it. Third, you must understand that the reason you need to be in good health is not just for yourself, but also for others, to be able to contribute vigorously to the great goal of the happiness of humanity and world peace. I will surely continue trying my best from now on based on these principles.

After the interview, my wife and I were concerned that Masako would be tired and would have difficulties finding her way home, so we tried to accompany her, at least towards the exit. She firmly stopped us: 'I will be fine, really. I am going to go shopping now, so we'll talk again later.' She then bowed in the traditional Japanese way and walked vigorously towards the elevator.

Human revolution and inner transformation in Ikeda's novels

This section focuses on passages from Ikeda's novels *The Human Revolution* and *The New Human Revolution* which show the constant dialogue between the terms 'human revolution' and 'inner transformation.' Human revolution is a specifically Buddhist form of inner transformation, and while following the general contours of inner transformation, human revolution is predicated on a specific practice. Part of Ikeda's humanization of religion is that he has deliberately made the boundary between the Buddhist and non-Buddhist, the religious and the secular, more porous. By keeping these two realms in dialogue he counteracts the tendencies toward closing off from the world that typically mark religious movements with a high degree of commitment and enthusiastic energy.

The two novels depict the rebirth and growth of the Soka Gakkai in Japan after World War II, and the developments leading to the establishment of the SGI abroad. They were originally published daily in the Soka Gakkai's newspaper, the *Seikyo Shimbun*, which today has a circulation of about 5.5 million in Japan. Their subsequent publication in book form in Japanese and in several other languages proved to be highly popular with Soka Gakkai and SGI members, but also attracted the attention of many other readers.

The process of planning, and then writing *The Human Revolution* took several decades, and the serialization of *The New Human Revolution* is an ongoing endeavor. In the spring of 1951 Toda had completed the first installment of his own autobiographical novel, also entitled *Human Revolution*, depicting the history of the organization from its founding in 1930 through its wartime suppression and Toda's own religious awakening in prison. Toda's work was to be serialized in the *Seikyo Shimbun*, with the first installment in the inaugural issue.

Toda had shown the manuscript to Ikeda, who was deeply moved and decided to one day write a sequel to his mentor's novel. Ikeda reaffirmed this determination when he visited Toda's old home in Atsuta village together with his mentor in the summer of 1954 (Ikeda 2004a, 1724–25). Toda's novel was published as a single volume in 1957, and after reading it Ikeda began planning the writing of his own sequel in August. Toda passed away on 2 April 1958, and six years later Ikeda announced his intention in public. The first installment of Ikeda's *The Human Revolution* was published in the *Seikyo Shimbun* on 1 January 1965. The final episode appeared on 24 November

1992, and by then the entire work consisted of 12 volumes. Ikeda then started writing *The New Human Revolution* in 1993, and almost 20 volumes have been published in English so far, out of a planned total of 30 volumes (Ikeda 2004a, xi). Ikeda describes his main motivation for this literary endeavor as follows in the preface of a 2004 English edition:

> The twenty-eight years during which I was engaged in writing *The Human Revolution* were very busy and active ones for me. I utilized every spare moment I could find to push forward with my narrative page by page, for I was convinced that the life of my mentor constituted a model for the manner in which an individual could carry out a splendid human revolution within his or her own life. If I could capture in writing Mr. Toda's spirit of sincerity and truth, I was sure it would open the way for a human revolution in the lives of all persons (Ikeda 2004a, viii).

Ikeda then continues with the quote mentioned at the beginning of this chapter, asserting that the human revolution of a single human being can 'cause a change in the destiny of humankind' (viii).

Ikeda chose to start writing the novel in Okinawa, the part of Japan where the civilian population had suffered most from the Pacific War, victimized by both US and Japanese troops. He wrote about his outrage concerning the Vietnam War in the 2007 peace proposal, in connection with the novel:

> During this trip through Asia, I directly sensed the dark shadows cast over the region by the deep divisions of the Cold War. Soon after this visit, the Vietnam War expanded to engulf the entire country with the start of US aerial attacks against the North in February 1965.
>
> This was just two months after I began writing what would become a major undertaking in my life, the novel *The Human Revolution*, in Okinawa, which at that point was still under American occupation. The novel begins with the words: 'Nothing is more barbarous than war. Nothing more cruel.' When I heard of the escalation of the war in Vietnam, I was filled with a profound anger that this very tragedy was being repeated once more in Asia (40).

Two types of concept can be distinguished in Ikeda's novels: inner transformation, which can be accomplished by various means, and human revolution, which is the specific way in which SGI members accomplish inner transformation through their practice of Nichiren Buddhism. The latter also refers to the fact that Josei Toda underwent a spiritual transformation in prison based on his understanding of the Lotus Sutra and of Nichiren Buddhism, and was able to share it with hundreds of thousands of people within 13 years (1945–58). Further it means that Ikeda continued this expansion of the human revolution movement through the propagation of Nichiren Buddhism, with the result that 10 million people in Japan and about 2 million individuals outside Japan are practicing within the Soka Gakkai and SGI today.

Behind these numbers indicative of a numerical expansion are countless concrete experiences of ordinary people who have overcome diverse difficulties through their practice of Buddhism. Soka Gakkai and SGI publications worldwide abound with such accounts of the personal victories of members. They have overcome hardships due to ill health, financial difficulties, bad relationships, addictions, failures and many other types of disaster, as Masako Tanimura's experience has shown above.

Concerning inner transformation, I define it in this work as the personal efforts of individuals to enhance their own courage, wisdom and compassion through any spiritual or philosophical tradition or means available. This definition also encompasses human revolution. The two definitions coexist throughout the two serial novels, and in the following passage Ikeda gives both of them. The first paragraph provides the 'Buddhist' version, whereas the second rephrases it in 'general' terms:

> Toda's charm seemed to sparkle brighter each day. The change in the man was incomprehensible, but others could not deny it – it was right before their eyes. Toda simply said it resulted from practicing the essence of Buddhism, the Daishonin's philosophy of the oneness of body and mind. He proceeded to teach them about human revolution, the change of destiny achieved by practicing the correct teachings of Buddhism with sincerity and courage.

> The transformation of a human being – the recognition of one's own dignity and individuality and the full flowering of his or her potential – is the shortest road to the transformation of society, education, science, government, culture and indeed, the whole of life. Toda stressed this over and over (Ikeda 2004a, 122).

There is a high degree of fluidity between the two concepts in these novels, and the text crosses effortlessly over boundaries that I think have been too much emphasized by Western rationalism. I believe the main reason is that for Ikeda there is no difference between the two. It seems clear that he is motivated by a powerful desire to encourage others, whether through Buddhism or other means. These two serial novels have a dual purpose: Ikeda provides a historical record of the human revolution movement (concretized by the development of the Soka Gakkai and the SGI), and he affirms his conviction that the starting point of world peace is to be found in the personal transformation of individuals, based on the belief that all people possess unlimited resources of positive qualities (concretized through his dialogues and activities to popularize the idea of inner transformation).

In *The Human Revolution* there are about 20 passages related to the human revolution, and also 20 passages concerning inner transformation. The following passages describe the very beginning of the human revolution movement, the spark that started the development of the Soka Gakkai and the SGI. On 3 July 1945 Toda was released from prison after almost two years of captivity for opposing the military government. Ikeda describes Toda's feelings immediately upon being freed:

> The night sky stretched out endlessly; not a star could be seen in the dark heavens. Yet Toda was conscious of a light that burned in the depths of his being. No one else could see it, nor had he the means to impart it to others. It was a flame kindled in the darkness of his solitary cell, and as long as he lived, it would never be extinguished. It was a flame that would never waver, even in the winds of an unstable world. He reaffirmed this to himself and felt satisfied (Ikeda 2004a, 8).

The mere fact that Toda had a burning sense of mission would not have been sufficient for the human revolution to spread like wildfire throughout postwar Japan. The time and the social circumstances were ripe, and Ikeda succinctly describes the spiritual hunger in people's hearts in the next passage. On 15 August 1945 the emperor announced Japan's defeat.

> The blackout had not been lifted officially on the night of the 15th, but houses were aglow with lights. Yet no joyous feelings of peace welled up in people's hearts. The war was over, but they'd sacrificed too much. From this day on, the next battle began in each citizen's mind. By now, they distrusted all authority. Some suddenly became fatalists, while others resolved to die for their convictions (48).

The next step in the development of the Soka Gakkai is described in the following passage, which provides a mixture of the two concepts. Ikeda gives voice to the conviction Toda felt in autumn 1945, when the US authorities were establishing a democratic political framework in a destroyed and starving nation:

> Above all, he [Toda] knew humankind must be absolutely convinced of the dignity of life, *based on Buddhism*. The magnificent life force of each individual must be made to gush forth through the power of the supreme Law. Individual self-awakening, human rebirth and human revolution would then follow, giving rise to a flowering of education, politics, science, culture and every other human activity. This was the true democracy people have dreamed of (98) (Italics added).

The following passage provides an example of the general meaning of inner transformation. Ikeda describes Toda's conviction that if people fail to change, no economic or political system will bring about peace:

> No matter what social system we adopt in the future, no matter how democratic its political structure, it's *bound to be ineffective as long as human beings themselves fail to change.* We're threatened by nuclear holocaust, but we still don't have the guts to renounce war (172) (Italics added).

One young man asked Toda about the corruption in public office that was rampant in Japan after the war, and he answered in terms of inner transformation in the general sense:

> Social evils like the present one are not new. Haven't they been around for thousands of years since the origin of human society itself? Right-minded people of justice have made every possible effort to end evil through legal sanctions, moral education, the reformation of the social structure and even political revolution, but all these efforts have proved abortive (345).

Here Ikeda shows Toda reaffirming what he said in the previous passage, that all political, societal or other external transformations are 'bound to be ineffective as long as human beings themselves fail to change.'

In the first 12 volumes[6] of *The New Human Revolution*, there are about 30 passages providing a definition or illustration of both concepts. In the next three passages, the first illustrates the human revolution, the second a mixture of both and the third passage inner transformation. This shows again the fluidity with which the text makes use of these two meanings.

In the first passage the echo from the 'flame' in Toda's heart right after his release from prison on 3 July 1945 is noteworthy. Here, on 2 October 1960, Ikeda flies to Hawaii to start the worldwide development of the SGI (officially established later in 1975), continuing the work of his mentor. This illustrates the propagation of the human revolution:

> Shin'ichi [Ikeda]'s voyage for world peace thus began by lighting a flame of courage in those who had lost hope and were being crushed under the weight of life's vicissitudes. Though such efforts might seem insignificant and far removed from the goal of world peace, the essential basis for peace lies only within the human being. Shin'ichi was deeply convinced that genuine peace could not be achieved without the revitalization of all individuals and the establishment of true joy and happiness in their lives (Ikeda 1995–1, 10).

The following passage relates the way Ikeda explained the concept of human revolution to Count Richard Coudenhove-Kalergi, the founder in 1923 of the Pan-European Movement and Secretary-General of the European Parliamentary Union in 1947, during their dialogue held on 30 October 1967. It is a blend of both definitions, the very first sentence illustrating the Buddhist sense, and the very last the generally applicable concept of inner transformation.

> Our movement aims for what we call human revolution, the inner transformation of the individual through the teachings of Nichiren Buddhism. Society is made up of human beings, we are the creators of our reality. As a result, we believe that by cultivating our lives, our hearts, we can change society. The purpose of the Soka Gakkai is to help people forge their character on a fundamental level, thereby bringing the fragrant flowers of peace and culture to bloom. We emphasize the view that all things arise from the human heart, the human spirit (Ikeda 2006–12, 246).

I would like to suggest that based on his personal experience of helping transform Western Europe, Coudenhove-Kalergi had no difficulty agreeing with Ikeda concerning the power of one individual to change the world.

Finally, the next passage provides an example of the general definition of inner transformation, without reference to any particular ideology or religion:

> World peace is not something given to us. It is something that we human beings must create, through our own effort and wisdom. It is something we must struggle for and win.

The key, therefore, to building peace is for individuals to develop themselves as human beings, and to challenge their weaknesses and triumph over them. In other words, peace can never be achieved without the struggle of human revolution, the struggle to develop and elevate our state of life.

Furthermore, if war is a realm of the fear of death, then peace must be a realm of the joy of life (Ikeda 2006–12, 233).

Concluding comments

The concept of inner transformation, meaning that a change in one individual can start a process leading to a transformation of society, can be found in many spiritual traditions, as well as in philosophy, social science and psychology, in the forms of a religious conviction in the strength of the spirit, the principles of Gandhian nonviolence, the emphasis on individual responsibility of Methodological Individualism, in Aristotle's Virtue Ethics or in the values of Humanistic Psychology. When inner transformation is based on the practice of Nichiren Buddhism in the SGI, it is called human revolution.

Whereas Buddhism, with its emphasis on the inner life, generally has the reputation of leading to passivity and quiet meditation, Toda and Ikeda's philosophy of peace, following the example of Nichiren, is committed to a full and vigorous engagement with the problems of daily life and society, a characteristic that has allowed the human revolution movement of the Soka Gakkai and the SGI to mobilize millions of people around the world.

Ikeda continuously crosses semantic boundaries between the religious and the mundane, as illustrated by the way he freely uses both the concepts of human revolution and inner transformation. I believe that this shows that he has been able to translate the concept of human revolution into an integral part of an inclusive philosophy of peace, which can be used by people of all backgrounds even without its original religious basis.

CHAPTER 6

Dialogue and Dialogical Methods for Peace: Socrates, Montaigne, Büber, Habermas and Ikeda

> For as there are misanthropists or haters of men, there are also misologists or haters of ideas, and both spring from the same cause, which is ignorance of the world.
>
> Socrates, as quoted by Plato (1892, 90)

> My thought sketches out the matter for a while and dwells lightly on the first aspects of it: then I usually leave the principal thrust of the task to heaven.
>
> Michel de Montaigne ([1580] 2003, 1058)

> I require a You to become; becoming I, I say You. All actual life is encounter.
>
> Martin Büber ([1923] 1996, 62)

> This concept of communicative rationality carries with it connotations based ultimately on the central experience of the unconstrained, unifying, consensus-bringing force of argumentative speech (. . .).
>
> Jürgen Habermas (1981, 10)

> Our efforts are based on the belief that it is dia-
> logue, first and foremost, that opens one heart to
> another. However slow this process may appear,
> we are convinced that it is the most certain path
> to world peace.
>
> Daisaku Ikeda (2009–PP, 13)

Among the five thinkers quoted above, only Ikeda makes an explicit link between dialogue and peace. In the process of attempting to systematize his philosophy of peace, I have come to consider that dialogue is the axis around which the whole system revolves. Inner transformation may be the starting point, but I believe that the most courageous, wise and compassionate person would not be able to contribute fully to peace without dialogue.

Dialogue with oneself can be one of the ingredients of inner transformation, as when one makes personal efforts to control greed, anger and foolishness and to enhance courage, wisdom and compassion. Self-scrutiny and introspection, when used for inner transformation, can be considered as forms of silent dialogue within the self. In order to overcome the challenges that inevitably arise in the process of attempts to pursue dialogue with others, one can find answers by practicing self-reflection and self-improvement. Ikeda recommends dialogue as a way to 'positively transform our own life as well as that of others':

> A journey of a thousand miles begins with a single step, as they say.
> We can never achieve victory in a journey toward a distant aspiration
> if we don't take that first step. Similarly, human revolution, or an
> inner transformation in people's hearts, which we of the SGI espouse
> as the way to lasting peace, starts with sincere dialogue with a single
> individual. Engaging in dialogue is a struggle to positively trans-
> form our own life as well as that of others. It is the act of breaking
> out of the shell of our lesser self, surmounting the wall of our callous
> ego, and creating and expanding positive connections with others.
> When we have the courage to meet and talk with people about our
> ideals, we are taking the first and surest step in our human revolu-
> tion (Ikeda 2009b, 91–92).

He has also stated:

> [D]ialogue is a kind of light to illuminate one's footsteps. The
> whole thing begins with one human being talking with another.

> Inter-civilizational dialogue is currently the focus of attention, but the point of departure or the prototype is human-to-human rapport (Ikeda and Tehranian 2003, 9).

I believe that one effective way to enhance global citizenship is to hold sustained dialogues with people of different backgrounds and convictions. I also think that unless it is leavened by dialogue, by a deeply integrated commitment to deliberative democracy on all levels, any vision of global civilization is likely to be suspected as the attempt of dominant cultures to impose their values and interests on the world.

Ikeda's concept of dialogue: a Habermasian interpretation

Since the earliest days of our species, humans have used language to share information, communicate feelings, express disagreement or reach understanding. Dialogue was used in Ancient India and Ancient Greece as a form of literature, for entertainment or instruction. The Lotus Sutra was written in the form of a dialogue, and Nichiren continued this tradition in Japan, writing some of his most important treatises in dialogical form. For instance 'On Establishing the Correct Teaching for the Peace of the Land' takes the form of a dialogue between a host and a traveler. It is quite possible that Ikeda's philosophy of dialogue was inspired by its Indian and Japanese roots, but because of his admiration for the early Greek philosophers his taste for this particular form can be placed at the confluence of both Eastern and Western traditions.

The *Compact Oxford English Dictionary* defines the second meaning of the noun 'dialogue' as a 'discussion directed towards exploration of a subject or resolution of a problem' (Compact Oxford 2008). The word comes from the Greek *dia*, meaning 'through,' and *logos*, meaning 'word or speech.' It is thus a method for human beings to explore a topic or come to a joint solution, using language. This in itself is not always conducive to nonviolence and harmony, and in this book I use the concept of dialogue as meaning communication using speech and reason for the sake of peace.

Ikeda offers the following definition of dialogue:

> The English word *dialogue* derives from the Greek *dialogos*, meaning 'through discourse meaning is shared.' Dialogue is not simply two people asserting their opinions, nor is it just a simple exchange of words. Through conversing, we can gain a shared insight into each other's point of view and intent. It is also a process of creating something of new and positive value (Ikeda 2009b, 86).

I would like to suggest that Ikeda's main purpose in using dialogue is to bring out the best in self and other, to let people's common humanity shine despite – or rather through – differences in backgrounds, lifestyles and world-views. In my opinion, Ikeda has been consistent throughout the years in his use of dialogue as a way to reach a deeper mutual understanding, reminiscent of Kant's injunction never to consider people as a means, but always as an end. In his dialogue entitled *A Passage to Peace* (2009), with Nur Yalman, a leading Turkish social anthropologist and professor at Harvard University, Ikeda said:

> I have always acted in the belief that enlightening others about humanism is the humane and social mission of the religious. With whatever strength is at my command, I have consistently under-taken the task of illuminating the humanistic philosophy and spirit deep within various cultures. The dialogues I have published with thinkers from all over the world, and the speeches I have delivered at Harvard University and many other institutes of higher education, are part of my work to this end (116).

In the following passage concerning successful dialogue, Ikeda mentions that the Buddhist concept of the 'four sufferings' is helpful because it defines what is common to all human beings:

> Last year (2008) I was interviewed by the popular Korean magazine *Wolgan choson* (Monthly Chosun). One of the questions I was asked was, 'What is the key to a successful dialogue?' I replied that all human beings, no matter what their social standing or their beliefs, experience what Buddhism describes as the sufferings of birth, aging, sickness, and death. When we engage in dialogue, we should bear in mind that we are talking to another person who, like our-selves, inevitably faces these sufferings. If we can do so, I said, we can communicate with anyone (Ikeda 2009b, 88).

Among the contemporary thinkers I have studied, I find that Jürgen Habermas's concept of 'communicative rationality' resonates most fully with Ikeda's conviction that the goal of dialogue is to illuminate 'the humanistic philosophy and spirit' within each person, and while keeping in mind that we all experience the same sufferings, to bring out the best in self and other. Some echoes of this concern found in Socrates, Michel de Montaigne and Martin Büber, whom Ikeda sometimes quotes, will be examined later.

Jürgen Habermas is mentioned in the dialogue entitled *Global Civilization* (2003) between Ikeda and Iranian-born peace scholar Majid Tehranian.

They agree that Habermas's 'communicative rationality' based on 'discourse without dominance' is a crucial ingredient for dialogue, because it recommends that communication not be used 'exclusively as a tool of strategy':

> **Tehranian:** Habermas's communicative rationality, by contrast [with instrumental rationality], does not begin with ideal constructs except for one that he calls 'ideal speech community,' characterized by the absence of force and the presence of equality in communicative access and competence of all participants in dialogue. Obviously, such conditions do not exist in the real world. But we can approximate them by creating the conditions of freedom and equality in communication. Despite the barriers of time, space, and culture, our own dialogue is a clear example of such communicative rationality (. . .).

> **Ikeda:** Habermas writes that a sincere speaker is obligated, by the tacit premise that he speaks with seriousness, to be responsible for the consequences of his verbal commitment. As you have pointed out, sincerity and open-mindedness on both sides are indispensable for genuine dialogue. In that sense, Habermas' thesis for 'discourse without dominance' merits a positive evaluation. He took exception to the thinking that treats communication exclusively as a tool of strategy (91).

In this section the relevance of Habermas's concept of communicative rationality in the practice of dialogue will be explored, as well as his 'communicative action theory' which has practical implications for the construction of a more dialogical society. These two concepts allow Habermas to make the transition between the art of dialogue and the construction of elements of a global civilization characterized by 'deliberative democracy.'

I believe that Ikeda's philosophy of dialogue points to the same vision of a more free and fair society. By becoming experts at dialogue, more and more people can hold discussions on increasingly complex topics, allowing deliberative democracy to flourish. This can empower an increasing number of people to develop their identities as global citizens, and to actualize elements of a global civilization of harmony and interdependence. In the two following passages, Ikeda emphasizes first the importance of bringing out our common humanity and second the fact that everyone's participation is crucial:

> Whenever I visited socialist or communist countries during the Cold War years, I was always guided by the conviction that 'because there are people to talk with' it must be possible to build a bridge

of friendship. We must somehow break through the 'friends vs. foe' pattern of relationship and talk with each other honestly and openly *on the common ground of humanity*. That, I was firmly convinced, would break the ice and lead to problem solving in the end (Ikeda and Tehranian 2003, 9–10) (Italics added).

If one drop of the water of dialogue is allowed to fall upon the wasteland of intolerance, where attitudes of hatred and exclusionism have so long prevailed, there will be a possibility for trust and friendship to spring up. This, I believe, is the most trustworthy and lasting road to that goal. Therefore, I encourage the flow of dialogue not only on the political plane but also *on the broader level of the populace as a whole* (xiv) (Italics added).

Habermas can be misquoted easily and grasping the essence of his voluminous writings represents quite a challenge. I will rely on two experts for a summary of Habermas's main themes: Eriksen and Weigard (2003) explain how Habermas attempts to save the enlightenment project of building a peaceful world based on human reason using the concept of communicative rationality.

According to them, taking Descartes as its point of departure, European rationalism has developed into logical positivism, bringing the benefits of modern science to humanity. European rationalism soon had its opponents in the Romantics who believed in the primacy of the emotions. Logical positivism has been vigorously opposed by the post-modernists who believe that skepticism and doubt are preferable to the naive confidence of the scientific mind, which brought unspeakable catastrophes to twentieth-century humanity. European rationalism is mostly characterized by 'purposive rationality,' the human ability to use reason to achieve specific goals, but this has been criticized by Max Weber (1904–05) as leading to dehumanization. Max Horkheimer (1937) and Theodor W. Adorno (1976) have attacked it for leading to manipulation.

Eriksen and Weigard (2003) then assert that the logical conclusion of what precedes – a negative evaluation of European rationalism and the Enlightenment project – is that there is no hope for rational dialogue, for achieving common goals through the logos, through human language and reason. Dialogue based on emotions (Romanticism) or on skepticism (post-modernism) is doomed to fail. Dialogue using purposive/instrumental rationality will lead to dehumanization (Weber) or manipulation (Adorno). In this context, Habermas wants to find a means to save the Enlightenment project by using rationality in a way conducive to meaningful dialogue.

In order to do this, he creates a distinction between two main types of rationality. The problem is not rationality itself but the fact that only one type of rationality, purposive rationality, has prevailed so far in European and Western culture. The other, underused type of rationality is what allows Habermas to continue the Enlightenment project, and he calls it 'communicative rationality' (Habermas 1981, 75).

I would like to assert that rationality is, of course, not a European invention, and that the human capacity for reasoning can be found in all civilizations. Moreover, using communicative rationality, people everywhere, at some time or another, have applied their reasoning powers to the practice of communication and dialogue, avoiding the pitfalls of emotionalism, skepticism, dehumanization and manipulation associated with purposive rationality.

Habermas wrote in *The Theory of Communicative Action* (1981):

> [I]f we start from the communicative employment of propositional knowledge in assertions, we make a prior decision for a wider concept of rationality connected with ancient conceptions of the logos. This concept of communicative rationality carries with it connotations based ultimately on the central experience of *the unconstrained, unifying, consensus-bringing* force of argumentative speech (10) (Italics added).

I consider the words 'unconstrained, unifying, consensus-bringing' as pointing to a use of dialogue conducive to peace. Habermas likewise emphasizes the potential role of this concept in conflict resolution:

> A greater degree of communicative rationality expands – within a communication-community – the scope for *unconstrained coordination of actions and consensual resolution of conflicts* (at least to the extent that the latter are based on cognitive dissonance) (15) (Italics added).

Ikeda points in the same direction in an editorial written for the *Japan Times*:

> [I]t is for just these reasons that dialogue is a choice requiring genuine courage and strength. Dialogue starts by clearly recognizing the positions and interests of the respective parties and then carefully identifying the obstacles to progress, patiently working to remove and resolve each of these. It is the ultimate constructive undertaking of the human spirit. And it is for just this reason that conflict resolution through dialogue – unlike military force whose

essence is destruction – holds the promise of a genuine and lasting solution (Ikeda [2007] 2008, 78).

I believe that Habermas's concept of communicative rationality is useful when attempting to explain why rational discourse can still be used successfully as a tool for dialogue between people of different backgrounds despite the catastrophic tragedies and disappointments of the twentieth and early twenty-first centuries. In a post-modern world, this trust in the inherent capacity of people to use reason will only make sense if the *dia-logos*, 'the use of language and reason/meaning/ideas' Ikeda is advocating, corresponds to Habermas's communicative rationality as opposed to purposive, or cognitive/instrumental rationality.

In the same editorial, Ikeda emphasizes once more that the goal of dialogue, the purpose of using language, reason, meaning and ideas to communicate, should first and foremost be to enhance our common humanity, not to obtain some advantage:

> From my own experience of having engaged in dialogue with many people from a wide range of political, religious, ethnic and cultural backgrounds, I am equally convinced that when we speak frankly on the basis of our common humanity it is always possible to see our way to the next step forward (79).

Moreover, Habermas also believes communicative rationality has practical applications in the organization of society. He articulates his thoughts in his concept of communicative action theory. I believe that the kind of deliberative democracy Habermas has in mind, which is based on a communicative use of rationality, is one essential component of Ikeda's vision for a new global civilization, which is a resolutely dialogical project.

According to Habermas, the public sphere is under constant threat of being colonized by the administrative system. Communicative action theory can be used to protect society against dehumanization, to protect the public sphere against the inhumane struggle for power that often characterizes the administrative sphere. He wrote:

> Many different occasions for discontent and protest arise wherever a one-sided process of modernization, guided by criteria of economic and administrative rationality, invades domains of life which are centered on the task of cultural transmission, social integration, socialization and education, domains orientated towards quite *different* criteria, namely towards those of communicative rationality (Habermas [1980] 2007, 365).

Here I see similarities with Ikeda's calls for UN reforms, when he emphasizes that the UN should have a human face, that human security should take precedence over narrowly defined national security, and that cultural and educational endeavors should receive at least as much attention as economic and administrative concerns.[1] In reality, both the administrative and public spheres are inextricably mixed in the same societal fabric, but for the sake of argument I will here establish a clear dichotomy between the two. It remains true that people can always decide which aspects of society they want to emphasize through thought, word and action: the public or the administrative sphere.

In order to bring out the contrast between the two, I would say that Machiavelli's political philosophy and the world defined by Habermas as the administrative sphere are where power, manipulation and domination can be given free expression. On the contrary, the public sphere characterized by communicative action is where people can bring out the best in themselves and others, accepting the challenges presented by dialogue, discussion and deliberation.

In the same *Japan Times* editorial, Ikeda wrote:

> Today we confront the unique opportunity to begin building a new civilization – one based on a consistent commitment to dialogue on all levels. The vital, vibrant currents of dialogue have the capacity to shake even the most stubborn allegiance to the use of force. Dialogue is not limited to the exchange of pleasantries, but includes the sharing of sharply differing perspectives. Courage and endurance are essential if we are to continue the painstaking work of loosening the knots of attachment that bind people to a particular point of view. The impact of this kind of humanistic diplomacy can move history in a new direction. In a world of richly diverse cultures, we cannot afford a regression to shuttered isolationism. It is crucial to revive the spirit of dialogue and to unleash a creative search for peaceful coexistence. To have faith in the promise of dialogue is to believe in the promise of humanity (81–82).

Using Habermasian language, I want to assert that Ikeda's vision for a global civilization of interdependence and harmony includes a flourishing of the public sphere and a defense of humanity against the excesses of the administrative sphere, using dialogue as a vehicle for communicative rationality, in order to let deliberative democracy flourish, thereby strengthening the public sphere towards more peace and justice. Since the use of communicative rationality implies a constant effort to respect human life, in line with the Kantian imperative to always consider people as an end and never as a means, I think the Habermasian concepts explored here provide philosophical support to the thesis that inner transformation, dialogue and global citizenship form a coherent system leading to peace. Lokesh Chandra, the scholar of Buddhism and Indian art already mentioned in Chapter 4, describes Ikeda's educational endeavors in quasi-Habermasian terms. I find striking similarities between what Chandra calls 'participative global order' and Habermas's public sphere on the one hand, and the 'depersonalization and bureaucratization of society' and the negative aspects of the administrative sphere on the other:

> As a poet, as a sage, as a thinker, you [Ikeda] endow the younger generation with a vision, with a transfiguration to awaken the immanent in them. You provide a value system for the psychosphere wherein nature and needs, aspirations and inadequacies can be endowed with a sense of purpose in a *participative global order*. A new order with a value system of caring as well as duty or responsibility towards others can serve society. It has to reverse the *depersonalization and bureaucratization of society*. The Bodhisattva ideal represents the imperative of duty, in the permanence of fundamental human values (Ikeda and Chandra 2009, 217) (Italics added).

To conclude this section on Habermas, in the following excerpt from Ikeda's contribution to the volume *From the Ashes* (2001c), he establishes a distinction between 'hard power' on the one hand and 'words spoken from the heart' on the other. Here again I find echoes of Habermas's distinctions between purposive/instrumentalist and communicative rationality, and between the administrative and the public spheres:

> Unless we can achieve a fundamental transformation within our own lives, so that we are able to perceive our intimate connection with all our fellow human beings and feel their sufferings as our own, we will never be free of conflict and war. In this sense, I feel that a *'hard power'* approach, one that relies on military might, will not lead to a long-term, fundamental resolution.

> I believe that dialogue holds the key to any lasting solution. Now, more than ever, we must reach out in a further effort to understand each other and engage in genuine dialogue. *Words spoken from the heart* have the power to change a person's life. They can even melt the icy walls of mistrust that separate peoples and nations. We must expand our efforts to promote dialogue between and among civilizations (Ikeda 2001c) (Italics added).

A reinforcement of the administrative sphere does not always lead to violence and the use of military might, but I believe it opens the gates to the pathways leading in that direction. In contrast, a strengthening of the public sphere and deliberative democracy has the power to pull society towards more peace and harmony. For Ikeda, it is 'words spoken from the heart' that will lead to the development of a 'participative global order.'

Learning from the Masters: Socrates, Montaigne and Büber

Socrates and Plato's views on *misologos* and *misanthropos* are highlighted in the 1989 peace proposal, where Ikeda says: 'To abandon dialogue is in fact to abandon being human' (Ikeda 1989–PP, 5). He develops this theme in more depth in his 1993 lecture at Claremont McKenna College. I believe that this link between the inability to love language and the incapacity to love people is a crucial element of Ikeda's philosophy of dialogue, the art of reaching mutual understanding *'dia-logos'* through language and logic/meaning/reason:

> I am reminded of the beautiful and moving passage in *Phaedo* in which Socrates teaches his youthful disciples that hatred of language and ideas (*misologos*) leads to antipathy toward humanity (*misanthropos*). The mistrust of language that gives birth to a misologist is but the inverse of an excessive belief in the power of language. The two are different aspects of the same thing, which is a frailty of spirit unable to cope with the stresses of human proximity brought about by dialogue (Ikeda 1996c, 173).

This link between *misologos* and *misanthropos* is found in the following passage from the dialogue entitled *Phaedo* in which Plato relates the last moments of Socrates before he is forced to end his own life by drinking the poisonous hemlock:

> Lest we become misologists, he replied: no worse thing can happen to a man than this. For as there are misanthropists or haters of men, there are also misologists or haters of ideas, and both spring from the same cause, which is ignorance of the world. Misanthropy arises out of the too great confidence of inexperience; – you trust a man and think him altogether true and sound and faithful, and then in a little while he turns out to be false and knavish; and then another and another, and when this has happened several times to a man, especially when it happens among those whom he deems to be his own most trusted and familiar friends, and he has often quarrelled

with them, he at last hates all men, and believes that no one has any good in him at all. You must have observed this trait of character? (Plato 1892, 90).

In my opinion, this passage confirms the importance of enhancing courage, wisdom and compassion in order to be able to hold fruitful dialogues. 'Ignorance of the world,' which gives rise to hatred of both ideas and people, must be overcome with an increase of wisdom, and the resulting love of ideas and people enhances one's compassion. All these efforts require courage.

I also see a link between Socrates's way of using dialogue as a tool to improve oneself, and Ikeda's capacity to learn from each encounter, mentioned by Seager below. The 'Socratic method' or *elenchus* is a dialectic method of inquiry, first presented by Plato in the Socratic dialogues. It is an essential methodological contribution that makes Socrates one of the founders of Western philosophy. By identifying and eliminating the hypotheses which lead to contradictions, dialogue partners are brought to examine the validity of their own beliefs. Similarly, according to Richard Seager, it is the educational power of dialogue that has most benefited Ikeda in his search for humanism. By using *elenchus* and other methods, while relentlessly pursuing dialogues with partners from diverse backgrounds, Ikeda has been able to refine his philosophy and make it global:

> These meetings serve a number of constructive ends, most basically that of satisfying Ikeda's passion for self-education. They have played a crucial role in his personal journey into cosmopolitan complexity (. . .). In this capacity, they have helped him to shape his emergent humanism, even as they enable him to carry Nichiren's Buddhism around the world (Seager 2006, 114).

Michel de Montaigne is mentioned in several peace proposals.[2] Ikeda quotes a passage from 'On the Art of Conversation': 'To my taste the most fruitful and most natural exercise of our minds is conversation. I find the practice of it the most delightful activity in our lives' (Montaigne 2003, 1045 quoted in Ikeda 2006–PP, 23). In the collection of poems entitled *Fighting for Peace* (2004b), Ikeda agrees that conversation is one of the greatest delights in life:

> Our desire is to walk
> with our intimate friends
> beneath the cherries' full bloom,
> inhaling the fragrance of peace,

caressed by warm breezes
and sharing our hopes
in pleasant conversation (113).

In 'On three kinds of social intercourse,' Montaigne wrote:

> What I would praise would be a soul with many storeys, one of
> which knew how to strain and relax; a soul at ease wherever for-
> tune led it; which could chat with a neighbour about whatever he
> is building, his hunting or his legal action, and take pleasure in
> conversing with a carpenter or a gardener. (Montaigne 2003, 925
> quoted in Ikeda 2006–PP, 24).

In this proposal, Ikeda notes that Montaigne loved holding discussions with
members of the elite and with ordinary people alike, and one of his methodological tools was to avoid imposing a conclusion.

For Montaigne it was important to launch an exchange without deciding
the outcome in advance. I see a link here with Habermas's distinction
between purposive and communicative rationality mentioned above. Ikeda
quotes Montaigne in one of the key passages concerning this method: 'My
thought sketches out the matter for a while and dwells lightly on the first
aspects of it: then I usually leave the principal thrust of the task to heaven'
(Montaigne 2003, 1058 quoted in Ikeda 2006–PP, 24). It is this willingness to be open-minded, and to let the dialogue do its work, that makes
Montaigne a champion of dialogue. The three volumes of his *Essays* show a
willingness to explore issues without deciding on the conclusion in advance,
and the French title *Essais*, which can be translated as 'attempts,' adequately
expresses Montaigne's open-mindedness.

I believe that one of the sources of Montaigne's passion for moderation and
dialogue can be found in his experiences with the fanaticism of the religious
wars in sixteenth-century France. A Roman Catholic, his efforts to become a
moderator between the two camps gained him the trust of both the Protestant
Henry of Navarre and the Catholic King Henry III. Montaigne had a direct
influence on such writers as Shakespeare, Emerson, Stephan Zweig, Nietzsche
and Rousseau, and owing to his humanistic refusal of dogmatism he is considered one of the founders of the anti-conformist tradition in French literature.

Martin Büber's concept of dialogue is mentioned in Ikeda's 2005 peace
proposal. He agrees with his distinction between relations based on 'I–It' and
those characterized by the 'I–You' perspective. I–It emphasizes the dichotomy
between the subjective and objective worlds, whereas 'I–You refers to the
kind of encounter and relations that escapes that superficial level to engage

the complete being on a far more essential dimension' (Ikeda 2005–PP, 28). Ikeda sees a direct link between the Buddhist concept of interconnectedness and Büber's philosophy: 'This way of thinking closely resembles the Buddhist concept of dependent origination (Jpn *Engi*), demonstrating the universality of Büber's vision of dialogue' (Ikeda 2005–PP, 28).

Martin Büber was an Austrian-born essayist, editor and translator who later moved to Israel. His work was mostly dedicated to three endeavors. He enhanced the revival of religious consciousness among the Jews with a German translation of the Bible and a retelling of Hasidic tales. He emphasized the importance of culture and spirituality, as opposed to Herzl's movement to create a nation-state where such elements were peripheral. He offered a philosophical exploration of the dialogic principle which is briefly introduced here.

In *I and Thou* (original German version 1923) Büber makes a simple distinction between the I–You and the I–It relationship as mentioned above. I–It is basically a monologue, in which a person considers the outside world and other people as objects, and assigns values to beings and things based on how they can be used. On the contrary, the I–You relationship considers the world and other people as important in themselves, in a holistic manner. Büber explained that the I–You relationship is about grasping the essence of the other person; something that is beyond words. This kind of relationship avoids superficial judgments and trappings to go straight to the essence of the other, and to people's common humanity. I believe the following passages are especially relevant:

> The world as experience belongs to the basic word I–It. The basic word I–You establishes the world of relation (Büber [1923] 1996, 56).

> The basic word I–You can be spoken only with one's whole being. The concentration and fusion into a whole being can never be accomplished by me, can never be accomplished without me. I require a You to become; becoming I, I say you. All actual life is encounter (62).

> Love is responsibility of an I for a You (66).

A conceptual link can be made with Habermas's distinction between communicative rationality (similar to I–You) and purposive rationality (similar to I–It), with both Büber and Habermas favoring the first mode of communication. I believe that for Ikeda also, dialogue is a way to reach our common humanity through the logos, putting human reason at the service of a more humane world, a way to ensure that the 'I' pays full attention to, and brings out the best in, the 'You.'

For Ikeda, this is a very serious endeavor that cannot be accomplished with a casual attitude:

> The real essence and practice of humanism is found in heartfelt, one-to-one dialogue. Be it summit diplomacy or the various interactions of private citizens in different lands, genuine dialogue has the kind of intensity described by the great twentieth-century humanist and philosopher Martin Büber (1878–1965) as an encounter 'on the narrow ridge'[3] in which the slightest inattention could result in a precipitous fall. Dialogue is indeed this kind of intense, high-risk encounter (Ikeda 2005–PP, 12).

Dialogical strategies

This section introduces several methods of ensuring a productive dialogue encountered in Ikeda's works: (1) Preparing the exchange thoroughly by studying the life and work of the dialogue partners in advance; (2) Creating intimacy with the dialogue partners by asking personal questions; (3) Moving towards more and more abstract and general topics; (4) Highlighting an important principle, in the case of Ikeda often a Buddhist principle, which can be made explicit using the interlocutor's own words; (5) Using even a disagreement as the starting point to finding common ground; (6) Giving the partners one's full attention, in person or in writing.

First, Ikeda always seems to know so much about the dialogue partners and their subject of expertise that it must be assumed that he prepares these exchanges thoroughly. A few examples of Ikeda's statements in the course of several dialogues about various topics such as nuclear abolition, the history of Islam, cancer research and art history will suffice to illustrate this point.

> Einstein knew that nuclear weapons development affects matters much more fundamental than mere techno-scientific progress. In April 1955, just before his death, he joined with Bertrand Russell and others to issue the Russell-Einstein Manifesto. This probing of how human beings should live in the Nuclear Age might be called their testament to humanity (Ikeda and Krieger 2002, 7).

> When he was still a merchant in obscurity, Muhammad was respected as a man of sincerity by people in Mecca. It was his personal integrity, then, that rescued him from extreme adversity and

provided him with a new setting for activity in Medina. The whole episode shows that his noble character was the great asset that supported him in crisis (Ikeda and Tehranian 2003, 20).

I understand that immunotherapy is being studied as a way of inhibiting cancer. Naturally, this would involve the body's natural defenses against illness, of which the immune system is the most important. What exactly is the role of white blood cells and lymphocytes within the immune system? (Ikeda, Simard and Bourgeault 2002, 47).

As you clearly indicate, the crisis that is deeply ingrained in material facts exerts a considerable influence on human morality. Many intellectuals have pointed out the crisis situation into which contemporary civilization has fallen. But, with their acute intuition, artists must have perceived it and the deep effect it has on our sensitivity earlier than others and no doubt expressed the insecurity and suffering associated with it. A specialist in art, like you, is in an excellent position to analyze this situation (Ikeda and Huyghe [1991] 2007, 39).

Second, Ikeda often asks personal questions at the beginning, and this propels the dialogue to a more profound level. Examples are selected from the dialogues with futurologist Hazel Henderson, nuclear physicist Joseph Rotblat, peace researcher Johan Galtung and chemist and vitamin C discoverer Linus Pauling. The exchanges might seem trivial in themselves, but their significance lies in the sense of intimacy these personal details have created between Ikeda and his partners. The participants can then move to more general topics based on this understanding. This method could simply be called 'breaking the ice.'

In the dialogue with Henderson, the mention of one's place of birth soon leads to more intimate family memories:

Ikeda: To start then, I was born in the Omori district of Tokyo in January 1928. (. . .) Tell me about your hometown.

Henderson: I was born in southwestern England in the city of Bristol in 1933. (. . .) From childhood, my parents instilled in me the attitude to question everything, not just blindly accept what I was told. Accordingly, I always questioned authority. I always stopped and thought for myself before making judgments. I didn't realize then what a gift that was! I'm very grateful to them now.

Ikeda: What a fine attitude. You are fortunate to have had such excellent parents.

Henderson: My father was an accountant at a pulp and cardboard factory in Bristol. A rather typical father of the time – a little despotic and stubborn, he was often absent because of work. Really, my mother was the anchor of my life and taught me how to love and learn (Ikeda and Henderson 2004, 4, 7).

During their dialogue, Joseph Rotblat shared memories of the disappearance of his wife during the Nazi massacres for the first time in a work destined to be published:

Ikeda: During our discussion, I would like to explore your recollections of your upbringing and the difficult conditions of your young adulthood. I understand that you were born in Warsaw, Poland.

Rotblat: Yes. When I was born, Warsaw was under the rule of Czarist Russia. At that point, for over one hundred years, Poland had been divided into three parts that were subsumed within the territories of Russia, Germany (Prussia), and Austria. (. . .)

Ikeda: By this time, nearly a year had passed since you had returned to Poland to bring your wife back to England. It must have been a very, very long year for you. (. . .) What a heart-rending story. You have not discussed these personal details of your past publicly before. You must have kept this buried deep in your heart. (. . .)

Rotblat: This has been the saddest experience of my entire life. Stalin once said, 'A single death is a tragedy, a million deaths is a statistic.' Based on this perspective, my wife Tola's death is a statistical fact. Her death had become a statistic. She was one of six million who perished in Poland during World War II. Ironically, around that time, I busied myself in the design of weaponry that could increase that death rate many times (Ikeda and Rotblat 2007, 27, 36).

In the dialogue with Galtung, Ikeda invites him to speak of an episode that had already been publicized many times, but that keeps its significance as Galtung's starting point for his search for peace.

> **Ikeda:** I have heard that seeing your beloved father, Dr. August Galtung, a former deputy mayor of Oslo and a physician, taken away to a concentration camp by the Nazis when you were only 13 years old motivated you to devote yourself to humanitarianism and peace.

> **Galtung:** My motivations were twofold. On the private level, I was influenced by the violent madness that afflicted Norway in general and our own small family in particular during World War II. I wanted to find out how all that horror might have been avoided; how the karma of all Europe might have been improved; and, in honest, personal terms, how we could have kept father at home with us (Ikeda and Galtung 1995, 3).

In the dialogue with Pauling, again the simple mention of one's hometown leads to more intimate family memories, paving the way for an open exchange throughout the rest of the conversation:

> **Ikeda:** To begin, perhaps we might get to know each other better by sharing information about our childhoods.

> **Pauling:** I was born in Portland, Oregon, on February 28, 1901. For the next few years, I lived with my parents in Salem, Portland, and Oswego – all in Oregon. (. . .) I had long, golden curls, which my father decided to have cut off. No doubt regretting the loss of a baby who was already growing into a boy, when she first saw me after the haircut, my mother burst into tears (Ikeda and Pauling 1992, 1).

I believe the examples above show the challenges of striking a balance between the personal and the generally relevant, in order to be able to handle the dynamic tension between agreements, disagreements and compromises that is sure to appear in the course of the dialogues.

Third, one needs to move smoothly to more abstract topics, once an acceptable level of intimacy has been established. In the following exchange, Ikeda starts with personal details followed by war memories and soon makes a general statement about war:

Ikeda: Before we begin our discussion, I would like to ask you about your personal background. That will help deepen our mutual understanding and it will also be a good way to introduce you to our readers.

Tehranian: Well, I was born in 1937 in an Iranian city called Mashhad. Mashhad literally means 'a place of martyrdom.' This is where Imam Reza, the 8th Imam of the Shi'a Islamic faith, is buried. (. . .)

Ikeda: I hear that his tomb is now a holy site to which a great many Shi'a pilgrims from all over the world come to pay tribute. (. . .) I was born in 1928 in Tokyo's Ohta ward. Of many childhood memories I remember particularly well the sight of the beautiful blue sea from the seashore near my home. (. . .) The peaceful days of my childhood did not last very long. When I was eleven, that horrible war – World War II – broke out.

Tehranian: I was only three, then. (. . .) While walking along the streets of the city, I remember hiding behind my mother's *chadar* so that the Russian bombs would not hit me!

Ikeda: War completely destroys the happy life of people, reduces whole towns to ashes overnight, and deprives us of the lives of our loved ones and dear friends. The horror of war is beyond imagination unless you've experienced it yourself (Ikeda and Tehranian 2003, 2–3).

A fourth strategy often used by Ikeda is to carefully listen to the interlocutors, and to then highlight a Buddhist principle hidden in the underlying architecture of their discourse. I find this rather risky, because people could feel used and imposed upon unless a necessary level of intimacy and trust has been established between the interlocutors.

I do not recall one instance in which the result was not positive and I find Ikeda's capacity to bring the discussions to such levels quite inspiring. In the dialogue with Mikhail Gorbachev, the political philosophy called 'New Thinking' designed by the former General Secretary of the Soviet Communist Party and last President of the Soviet Union is highlighted as an illustration of the centuries-old Buddhist concept of dependent origination, or the interconnectedness of all things (Skt *pratitya-samutpada*):

Gorbachev: For us the New Thinking started with the recognition of what was evident and indisputable; that is, that socialism and capitalism are only different alternatives on the path of the development of human civilization. But the recognition of the world's essential heterogeneity and of diversity of values and means was only the first step. The second, which derives from the first, was recognition of the essential interconnections and mutual interdependence of everything in the world.

Ikeda: Your words hark back to the Buddhist conception of dependent origination as the source of all existence. Obviously, phenomena have particular meanings. But individual traits can manifest themselves in their full glory only because of the universal interconnectedness of existence. This extremely dynamic viewpoint resonates with your ideas of the essential interconnection and interdependence of the world. Because of this interconnection, coexistence is the key to the essence of the 21st century (Ikeda and Gorbachev 2005, 53).

A fifth strategy is to use a disagreement as a source for creating an even deeper understanding between participants. The dialogue in book form with British historian Arnold Toynbee entitled *Choose Life* (1976) is one of the very few dialogues in which disagreement actually comes to the surface, probably because so much of it was direct and 'live.' It contains a difference of opinion between the two partners about the future of the world, which is somehow resolved by lifting the dialogue to a higher level.

Toynbee thinks the greatest problem of humanity is greed, which causes all kinds of suffering and catastrophes. He agrees with Ikeda that inner transformation allowing people to overcome their greed through self-mastery is needed. However, Toynbee believes that this movement of inner transformation will be too slow, and that a world dictatorship will have to appear in order to prevent a global disaster. He bases his conviction on three historical examples of long and stable dictatorships that were established in the wake of three shorter and more brutal ones. Ikeda does not agree, and both are able to overcome this difference by seeing eye-to-eye again on the specific point of 'self-mastery.' Selected passages from this exchange are presented and analyzed below.

Toynbee: I suspect that a worldwide totalitarian movement of the communist-fascist kind may overthrow existing institutions (. . .). The global party platform will probably be stabilization in all departments of life at any price. When this revolutionary work has been accomplished under the leadership of a ruthless world dictator (. . .) the necessary stabilization will be remodelled into a milder and therefore more durable form. This will be accomplished by a second world dictator who will be more tactful in his actions (. . .).

Ikeda: Your forecast is both bold and disturbing. (. . .)

Toynbee: Although I could give many more illustrations of my point, in fact I have in mind three cases taken from Japanese, Chinese, and Roman history. Tokugawa Ieyasu, who followed Toyotomi Hideyoshi, established the long-lived Tokugawa regime. Ch'in Shih Huang-ti founded the Imperial Ch'in, which lasted a brief fourteen years (221–207 BC). His successor, Han Liu Pang, however, created a Chinese imperial regime that lasted, on and off, for more than twenty-one centuries. Similarly, Augustus, who followed Julius Caesar, established a Roman imperial system that lasted from 31 BC until AD 284 in its original form and in a more autocratic form at Constantinople till AD 1204.

Ikeda: (. . .) Though obviously social questions are important, the true cause of abuse of power lies in the evil that – like good – is a basic element in human life (. . .).

Toynbee: I agree that the essential evil of power is an innate tendency in human nature and that we must search for means of mitigating this evil. I believe that the only effective means is the subordination of egotism or greed to altruism or love in the conduct of individuals. In other words, self-mastery is the only way to happiness for the individual and for all humanity (Ikeda and Toynbee 1976, 230–31).

To rephrase this exchange, first Toynbee presents his general theory that a ruthless and short-lived dictatorship must appear in order to stabilize the chaotic situation of the world today, to be followed by a milder but still dictatorial longer form of world government. Ikeda is diplomatically critical and this encourages Toynbee to give detailed examples of his theory. Ikeda insists that he believes in human revolution more than in world dictatorship, and finally Toynbee agrees, using his own vocabulary to describe the concept of human revolution: altruism, love and self-mastery.

It is to be noted that a dialogue can be productive and enhance the understanding between participants even if a disagreement persists. In the same work, Toynbee and Ikeda agree in their opposition to the death penalty and nuclear weapons, but their opinions differ concerning homosexuality, euthanasia and suicide, and they fail to reach a compromise concerning these three topics. Ikeda sees homosexuality as unproblematic and Toynbee supports euthanasia and suicide in specific circumstances, but they do not see eye-to-eye on these issues. Ikeda doesn't try to 'win' arguments, but to raise the level of the discussion to the plane of a higher synthesis, where the differences are resolved.

Toynbee: If you attempt to solve the problem of promiscuous heterosexual relations in coeducational institutions by segregating boys from girls, you find yourself with the equally serious problem of homosexual relations.

Ikeda: I believe that male and female homosexuality is a relative issue. Some societies accept it, as did ancient Greece; some condemn it. Sexual relations between male and female involve deeper issues since they lead to pregnancy and are therefore closely connected with the dignity of life itself. If I were forced to make a decision, I would say that probably homosexual relations among students are the lesser of the two evils (70).

(. . .)

Toynbee: I define euthanasia as the killing of a human being not in order to punish him and not in order to protect other people against him but as an act of mercy for him.

(. . .)

Ikeda: If we grant that euthanasia ought to be approved under certain conditions, your suggestion for a way to deal with it is convincing. Nevertheless, I cannot condone the shortening of life by physical, chemical, or any other external means. I do agree, however, that it is unnecessary to waste efforts on keeping alive hopelessly ill people (. . .) whose brains no longer function or whose bodies cannot take in nourishment unaided (. . .). While recognizing that freedom to assist another to escape unbearable pain by taking his life or to seek death for oneself is a logical conclusion of humanistic thought, I am afraid that, should this idea be regarded with less than maximum caution, it could degenerate into the kind of under-valuing of life that I have often condemned (163).

(. . .)

Toynbee: Both these friends [an artist who had had a stroke and a writer who was being overtaken by incurable blindness] had to make sure that they would be able to contrive to commit suicide without being detected and prevented. Both were successful, but the need to avoid being hindered was an aggravation of a tragic situation. I feel that this aggravation of their plight was an unjustifiable additional affliction for them. In cases such as these two, I hold that suicide is legitimate and that to put obstacles in the way of it is very wrong.

Ikeda: The cases of your friends arouse sympathy, but I still insist that one must regard one's own life with the same maximum respect that one must give the life of another person. Talents and the ability to reason are only a part, not all, of the total entity of life. To argue that once a person's abilities have failed, he can no longer live in a meaningful way is to put too narrow an interpretation on life itself. Should this attitude become widely accepted, talentless people might come to be considered unworthy of living (165).

I think that one reason Ikeda is successful in managing such differences of opinion, besides his capacity to establish a deep level of intimacy, is his use of Montaigne's method mentioned above. If I may paraphrase the French moralist, the important point is to 'sketch out the matter lightly, dwell lightly on the first aspects of it, and leave the principal thrust of the task to the dynamics of the dialogue itself.' Since the outcome of the dialogue is not pre-determined, and since the main goal is to bring out the best in oneself and others, disagreements can be considered as a natural, inevitable and even useful part of the process.

Finally, it is important to give the dialogue partners one's full attention. In his recent work entitled *The Living Dialogue: Socrates to Ikeda*, N. Radhakrishnan, the Chairman of the Indian Council for Gandhian Studies, sums up the main impression he keeps from his encounters with Ikeda, and I believe this passage describes the kind of wholehearted earnestness Ikeda brings to his dialogues:

I have been privileged to have dialogues with Dr. Ikeda on six different occasions in the last fifteen years. When I remember those occasions, I see that the manner in which Ikeda engages a person in dialogue is based on the profound worth he accords to each individual. (. . .) This is an important character of the dialogues Ikeda has been holding with persons of different tempers, from diverse cultural, political and ethnic origins (Radhakrishnan 2006, xix–xx).

Ikeda's whirlwind of dialogues

In the introduction to one of Ikeda's works, Joseph Rotblat wrote:

> For over forty years, Daisaku Ikeda has traversed the globe, engaging in dialogue with many of the world's leading thinkers, and carrying the message of hope and goodwill. He wishes to embrace all people and is determined to forge heart to heart bonds of mutual acceptance and respect which will ensure a lasting peace (Ikeda 2004b, ix).

Ikeda has met more than 7,000 scholars, political and opinion leaders from virtually all countries, has held longer dialogues with many of them and has published about 50 of these dialogues in book form. Twenty of them have been translated into English, and they serve as the main material for this chapter. Among Ikeda's dialogue partners, besides those introduced above, it is worth mentioning peace researcher Elise Boulding, Chinese philosophy expert Tu Weiming, former president of the Republic of Chile Patricio Aylwin Azocar, leading Korean academic Cho Moon-Boo and leading Chinese writer Jin Yong.[4]

The number of dialogues Ikeda has engaged in and published is therefore impressive,[5] as is the fact that his interlocutors include representatives of so many of the world's cultural, philosophical and religious traditions. This, considered in the light of the fact that he is clearly devout in his Buddhist faith, shows a capacity to combine a commitment to a specific belief system with the openness to connect with people holding different views, on the basis of a common humanity.

Ikeda has discussed a wide range of topics and concerns with his partners, including: the abolition of nuclear weapons (Krieger, Rotblat), the future of civilization (Peccei, Toynbee), humanistic governance (Aylwin, Gorbachev, Kissinger), ecological economics (Henderson, Swaminathan), peace research and activism (Boulding, Galtung, Pauling), spirituality and religions (Djourova, Tehranian, Wilson), health and bioethics (Bourgeault and Simard), astronomy (Wickramasinghe, Serebrov, Mourão) and literature and the arts (Huyghe, Malraux).

Once the dialogue partners have agreed to publish a book together, they have to meet in person at least once, often complementing their conversation with abundant written correspondence until they are both satisfied with the result. In many cases, it is after a first face-to-face meeting that they decide to pursue a more sustained dialogue and to have it published. René Simard, former rector of the University of Montreal and authority on cancer research, wrote that after his first meeting with Ikeda they 'came to the conclusion that an encounter between a philosopher and a biologist could produce an interesting dialogue' (Ikeda, Simard and Bourgeault 2002, 16).

Next follows an arduous process of refining the translation, editing, updating, adding introduction and final comments, until a complete agreement is reached by the parties. Generally, the dialogue is then first published in Japanese (with some exceptions), before being translated into different languages whenever possible, based on the book's popularity and other logistic considerations. For instance, the Toynbee Dialogue was published in 28 different languages and that with Aurelio Peccei in 17 languages, but the dialogues with Elise Boulding, Kenneth Galbraith and André Malraux only have a Japanese version (as of October 2009).

Besides the dialogues published in book form, many others are mentioned by Ikeda in other works. For instance the book *Wonderful Encounters* (2003) relates Ikeda's meetings and dialogues with such diverse figures as photographer Cornell Capa, violin virtuoso Yehudi Menuhin, peace scholar Glenn Paige and former Chinese Premier Zhou Enlai among others.

The first of Ikeda's dialogues with renowned scholars to be published in book form took place in 1970, a discussion with Count Richard Coudenhove-Kalergi who was one of the pioneers behind the realization of the European Union. They discussed such themes as the potential for a pan-Pacific civilization for a total of about ten hours. Published in 1972 in Japanese, this dialogue was not translated into other languages. It is the second one, with Arnold Toynbee, which has been published in 28 languages (as of October 2009), that has attracted worldwide attention.

The dialogue was held in person with Toynbee for a total of about 40 hours in 1972 and 1973, and the historian William H. McNeill writes how the dialogue was organized in the biography *Arnold J. Toynbee: A Life* (1989). Toynbee became a leading authority on history after the publication of his ten-volume *A Study of History* (1934–61) starting with the publication of the first three volumes in 1934, and even more after the next three in 1939. He became more and more recognized in the US until his reputation as 'sage for the American century' was secured by the 17 March 1947 cover of *Time* magazine (Seager 2006, 116).

By 1954 he was under attack by scholars who did not agree with his theory of the decline and rise of civilizations, but enthusiasm for Toynbee reached a climax in Japan after his third trip to that country in 1967. The success of that visit is probably due to the publication of an abridged version of *A Study of History* in Japanese in 1966, which offered an alternative to the Marxist view of history that dominated Japanese academia at the time. Toynbee was invited to publish a dialogue in 90 installments with Kei Wakaizumi in the daily *Mainichi Shimbun*. It was Wakaizumi, professor of international relations at Kyoto Sangyo University, who introduced Ikeda and Toynbee around that time, according to McNeill (1989). In the fall of 1969, the renowned historian invited Ikeda to come to the UK for a dialogue, with the following letter:

> When I was last in Japan in 1967, people talked to me about the Sokagakkai [sic] and about you yourself. I have heard a great deal about you. (. . .) I am going to read some of your books and speeches translated into English. (. . .) It is my pleasure, therefore, to extend to you my personal invitation to visit me in Britain in order to have with you a fruitful exchange of views on a number of fundamental problems of our times which deeply concern us all (Kelly 2002, 20 quoted in Seager 2006, 117).

As Seager writes, there were at least three common points between the philosophy of the 83-year-old British historian and the 42-year-old Japanese Buddhist leader: the belief in a spiritual dynamic underlying the great movements of history, the concept of challenge and response, explaining how creative groups are able to overcome obstacles, and 'a conviction that the next chapter in history was to be the emergence of global civilization, although Ikeda expressed more optimism than Toynbee about it being achieved through peaceful means' (Seager 2006, 118).

Toynbee also suggested to Ikeda that he should expand his networks, holding dialogues with many more thinkers. Toynbee gave Ikeda a list of a few leading intellectuals he should meet first, including Aurelio Peccei and Joseph Derbolav. Ikeda followed the historian's advice, meeting with these individuals and others. Ikeda also uses dialogue for informal citizen diplomacy, and in 1974 and 1975 he took action as a private citizen in order to contribute to the defusing of tensions among the main players of the Cold War, China, the Soviet Union and the United States.

During his first visit to China in May 1974, Ikeda became aware of the anxiety prevailing in the country when he witnessed the Chinese building a huge network of underground shelters in Beijing against the threat of Soviet attack. A few months later, Ikeda was in Moscow:

> In September the same year, I visited the Soviet Union for the first time, and met with Premier Aleksei N. Kosygin (1904–80). I spoke of China's deep concern about the Soviet Union's intentions, and asked him straight out whether the Soviet Union was planning to attack China or not. The premier responded that the Soviet Union had no intention of either attacking or isolating China (Ikeda 2007–PP, 42).

When he next visited China in December 1974, he brought this message from Kosygin with him. He also met with Premier Zhou Enlai and discussed the friendship between China and Japan:

> During our meeting, Premier Zhou stressed that China had no wish to be a superpower. Taken together with Premier Kosygin's words, this statement convinced me that an easing of tensions between the two countries was not far off. And indeed, this proved to be the case (Ikeda 2007–PP, 42–43).

Next Ikeda met Secretary of State Henry Kissinger in the US: 'When I told him of Premier Zhou's wish to conclude a Sino–Japanese peace and friendship treaty, Kissinger expressed his agreement and support for the idea' (Ikeda, 2007–PP, 43). On the same day, Ikeda met the Japanese Minister of Finance, Masayoshi Ohira, in Washington: 'I conveyed Kissinger's words to him and expressed my own sense of the absolute necessity of such a treaty. Ohira, who later served as Japan's prime minister, responded that he was fully committed to bringing such a treaty about' (Ikeda 2007–PP, 43). The Sino–Japanese Peace and Friendship Treaty became a reality three years later, in August 1978.

There have been a variety of ways in which Ikeda was able to meet his dialogue partners, and another example provided by Seager will illustrate this diversity. This is how Ikeda was introduced to Nelson Mandela, whom he met in 1990 and again in 1995:

> In the mid-1980's, Oswald Mtshali, a South African writer whose poetry was influential in the anti-apartheid movement, read Ikeda's *Glass Children* and was inspired by his remarks about empowering youth. He later praised Ikeda as a profound Eastern philosopher in a series of articles that Mandela read while imprisoned. Some years

later, Mandela requested a meeting with that philosopher during his visit to Japan (Seager 2006, 120).

Concluding comments: Ikeda's philosophy of dialogue for peace

One of the explanations for the huge number of dialogues and exchanges held by Ikeda, besides his love of human contact and his desire to learn, might be found in his idealism. Unconcerned by utilitarian calculations concerning the potential benefits to be reaped by specific dialogical efforts, Ikeda believes that holding dialogues is like planting seeds, like making good causes that will inevitably produce positive, yet undefined, results. I believe that the following passage, mentioned earlier in another context, captures the essence of this struggle:

> If one drop of the water of dialogue is allowed to fall upon the waste-
> land of intolerance, where attitudes of hatred and exclusionism have
> so long prevailed, there will be a possibility for trust and friendship
> to spring up (Ikeda and Tehranian 2003, xiv).

I would like to suggest that dialogue at its most meaningful is not possible between people who have not sufficiently elevated their consciousness through self-mastery and inner reformation. The latter can be the result of intense efforts at introspection for a few minutes or of a lifelong commitment to self-improvement, but I believe one should always prepare oneself in some way before trying to communicate deeply with another human being. Inner transformation therefore must precede dialogue, even though this does not mean that one must be 'perfectly transformed' before being able to hold productive dialogues. Rather, I believe that the most effective approach is a daily process including efforts at both inner transformation and dialogue. Even brief efforts towards self-scrutiny will immediately improve the quality of the dialogue one is engaged in.

At the same time, it is often through dialogue that we are inspired to start a process of inner transformation. As a result, to fully understand the importance of the concept of dialogue in Ikeda's philosophy of peace, several models showing the interdependence of the concepts of inner transformation, dialogue, global citizenship and global civilization might be useful.

This chapter has highlighted the coherence between several aspects of Ikeda's philosophy of dialogue for peace and their similarities with the ideas of dialogical thinkers. I believe that it is based on a decision to protect and enhance life that one can opt for a dialogical style characterized by open-mindedness, as Montaigne recommends. A large dose of courage, wisdom and compassion is helpful if one is to follow that route. One is then equipped with the tools to make Habermas's communicative rationality the basis of one's dialogical activities, resisting tendencies to use purposive rationality which too often leads to dehumanization (Weber) and manipulation (Adorno). One can then grasp the essence of the other person, enjoying what Büber calls an 'I–You' relationship. Repeating this type of dialogical exercise can enhance our identities as global citizens.

From this understanding of other people and a mastery of humane dialogical methods, it is possible to develop communicative action and deliberative democracy, and to reinforce the public sphere, protecting it from the negative sides of the administrative sphere. This in turn is fertile ground for the development of more humane global governance, with its tremendous potential to lead to the creation of elements of a global civilization of interdependence and harmony.

To paraphrase Socrates, the use of dialogue is indispensable to create a society characterized by love of language, of ideas and of people. I believe this is the kind of world Ikeda wants to bring about through dialogue.

CHAPTER 7

Global Citizenship and Elements of a Global Civilization of Interconnectedness in the Peace Proposals

To set out from immediate and concrete realities, creating with every step new neighbors in an expanding network of human solidarity – this is the true path to peace.

[T]he perspectives and principles that constitute what I refer to as 'inner universality' are rooted in the world of concrete realities and can only be developed from within. The truly important questions are always close at hand, in our tangible and immediate circumstances.

Dialogue presents infinite possibilities; it is a challenge that can be taken up by anyone – any time – in order to realize the transformation from a culture of violence to a culture of peace.

[I]f we search beyond the arbitrary, surface labels and engage with each other as individuals in dialogue, generating spontaneous and intense interactions of heart and mind, we will be able to give rise to the 'deeper, slower movements'[1] which Toynbee considered to ultimately shape human history.

Daisaku Ikeda (2009–PP, 12, 10, 24, 25)

In the context of the systematization of Ikeda's philosophy of peace presented here, the third main concept besides inner transformation and dialogue is global citizenship. For Ikeda, this idea does not imply arduous linguistic training or extensive travels, but rather an 'inner nobility,' a capacity to be 'genuinely concerned for the peace and prosperity of the world.' In his 1996 lecture entitled 'Education toward Global Citizenship,' he wrote:

> Over the past several decades, I have been privileged to meet and converse with many people from all walks of life, and I have given the matter some thought. Certainly, global citizenship is not determined merely by the number of languages one speaks, or the number of countries to which one has traveled. I have many friends who could be considered quite ordinary citizens, but who possess an inner nobility; who have never traveled beyond their native place, yet who are genuinely concerned for the peace and prosperity of the world (Ikeda 2001a, 100).

It is after this passage that Ikeda recommends courage, wisdom and compassion as the three most important qualities for global citizenship. I believe this concept is organically linked with the development of elements of a global civilization and that the more global citizens appear in society, the more our institutions will show the capacity to tackle global problems. Whereas the construction of elements of an inclusive global civilization requires expertise in such fields as politics, law and economics, I consider global citizenship as the human capacity to see the common humanity shining in all people. In this sense, this human quality is deeply linked with the efforts at inner transformation and constructive dialogue described in previous chapters, and it is therefore considered here as the third and final pillar of Ikeda's philosophy of peace.

In the children's tale entitled *Over the Deep Blue Sea* (1992), Ikeda narrates the story of Akiko and Hiroshi, two youngsters who find themselves on a new island with no friends. One of the locals, Pablo, resents the fact that their country attacked his island during the War. However, at the end he saves Hiroshi's life, and Ikeda uses the image of ocean rivers to symbolize the spirit of global citizenship in the following passage:

> It was one of those ocean rivers which had swept them out to sea. The ship's skipper told them so when he had brought them both safe home. 'They're longer than any rivers on dry land,' he said. 'They carried our ancestors' tiny boats all around the world, some to live here, some to settle there. . .'

'You mean that Pablo's ancestors and ours might have lived in the same place once?' exclaimed Akiko. 'Might have been brothers, even?'

'Well, of course! We're all just sailors come ashore off the same deep blue sea!'

'Maybe that's why I rowed out when I saw Hiroshi was in trouble,' said Pablo. 'How can brothers be enemies?'

'How can *anyone* be enemies,' said Hiroshi, 'if it's only the sea in between that makes us different?' 'Sometimes people forget,' said the skipper sadly. Like Pablo's Grandma, he could remember the War (22).

In this chapter I argue that Ikeda's peace proposals contain most of his ideas on global citizenship and on the way to make progress towards a better world by overcoming narrow interests. It also contains concrete ideas for the development of elements of a future global civilization of harmony and interdependence. The concept of humanitarian competition is also part of this vision for a more peaceful world.

First, the overall background and origins of the peace proposals will be addressed. Next, the methodology used to analyze them is explained, as well as the division of the proposals in three periods. I then trace the representation of the three main concepts explored in this work as they appear throughout the proposals, as well as some of the major issues that Ikeda consistently deals with in these writings. A discussion follows concerning the potential impact and intended audience of the proposals, as well as some of the SGI's activities for coalition building. The last section attempts to paint a picture of Ikeda's vision for a future inclusive and harmonious global civilization mostly based on the 27 proposals, with some relevant additions from his other writings. A comparison with the 'liberal peace' theory and Daniele Archibugi's concept of 'cosmopolitan democracy' is also presented.

Background and origins of the peace proposals

On 26 January every year since 1983, Ikeda has released an extensive essay called a peace proposal (PP), which is published in several news outlets and forwarded to key personnel of the United Nations and other leading peace organizations. These 27 proposals (1983–2009) outline Ikeda's vision for a more peaceful and harmonious world based on interdependence, creative coexistence and cooperation, a new global paradigm in which the UN plays a central role.

They are usually divided into two parts, one exploring philosophical themes (such as inner transformation, dialogue, global citizenship, elements of a global civilization as well as Makiguchi's concept of humanitarian competition) and the other offering concrete proposals concerning global issues (such as abolition of nuclear weapons, UN reform, peace in East Asia and the environment).

When Ikeda penned his first peace proposal in 1983, he was no novice in the promotion of peace through words and actions. One important starting point of his activities and of the SGI peace movement was the 1957 declaration against nuclear weapons by Josei Toda. Another important milestone was Ikeda's declaration[2] in favor of better relations with China in 1968. Leading up to the first peace proposal, three speeches by Ikeda in 1975, 1978 and 1982 are also examined below.

The first time Soka Gakkai members were collectively exposed to an issue decisively outside the scope of what would normally be considered religious activities was through Toda's 1957 Declaration Calling for the Abolition of Nuclear Weapons.[3] This declaration became the basis for the first petitions, exhibitions and publications of the Soka Gakkai concerning peace, and has been analyzed in depth in Chapter 3.

Ikeda's 1968 declaration in favor of the normalization of Sino–Japanese relations attracted the attention of the Chinese leaders, but it was severely criticized by many more rightwing Japanese politicians. Ikeda affirmed that mainland China should be invited to become a member of the UN and encouraged the restoration of diplomatic ties between Japan and China. These two ideas became a reality soon after, in 1971 and 1972 respectively. Chinese leaders and ordinary people have expressed gratitude for Ikeda for his 1968 declaration and subsequent efforts for Sino–Japanese friendship, in the form of academic degrees,[4] the establishment of research centers[5] devoted to the study of Ikeda's philosophy, invitations to meet such leaders as Zhou Enlai, Deng Xiaoping and others, and visits by Chinese leaders who are keen to hold dialogues with Ikeda during their trips to Japan. The proverbial phrase, 'when you drink water, remember those who dug the well,' has been used by many Chinese figures to express their appreciation for Ikeda's efforts.

Some Japanese politicians and scholars who were in favor of the improvement of Sino–Japanese relationships have also expressed their support for Ikeda's 1968 declaration as an important historical event. For instance Kenzo Matsumura, at different times Minister of Health, Education and Agriculture and Forestry, as well as scholar of Chinese literature Yoshimi Takeuchi, shared the impact the 1968 declaration had on them personally, and on Sino–Japanese relationships at the time.[6]

On the Chinese side, Ms. Lin Liyun, who served as the personal Japanese interpreter of former premier Zhou Enlai, remembers vividly that the former premier considered Ikeda's 1968 declaration as an event of great significance. When Kenzo Matsumura met Zhou Enlai in March 1970, he told Zhou that he wanted to entrust the future of Sino–Japanese friendship to Ikeda. Zhou replied that he was ready to welcome Ikeda to China at any time (*Seikyo Shimbun* 2008, 3).

In the local newspaper *Akita Sakigake* of 4 September 2008, Kazuteru Saionji, director of the Kogakuin University Confucian Academy and author of numerous books about Chinese history, mentioned that the 1968 Ikeda declaration was of great historical significance due to its timing. In the 1960s China was in the middle of the Cultural Revolution, the country was isolated and Sino–Japanese relations were in crisis. Ikeda's call for the restoration of diplomatic relations between the two countries and for the inclusion of China in the UN was a dramatic move in favor of China (*Akita Sakigake* 2008, 7).

One last example is found in an article from the *China Daily* entitled 'Praise for Man who Called for Friendship,' reporting comments made by Chinese President Hu Jintao during his visit to Japan on 8 May 2008:

> President Hu Jintao yesterday spoke highly of Daisaku Ikeda (. . .) for his contribution to the friendship between China and Japan. (. . .) In 1968, Ikeda called for restoring Sino–Japanese ties before 20,000 Soka Gakkai university students. He also called for the normalization of Sino–Japanese diplomatic relations (. . .). At the time, China was perceived as an enemy by many in Japan and was isolated from the international community.

> Ikeda's proposal drew condemnation, but also caught the attention of those who were interested in restoring relations between the two [countries], including Chinese Premier Zhou Enlai. One person who supported the normalization of relations was Kenzo Matsumura, a member of the House of Representatives, the Lower House of Japan's Diet. He approached Ikeda following his speech and urged him to visit China. Ikeda felt this was a matter for politicians and suggested representatives of the Komei Party should make the visit.

> Thus, a chain of events was set in motion, culminating in the restoration of diplomatic ties in 1972 (*China Daily* 2008).

In order to understand the origins of the first peace proposal released in 1983, it is necessary to examine three preliminary documents written by Ikeda: the 1975 speech establishing the International Buddhist League,[7] the 1978 nuclear abolition proposal submitted to the First Special Session on Disarmament (SSOD-I) of the UN and the 1982 nuclear abolition proposal submitted to the Second Special Session on Disarmament (SSOD-II). The 1983 peace proposal explicitly refers to the 1975, 1978 and 1982 documents, ensuring the consistency of Ikeda's position in this first appeal.

Concerning the establishment of the International Buddhist League (IBL) on 26 January 1975 in Guam, Ikeda and several Japanese Soka Gakkai leaders had planned to launch it together with representatives of different national Soka Gakkai organizations. However, the participants proposed to name the new organization the Soka Gakkai International (SGI) instead. Ikeda accepted their request, and became the first president of the SGI. Ikeda's speech can be considered as the point of departure of the worldwide lay Buddhist movement of the SGI.

The two main ideas of the 1975 IBL/SGI text are present in the 1983 proposal, the first being that Buddhist humanist ideals must first spread throughout society in order for an international solidarity of awakened citizens to be created. This point was discussed during Ikeda's dialogue with the historian Arnold Toynbee. The second idea is that Buddhist principles need to be shared with the UN. This is Ikeda's response to a request Kurt Waldheim (the then UN Secretary-General) made to Ikeda in 1975:

> A few days ago, I took part in a meeting with the Secretary General of the United Nations, Kurt Waldheim, a man who is deeply serious and concerned about the peace of the world. At the conclusion of our meeting, he said – perhaps by way of encouragement – that he would like to know more about the principles of our movement and to use the knowledge gained from them, in a reconsideration of the management of the United Nations as a substantial organ for peace. We must respond to his request (Ikeda 1975, 23).

In his 1978 UN proposal on the occasion of SSOD-I, Ikeda mentions the essence of Toda's 1957 declaration and presents ten points[8] for the abolition of nuclear weapons. It suggests that the path towards a solution to the nuclear arms issue is dialogue and a focus on humanity in general, not only on nations. This can be considered as an early expression of the concept of 'human security'[9] based on the spirit of global citizenship. Ikeda also suggests the establishment of a 'Council of World Citizens for the Protection of the UN.'

Among the ten points of this text, six were rarely mentioned afterwards by Ikeda. However four of the points reappear often in the proposals. They are: the creation of more Nuclear-Weapons-Free Zones, the creation of an Arms-reduction Research and Information Center, the encouragement for more anti-war exhibits and more movies about nuclear weapons and the transfer of money from military activities to peaceful ones, and from national budgets to the UN.

In the 1982 UN proposal at SSOD-II, Ikeda reasserts his position against nuclear deterrence and the Buddhist philosophy at the basis of that position. To create a world without war, people need mutual trust and collaboration, not horribly destructive weapons and deterrence, which is a euphemism for massive death threats. He repeats his 1978 call for ordinary people to stand up and act against nuclear weapons, his 1978 proposal for the creation of a 'Council of World Citizens Association to Support the UN,' as well as all 10 points of the 1978 text.

Ikeda reaffirms the importance of the Buddhist ideals of respect for all life and his conviction that nuclear weapons are an absolute evil in his first annual peace proposal (1983). He encourages the activities of ordinary people, non-governmental organizations (NGOs), networks of universities and of research institutions, and stresses the need to create a global network of ordinary people for peace between the US and the USSR; an idea already found in the 1982 text.

The initial peace proposal of 1983 can therefore be considered as the crys-tallization of Ikeda's thoughts about peace as expressed in his writings since 1975, and also as the point of departure of all subsequent proposals and some other texts, such as his proposal for UN reform entitled *Fulfilling the Mission: Empowering the UN to Live up to the World's Expectations* (Ikeda 2006c) and his proposal for nuclear disarmament entitled *Building Global Solidarity Toward Nuclear Abolition* (Ikeda 2009a).

Inspired by these numerous writings, the members of the Soka Gakkai and of the SGI have promoted peace by organizing petitions, exhibitions and other events. In 1973 youth members of Soka Gakkai collected 10 million signatures in support of nuclear abolition, and this petition was presented to Secretary-General Kurt Waldheim at the UN in 1975. Along the same lines, in 1997 the youth members collected 13 million signatures for Abolition 2000, and the petition was presented to the Preparatory Committee of the Nuclear Non-Proliferation Treaty (NPT PrepCom) in 1998. These efforts were widely recognized in the nuclear disarmament community, for instance in March 2000 when Ikeda received the World Citizen Award from the Nuclear Age Peace Foundation (NAPF).

The first major exhibition was 'Nuclear Arms: Threat to Our World' in 1982 at the UN Headquarters in New York. It was organized to coincide with the Second Special Session on Disarmament (SSOD-II) in cooperation with the UN Department of Public Information (UNDPI) and the cities of Hiroshima and Nagasaki. The exhibition was viewed by 1.2 million people in 25 cities in 16 different countries, including the US, France, China and the Soviet Union, which were four nuclear powers on different sides of the Iron Curtain. This was 25 years after Toda's 1957 declaration and can be considered as one of several concrete responses to Toda's call. The exhibition consists mainly of photographic panels depicting the horrific destruction of Hiroshima and Nagasaki, and the death, injury and suffering endured by its inhabitants. An updated version entitled 'Nuclear Arms: Threat to Humanity,' launched in 1996, was viewed by half a million people in 14 cities in eight Latin American countries.[10]

The Youth Peace Conference (YPC) was established in 1979, and this group of young people became the driving force for the Soka Gakkai's activities for peace. The YPC wages various campaigns inspired by some of Ikeda's ideas found in the peace proposals and elsewhere, and actively supports the UN. They have participated in the promotion of Human Rights education (1995–2004) and from 2005 supported a 'World Program for Human Rights Education.' Between 1973 and 2001 they organized 21 campaigns to support UNHCR and other humanitarian relief organizations. In 1991 and 1992 they collected 300,000 second-hand radios for the UN Transitional Authority in Cambodia (UNTAC), to ensure that the Cambodian people, many of whom were illiterate, were able to understand the issues and logistics of the 1993 UN-sponsored elections by listening to the radio.

There have been many other SGI exhibitions since then, and only a few more are mentioned here. The 'War and Peace' exhibition was first held in 1989 at the UN headquarters in New York, and it toured five countries in four years, including the US and the USSR. 'Linus Pauling and the Twentieth Century' toured seven cities in the US and five cities in Japan, and was viewed by more than one million people. 'Toward a Century of Humanity – Human Rights in Today's World' toured 40 cities in eight countries. Among many other topics, there were also exhibitions about Education for Sustainable Development and against bullying in Japanese schools. The exhibition 'Anne Frank: the Courage to Remember' organized in collaboration with the Simon Wiesenthal Center was the first in Japan about the Holocaust. Since 2002, the exhibition 'Seeds of Change: The Earth Charter and Human Potential' has highlighted the links between the individual and the global in humanity's struggle to preserve the environment. 'From a Culture of Violence to a Culture of Peace: Transforming the Human Spirit' was launched on 8 September 2007 to commemorate the 50th anniversary of Toda's 1957 declaration. It is based on Ikeda's call issued in the August 2006 proposal on

UN reform for an 'International Decade of Action by the World's People for Nuclear Abolition.' In April and May 2008, it was held at the United Nations Office in Geneva in conjunction with the Second Preparatory Committee (PrepCom) for the 2010 NPT Review Conference.

The methodology used to analyze the peace proposals

Considering all the proposals from 1983 to 2009 as a single body of text totaling around 1,000 pages, a coding and tracking of the main concepts found in the 27 peace proposals has revealed that five themes and six issues appear most often. For a theme or issue to be counted as relevant, it had to be found in a minimum of ten proposals.

The coding and tracking had to be done manually, and not using keyword-tracking software, since the same concept is sometimes expressed in different ways. For instance 'inner transformation' may be described as the 'awakening of determination,' or self-discipline, self-restraint, self-control, self-renewal, the perfection of a person's character and human revolution. It was important to thoroughly understand the context in order to do this coding.

The initial results of this research are as follows, with the themes and issues ranked based on the number of peace proposals in which they appeared: nuclear weapons (27), UN reform (27), inner transformation (21), peace in East Asia (20), dialogue (19), global citizenship (17), human rights (12), human security (11), humanitarian competition (11), global civilization (11), and the environment (10).

Next these 11 topics were divided into five themes and six issues, with the interesting result that inner transformation (21), dialogue (19) and global citizenship (17) appeared as the top three themes, confirming their importance in Ikeda's philosophy of peace. Nuclear weapons (27), UN reform (27) and peace in East Asia (20) were the top three issues.

Since some themes and issues appear more often during certain years, a division into three time periods was established. For instance, out of a total of ten times, the environment appears in 1990, in 1992 and in 1997, and then seven times in the last nine years. To reflect the fact that the environment appears in almost each one of the more recent peace proposals, it was necessary to create a division into periods. Another example is the fact that humanitarian competition did not appear at all before 1996.

Two of the major events that affected the world situation between 1983 and 2009 were the collapse of the Soviet Union, signaling the end of the Cold War in 1991, and the attacks on the US in 2001, signaling the beginning of the subsequent 'war on terror.' An exact division based on these events did not prove to be useful, but three periods of nine years do correspond roughly to the shifts in the world situation caused by these events, and make it possible to highlight some interesting data. For the purposes of this research on the peace proposals, a division in three equal periods of nine years was therefore adopted. The first time an issue appears in the proposals is also of relevance, and as a result the following table was created and used to understand when specific themes and issues have appeared in all of them.

Topic	First time	1983–1991	1992–2000	2001–2009	Total
Theme					
Inner transformation	1984	3	9	9	21
Dialogue	1986	4	6	9	19
Global citizenship	1984	5	7	5	17
Hum. Competition	1996	0	4	7	11
Global civilization	1989	3	4	4	11
Issue					
Nuclear weapons	1983	9	9	9	27
UN reform	1983	9	9	9	27
Peace in East Asia	1985	6	6	8	20
Human rights	1984	3	5	4	12
Human security	1988	2	3	6	11
Environment	1990	1	2	7	10

A few conclusions can be drawn from the above table:

— Inner transformation has appeared in all the peace proposals since 1992.
— Dialogue is of increasing importance and has appeared each time since 2001.
— Humanitarian competition first appeared in 1996 and now appears frequently.
— Nuclear weapons and UN reform appear in all the peace proposals.
— Peace in East Asia is of increasing importance.
— The environment has become a prominent issue since 2001.

Ikeda consistently emphasizes the themes of inner transformation, dialogue, global citizenship, global civilization and Makiguchi's concept of humanitarian competition in the first part of the proposals. In the second part, his position on specific issues sometimes changes according to world events. For instance, his initial calls for a meeting of the top leaders of the US, Russia and other countries were not made any more from 1990 to 2008, since they had lost their relevance with the end of the Cold War. Then the idea came back in 2009, when Ikeda proposed the idea of a US–Russia summit, which did happen in the form of a meeting of the heads of state of the two countries a few months later in April. Despite these fluctuations, the issues of nuclear disarmament, UN reform, peace in East Asia and the environment have appeared consistently in the last nine peace proposals. The next two sections explore the themes and issues mentioned above.

The main themes: inner transformation, dialogue, global citizenship, global civilization and humanitarian competition

Inner transformation

The idea of inner transformation appears in the peace proposals in many different forms, as mentioned above. A first reading through the proposals to find the main ideas on inner transformation reveals some apparent contradictions, which are resolved later in this section through a deeper analysis. For instance, Ikeda recommends rationality as an important ingredient in endeavors towards peace:

> The reason I have discussed Plato in such detail is because I believe his idea of the ordering of the soul so that the rational part governs is a key point in establishing, firmly and widely, the age of the people's will and the tide of democracy (1990–PP, 12).

On the other hand, he affirms that spirituality is essential:

> One of the major functions of religion, I believe, is to foster the kind of self-control and self-restraint I have discussed here. (. . .) [T]he building of lasting peace depends on how many people capable of self-restraint can be fostered through religious guidance. If a religion is worthy of the name, and if it is one that can respond to the needs of contemporary times, it should be able to nurture in its followers the spiritual base for becoming good citizens of the world (1990–PP, 19–20).

Also while recommending rationality, which contains a certain level of abstract thinking, he condemns the spirit of abstraction as being destructive. These apparent contradictions can be resolved by clarifying Plato's defini- tion of rationality as it is used by Ikeda (1990–PP). Moreover, Ikeda does not consider the religious and the secular as two strictly separate spheres, as mentioned in Chapter 5. By the same token, Ikeda has made the boundaries between the rational and the spiritual more porous.

Important concepts related to the theme of inner transformation are the primacy of introspection versus external changes, the importance of people versus abstractions, the usefulness of Plato's concept of rationality and of Buddhism's view of human psychology for the practice of self-mastery. The personal inner reformation of individuals is considered the starting point of the process towards peace. It is contrasted with its opposite, attempts at external reforms based on an abstract search for absolute principles. In the context of efforts at inner reformation, both good and evil can be found within the human heart, whereas an obsession with external reforms will find good within, and evil outside, in a 'bad ideology' or in 'bad people.' According to Ikeda, the tendency to locate evil outside oneself has caused great suffering to humanity, and its potential for violence and bloodshed has been demonstrated time and again throughout the darkest episodes of human history, such as violent revolutions, civil wars, organized warfare and other social upheavals.

Ikeda draws upon several European thinkers to illustrate his point (1992–PP). He mentions that in *Les Dieux Ont Soif* (*The Gods Are Thirsty*) Anatole France denounces the excesses of the 1789 French Revolution and the ensuing reign of terror, during which countless lives were sacrificed in the name of such abstractions as 'liberty, fraternity and equality.' Similarly, in *Dr. Zhivago*, Boris Pasternak condemns the same tendency to slaughter huge numbers of people for an abstract idea, in this case the massacres of the 1917 Russian Revolution and its aftermath, for the sake of the dream of a 'classless society.' The human propensity to give priority to immaterial concepts over real people is referred to by Gabriel Marcel as the 'spirit of abstraction' in *Man against Mass Society* (1992–PP). This is also one of the main themes of the 2008 and 2009 peace proposals.

Having clearly illustrated the dangers inherent in the tendency to find evil outside oneself and to sacrifice real life for an abstract ideal, Ikeda then elaborates on the validity of starting with inner reformation, an idea which echoes Spinoza's definition of peace, quoted and espoused by Ikeda: 'a virtue that springs from force of character' (2000–PP, 18).

Ikeda also uses the interpretation of Plato by Alain, who considered *The Republic* as 'the individual's guide to inner self-control' (1990–PP, 11). Plato declares that democracy inevitably leads to anarchy, because it allows people to indulge in too much freedom and pleasure, making them weak and unable to discipline themselves. They then need a tyrant to lead them out of the chaos they have created for themselves. Ikeda, following Alain, interprets this as an encouragement to find the true Republic within oneself, in the capacity for self-mastery and inner transformation. In this sense, for Plato rationality means the capacity to control oneself through willpower, and this mental faculty is therefore clearly distinct from the tendency to cling to abstract concepts against which Gabriel Marcel had warned.

Real progress towards peace then starts with self-mastery, identifying evil as a personal, inner tendency that needs to be overcome through inner transformation. Ikeda highlights the similarity between the preamble of the UNESCO constitution, Buddhist principles and calls for inner transformation by rationalists and humanists of all backgrounds: 'Therefore, from the Buddhist point of view, the issue of how to build, as the UNESCO Constitution says, the "defenses of peace" within the hearts[11] of such individuals takes precedence over any external systemic factors and represents both the wellspring and the core of any attempt to build world peace' (1995–PP). This priority placed on the human mind sets his philosophy apart from Marx's theory of the 'substructure/superstructure' and Galtung's focus on 'structural violence.'

As mentioned in Chapter 5, Ikeda's philosophy can be placed firmly on the agency side of the agency–structure debate. No matter what structural challenges people face, they will only be able to solve them if they first have enough courage, wisdom and compassion to transform the situation in the best way possible. For Marx, the conscience of individuals is shaped by the society in which they live and work, and it is necessary to implement structural changes first. The position of Galtung is analyzed in depth in Chapter 8.

In this context, the definition of good and evil proposed in the dialogue with Toynbee becomes illuminating. 'Good' is associated with the 'longing to unite one's life with the life of the universe and to draw vital energy from the universe' (Ikeda and Toynbee [1976] 1989, 332). This idea is close to Jung's concept of the cosmic self, as well as Emerson's 'universal beauty' or 'eternal One,' and Whitman's longing to fill the 'vastness of space,' all mentioned by Ikeda in his lecture at Harvard University in 1993 (Ikeda [1993] 1996, 161–62).

In the dialogue with Toynbee, 'Evil' is associated with 'the diabolical desire (. . .) to control others' (Ikeda and Toynbee [1976] 1989, 333) and is a product of the small ego obsessed with the satisfaction of selfish needs. Evil is also defined numerous times in Ikeda's writings as that which destroys and disrupts cooperative and collaborative relations among people: 'the basis for the kind of dialogue required in the twenty-first century must be humanism – one that sees good in that which unites and brings us together, evil in that which divides and sunders us' (2005–PP, 12).

I would like to suggest that the apparent contradictions mentioned at the beginning of this section can be resolved by reorganizing the main concepts found in the peace proposals around the following narrative. The small ego, the smaller self, finds evil outside, creates some abstract idea explaining all the wrongs of the world, and is ready to sacrifice countless people considered as embodying this evil, convinced that in doing so it is fighting on the side of justice or 'good.' The small ego is actually only attempting to satisfy its own needs for self-righteousness and control of others, and this is how real evil is perpetrated through violence and bloodshed. In contrast the greater self, striving for unity with the cosmic life-force, will consider both good and evil as inherent, and will use tools for self-control such as Plato's rationality, Buddhist introspection or other means toward inner transformation, to bring out the best in oneself and others, making a solid start on the path towards world peace.

As mentioned above, Ikeda does not make a clear distinction between the rational and the spiritual, considering both of them as inherent functions of the human heart and mind. In the following passage, Plato's philosophy and the behavior of Bodhisattva Jofukyo (also Fukyo, Skt *Sadaparibhuta*, meaning Never Disparaging) are both considered as advocating self-control as a universal virtue, further blurring the separation between the rational and the spiritual:

> Bodhisattva Jofukyo's unshakable belief that humanity should never be despised exemplifies the kind of self-control we must learn to nurture in ourselves. In the Lotus Sutra, the story of Bodhisattva Jofukyo is a parable of the ultimate in Buddhist discipline, but it also is akin to Plato's contention that we must learn to place our souls under the control of our 'rational part' and illustrates the importance of self-control as a universal virtue of all humankind (1990–PP, 20).

After the attacks of 9/11, the main philosophical thrust of the proposals remains unchanged, and the necessity to start with inner transformation demonstrated in the previous proposals remains valid. However, in the 2002 proposal there is a new emphasis on the lack of self-control unleashed by the military attacks on Afghanistan. Ikeda condemns unilateralism and bloodshed as pointing in the wrong direction.

Ikeda believes that the adequate response to 9/11 is to be found in the power of the human spirit, and especially in the three qualities of courage, wisdom and compassion (2002–PP). Actions driven by a desire for revenge will only trigger more violence: 'Vengeance invites vengeance' (Ikeda

2002–PP, 4). Ikeda opposes violence in all its forms: 'Let me reiterate my absolute opposition to all forms of violence, terror and retaliation, from the intimate violence of bullying and domestic abuse to the mega violence of war. All violence is an unacceptable affront to human dignity' (2002–PP, 5).

He also asserts that war is the clear proof of the defeat of the human spirit, and recommends humanism based on self-mastery as the only way out of the quagmire. The 2002 peace proposal is therefore one of Ikeda's clearest responses to the tragedy of 9/11 and the violence unleashed in its aftermath in Afghanistan and elsewhere. Another is found in his essay 'The Evil over which we Must Triumph' in *From the Ashes: A Spiritual Response to the Attack on America* (2001c), in which Ikeda writes:

> It is the function of evil to divide; to alienate people from each other and divide one country from another. The universe, this world, and our own lives are the stage for a ceaseless struggle between hatred and compassion, the destructive and constructive aspects of life. We must never let up, confronting evil at every turn.
>
> This attack was an ultimate manifestation of evil and shows us the vilest depths to which human nature can sink.
>
> In the end, the evil over which we must triumph is the impulse toward hatred and destruction that resides in us all (106).

In the 2003 proposal, Ikeda condemns unilateralism, and emphasizes a definition of civilization as self-control made manifest. He asserts that the violent response shows a failure of the imagination, and that the military planners have fallen to the level of the terrorists (2003–PP). In 2004 he reiterates his calls for nonviolence made in 2002 and 2003. He gives the example of the Indian King Ashoka as a leader who understood how to move from a culture of violence to a culture of peace. In 2005 and 2006 he criticized fanaticism and dogmatism, asserting that dialogue and gradualism were more effective.

In 2007, based on Comte-Sponville's argument in *Le capitalisme est-il moral?*, he asserts that the main problem is not capitalism per se, but that people have lost their humanity: 'Without the qualitative elevation of individual human beings, neither social transformation nor the creation of a more positive society is possible' (2007–PP, 25). In 2008, Ikeda reaffirms his opposition to fundamentalism, and warns that any slogan, even 'freedom and democracy,' can become an empty abstraction used as an excuse to sacrifice people, and warns that among different types of fundamentalisms, there is also 'market fundamentalism.' In the 2009 proposal, inner transformation takes the form of a spiritual struggle to try to love people who are close at hand in our immediate environment:

> To love such people requires the kind of spiritual struggle that engages our entire being, a dramatic metanoia or turning of the soul such as is called for in the New Testament Sermon on the Mount. The single individual, undeniably present in our immediate circumstances, represents the crucible in which the true value of our commitment to love humanity is tested (2009–PP, 10).

In conclusion, the emphasis on inner transformation – self-mastery, self-scrutiny or human revolution – as the starting point of the peace process is omnipresent in the peace proposals. In the proposals from 2002 to 2005, Ikeda has clearly expressed his opposition to the violence unleashed since the tragedy of 9/11 and the military responses it triggered. By 2009, this aspect has given way to a warning concerning the dangers of the 'spirit of abstraction' denounced by French philosopher Gabriel Marcel, in response to the financial crisis of September 2008 which, according to Ikeda, was partly due to humanity's excessive worship of the abstract notion of currency.

Dialogue

Among the most important ideas found in the peace proposals, Ikeda points out the main obstacles on the path to meaningful dialogue as prejudice and closed-mindedness, and he quotes Western thinkers who confirm this point: 'Gabriel Marcel, Walter Lippmann and José Ortega y Gasset were contemporaries. Their writings illustrate the same profound concern: that closed-mindedness robs people of the ability to engage in dialogue and discourse with others (. . .)' (1993–PP, 13). As mentioned in Chapter 6, Ikeda often mentions thinkers such as Socrates, Montaigne and Büber as champions of dialogue.

Ikeda praises Montaigne in particular as an outstanding practitioner of the art of dialogue, a man who loved conversation and believed that there could be no meaningful debate without rebuttal. Ikeda states that the UN should reassert its original purpose and play a central role in ensuring that the different nations and regions of the world use dialogue to resolve their differences and transform their conflicts as members of the same global family (Ikeda 1993–PP).

Emphasizing that 2001 had been declared the 'Year of dialogue among civilizations' by the UN General Assembly, in the 2001 peace proposal Ikeda recommends the spread of open dialogue that brings forth such qualities as strength, wisdom, solidarity and our innate capacity for good. The twentieth century was characterized by a failure to base human society on dialogue, and Ikeda expresses his great hopes for the new century. Reality showed stubborn and spectacular refusal to reflect these ideals some eight months after Ikeda's statement with the attacks of 9/11 and the ensuing violent responses.

As was the case with the theme of inner transformation, the proposals from 2002 to 2008 express criticism of the violence that engulfed the world, this time because of the complete absence of dialogue in this situation. Ikeda warns that societies that refuse interaction fall into decline, even the most dominant, and reaffirms Ortega y Gasset's definition of civilization as the desire to live in common, a commitment that requires vibrant dialogue (2002–PP). In 2003 he asserts that a refusal of dialogue stems from a lack of humanity.

In 2004 and 2005 Ikeda refers to Shakyamuni and Socrates as great examples of self-knowledge and dialogue, and to his own efforts at citizen diplomacy through his numerous dialogues, for instance with Zhou Enlai, Kosygin and Kissinger in 1974–75. He highlights the similarities between Martin Büber's philosophy of dialogue and his own. As mentioned in Chapter 6, Ikeda agrees with Büber that dialogue is 'an encounter "on the narrow ridge" in which the slightest inattention could result in a precipitous fall.' He adds that '[d]ialogue is indeed this kind of intense, high-risk encounter' (2005–PP, 12).

He praises Montaigne once more in 2006 (as he did in the 1994 and 1995 peace proposals). One technique used by the French philosopher was to leave the conclusion open-ended, as mentioned earlier.

In 2007, the 50th anniversary of Toda's declaration against nuclear weapons, Ikeda reaffirms the mission of SGI as the creation of a more dialogical society, and gives a list of his own numerous dialogues and activities for cultural exchanges. In 2008, he reaffirms that he concurs with Socrates, according to whom (in the words of Plato): 'there is no worse evil that a man could suffer than this – hating arguments. Misology (hatred of language) and misanthropy (hatred of human beings) spring from the same source' (2008–PP, 14). In the 2009 peace proposal, Ikeda writes: 'Dialogue presents infinite possibilities; it is a challenge that can be taken up by anyone – any time – in order to realize the transformation from a culture of violence to a culture of peace' (2009–PP, 24).

Global citizenship, humanitarian competition and elements of a
global civilization of harmony and interdependence

In 2005 Ikeda stresses the importance of education for global citizenship, which he links with education for human rights and sustainable development.

Since human rights and sustainability have become global problems, building frameworks facilitating global responses will reinforce the capacity of global citizens to find appropriate solutions. He reasserts his support for the Universal Declaration of Human Rights (UDHR) in 2008, the year of its 60th anniversary, and suggests holding an international conference dedicated to human rights education that would involve civil society in a significant way for the first time.

In this section I have chosen to treat the themes of global citizenship, humanitarian competition and global civilization together. I consider them all parts of a vast puzzle leading to a better society. As global citizens try to tackle global problems, they will need to reform international institutions, such as the UN. This will be made difficult by the spirit of competition between opposing countries at the military, economic and political levels. A new paradigm, namely *humanitarian competition*, will have to influence relations between nations if a more inclusive and global society is to appear. More elements of a global civilization, similar to the now existing International Criminal Court (ICC) or the International Atomic Energy Agency (IAEA), which are able to tackle global issues more effectively, will then start appearing. In his peace proposals, Ikeda makes detailed suggestions concerning new elements of a future global civilization, but in my opinion the main goal is not to unify the world administratively, but rather to implement the vision of his mentor Toda, which was to 'rid the world of misery.'

It is therefore essential to understand that the kind of global civilization Ikeda has in mind is more like a flexible framework than a set of cultural practices to be imposed on the world. In *For the Sake of Peace*[12] (2001b), Ikeda differentiates between two aspects of culture, favoring the first one:

> Let it suffice to say that culture manifests two contrasting aspects. One resonates with the original sense of the word *culture* – that is, to cultivate – and involves the cultivation of the inner life of human beings and their spiritual elevation. The other is the aggressive, invasive imposition of one people's manners and mores on another (. . .) (Ikeda 2001b, 102).

He mentions European colonial policy as a typical example of the second aspect, namely cultural imperialism, quoting Palestinian-born literary theorist and cultural critic Edward Said:

> [He] writes in his book *Culture and Imperialism*, regarded by many as a key work of postcolonial analysis: '[T]he meaning of the imperial past is not totally contained within it, but has entered the reality

of hundreds of millions of people, where its existence as shared memory and as a highly conflictual texture of culture, ideology and policy still exercises tremendous force'[13] (2000–PP, 12).

Ikeda continues:

> As we follow Said's carefully developed and copiously illustrated argument, we discover the depth to which the ideology of cultural imperialism has taken root in the hearts and minds of 'decent men and women' – the educated classes of the imperial powers. (. . .) He reveals how (. . .) great thinkers, consciously and unconsciously and with an astonishing freedom from any sense of culpability, supported the goals of cultural imperialism (13).

The future global civilization Ikeda envisions must first and foremost be inclusive and allow all cultures to flourish:

> One necessary aspect of a culture of peace is that it must provide a basis on which a plurality of cultural traditions can creatively interact, learning and appropriating from one another toward the dream of a genuinely inclusive global civilization (Ikeda 2001b, 108).

It is therefore necessary to make a clear distinction between the mainstream use of the word globalization and Ikeda's definition of a global civilization. Globalization is mostly understood as the Western and mainly US-led attempts at imposing the same economic standards in every corner of the planet, first and foremost concerning the development of global markets for labor, goods and services. Whereas some see this process as benign, some consider it as a current form of cultural imperialism, imposed through violent force if necessary.

In contrast, Ikeda's vision for a global civilization can be described as a platform, a set of dialogical mechanisms, a framework allowing people of different backgrounds and ideologies to participate together in the construction of a better world. The creation of this global civilization will evidently depend on people's capacity for inner transformation, dialogue and global citizenship, but also on a series of mechanisms described below.

Ikeda's vision for an inclusive global civilization, based on a culture of peace, a concept that can be defined, in light of the above, as 'the cultivation of the inner life of human beings and their spiritual elevation' towards peace, has two major concepts at its core, and all the themes and issues contained in the peace proposals can be related to two major clusters of ideas, 'inner universalism' (1989–PP) and 'interconnectedness' (1996–, 1997–, 2003–PPs). The first is related to inner transformation and the second to dialogue, adding to the consistency of the underlying architecture of the system I present here as Ikeda's philosophy of peace.

Inner universalism is found in the Lotus Sutra (see Chapter 4) and finds value in each and every human being, affirming their intrinsic potential, an idea which is at the basis of the concepts of inner transformation and human revolution. In my opinion, inner universalism is a very rich and useful idea. I believe it counteracts both the imposed-from-without, one-size-fits-all universalism of Western models (such as economic globalization) and the post-modern counter-argument of incommensurable particularism, which I find paralyzing. It says that there are universal human values, but they are only meaningful and effective when they are discovered and developed from within.

Interconnectedness is a fundamental Buddhist concept which I interpret as affirming that people cannot live in isolation, and therefore need to reach out to each other, using different means of communication including dialogue. If Ikeda's idea of an inclusive global civilization is based on the two philosophical concepts of inner universalism and interconnectedness, how can they be operationalized in a concrete way?

The idea of human security, first mentioned by Ikeda in the 1995 peace proposal,[14] can be considered as one way to translate the concept of the fundamental worth of each human being, or inner universalism, into a concrete form. Without denying the functional importance of nations, proponents of human security try to place the emphasis on human beings rather than on states. Further, the desire to enhance and protect human security has to be translated into administrative and legal language and action, and Ikeda has made several proposals to that effect. The key point is to develop frameworks allowing for the protection of people, children, women and men, frameworks which can include, but also go above and beyond, preoccupations with national security.

The idea that all human beings are in close relation with all others and with other living beings and the environment (interconnectedness) is first translated in the peace proposals into the concept of humanitarian competition. This is one of the main ideas contributed by Tsunesaburo Makiguchi, Toda's mentor, in his book *Jinsei Chirigaku* (*The Geography of Human Life*) published in 1903. My understanding of this concept is that people, nations, ethnic groups, companies and all individuals and organizations which are in close relationship with each other cannot be prevented from competing. However, if they are vying for humanitarian competition, they will bring out the best in themselves and others. Many of Ikeda's proposals have this concept of humanitarian competition as their basis. Makiguchi wrote only about the competition between nations, but this concept can be broadened to include humanitarian competition between all actors in society: economic, financial, political, administrative or educational. Ikeda mentions Mandela and de Klerk as excellent examples of leaders who desired to create a society in which all people are victors (1996–PP), and I believe this idea was one of the keys to the rebuilding of post-apartheid South Africa. Instead of the win/lose options of traditional competition, Ikeda proposes the win/win solutions of humanitarian competition, with groups vying with each other to show the greatest proof of humane behavior.

Ikeda first emphasized the concept in a speech delivered in 1993, on the occasion of the 90th anniversary of the publication of Makiguchi's *Geography*. I think one of the reasons why the idea of humanitarian competition appeared in the proposals from 1996 was the failure to establish a more cooperative world after the end of the Cold War, and Ikeda's desire to find a 'third path.'

In 1989–90 the end of the Cold War allowed humanity to entertain hopes of a much more peaceful and collaborative world, based on such ideas as Gorbachev's 'New Thinking.' Unfortunately, the 1991 Gulf War and the triumph of the unilateralist, lone superpower trends in the US administration created a new, chaotic situation, with the US aggressively seeking to dominate the entire world. The post-Cold War failure to bring about a peaceful world system is described in Ikeda's book *For the Sake of Peace*:

> What we should pursue, therefore, is not a world order based on the universalization of certain specific values (as in Francis Fukuyama's *The End of History and the Last Man*) or one which sees cultures in ceaseless conflict (as in Samuel Huntington's *The Clash of Civilizations and the Remaking of the World Order*). Rather, we must seek the 'third path,' a global civilization whose core values are tolerance and coexistence (Ikeda 2001b, 124).

However, 'tolerance and coexistence' have passive connotations[15] that cannot compete with the (unwholesome) excitement generated by Fukuyama and Huntington's theses. In contrast, Makiguchi's concept of humanitarian competition is dynamic and engaging, recognizing the need of individuals and groups to compete, but proposing a humanitarian motivation conducive to peace. By 1996 it had become clear that the hoped-for new world order based on cooperation and mutual trust would not see the light, and this is probably why Ikeda decided to introduce Makiguchi's concept of humanitarian competition in the proposals as a viable alternative.

The global ethics called for by Makiguchi's idea is mentioned in Ikeda's 2006 proposal for empowering the UN already mentioned above (not an annual proposal):

> If the ideal of humanitarian competition is to take root in the international community, we must firmly establish the awareness that no society can found its security and well-being upon the terror and misery of another; we must create a new set of global ethics (Ikeda 2006c).

The 2009 peace proposal is entitled 'Toward Humanitarian Competition: A New Current in History.' Ikeda offers a full explanation of the concept, quoting from Makiguchi's 1903 work and showing the links with Joseph Nye's 'soft power' and Hazel Henderson's 'win-win world' in a passage worth quoting in full:

> In the closing chapters of this work [Makiguchi's *The Geography of Human Life*], published when he was just thirty-two, Makiguchi surveyed the grand flow of human history and identified the forms of competition – military, political and economic – that have prevailed in different periods.
>
> These are not clear and distinct historical demarcations. For example, economic competition often has a military backdrop, and the reverse is also true. In other words, these different forms of competition overlap and intertwine as they undergo gradual transformation. If we follow this process with both care and boldness, the trajectory of humanity's development becomes clear.
>
> Makiguchi concludes with a call for us to set our sights on the goal of engaging in what he termed humanitarian competition. He did not reach this conclusion from a suprahistorical perspective but rather by tracing the inner logic of historical development. Makiguchi describes humanitarian competition thus: 'To achieve the goals that would otherwise be pursued by military or political force through the intangible power that naturally exerts a moral influence; in other words, to be respected rather than feared.'[16]
>
> I am reminded here of nothing so much as the concept of 'soft power,' which has been defined by Joseph S. Nye, Jr., of Harvard University, whom I have had the privilege of meeting on several

occasions, as 'the ability to get what you want through attraction rather than coercion.'[17]

Likewise, there are resonances between the concept of a 'win-win world' put forward by the American futurist Hazel Henderson and the views Makiguchi expresses in the following passage: 'What is important is to set aside egotistical motives, striving to protect and improve not only one's own life, but also the lives of others. One should do things for the sake of others, because by benefiting others, we benefit ourselves.'[18]

I am fully convinced that the time has now arrived, a hundred years after it was originally proposed, for us to turn our attention to humanitarian competition as a guiding principle for the new era (2009–PP, 7–8).

Combining the concept of a flexible framework allowing different cultures to cooperate, the concept of human security and the idea of humanitarian competition, one can list the following elements as constitutive of a global civilization of peace: building a flexible framework for world global govern-ance, keeping a reasonable amount of sovereignty for national governments, placing the emphasis on human security and ensuring the participation of all individuals and groups.

For Ikeda the starting point of the process towards such an inclusive global civilization is personal relations, the willingness to 'build tolerant and enduring links' (Ikeda 2001b, 132). He also proposes a set of criteria as a way to monitor the progress towards a peaceful global civilization. He suggests Arthur Kaufmann's six prerequisites to build a peace compatible with justice as a good example:

First is the principle of equality. Based on recognition of the fundamental sanctity of life, it guarantees dignity equally to all individuals. Among nations, it assures equal opportunity and equal respect in economic and cultural relations. The second prerequisite is 'the golden rule' as expressed in the Bible: 'Do unto others as you would have them do unto you.' But Prof. Kaufmann translates the rule into an ethical principle and expands on it to include the negative proposition, 'Don't do unto others what you would not have them do unto you.' The categorical imperative is the third prerequisite, following Immanuel Kant's famous aphorism, 'Act only on that maxim through which you can at the same time will that it should become a universal law.' The fourth is the principle of fairness. As in sports where playing on a level field is the basic rule, in international relations all countries must be entitled to the same advantages and subject to the same disadvantages. The fifth is the principle of responsibility. No action should be taken the consequences of which might destroy, endanger or degrade people's lives or the environment in which they live, now or in the future. The sixth is the principle of tolerance. Even if your neighbor's thoughts run counter to your own interests, you should respect them (1991–PP).

Besides the establishment of a flexible framework respecting a degree of national sovereignty and a checklist for enduring prosperity, Ikeda also proposes disarmament as a characteristic of a future global civilization of interdependence and harmony. As will be explored in later sections, besides the abolition of nuclear weapons, he recommends a comprehensive ban on all weapons, big and small, conventional or WMD, and even the complete abolition of war as an institution.

All the ideas found in the peace proposals of 1983 to 2001 are also at the basis of the 2002 to 2009 peace proposals written after 9/11. If anything new has been added since 2002, it is the combination of specific issues such as human rights, nuclear disarmament or climate change with the idea of a reinforced and more effective international framework.

Ikeda reiterates his support for the establishment of the International Criminal Court (ICC) in 2002,[19] also hoping to see the UN play a central role in the strengthening of international law, with concrete proposals to prevent and combat terrorism by legal means. He repeats his support for the ICC in the 2004 peace proposal.

In the 2007 and 2008 peace proposals he suggests the creation of a UN international nuclear disarmament agency. Following the 2007 Intergovernmental Panel on Climate Change (IPCC) report concerning the threat to humanity's existence posed by climate change, Ikeda proposes to build an international framework of cooperation and solidarity for coping with climate change in his 2008 peace proposal. He reasserts the importance of Makiguchi's concept of humanitarian competition and its contemporary usefulness and relevance:

In a book published in 1903, Tsunesaburo Makiguchi called for 'humanitarian competition' among states. This was a vision of an international order in which the world's diverse states strive to positively influence each other, to coexist and flourish together rather than pursuing narrowly defined national interests at each other's expense. I feel that the work of solving the global environmental crisis provides a unique opportunity to move toward such a world (2008–PP, 21).

During the years 2002 to 2008, Ikeda therefore did not alter his former vision of a global civilization but enriched it with a renewed call for organized global solidarity concerning environmental problems, human rights and nuclear disarmament among other issues, as will be examined later. The attacks of 9/11 and the ensuing 'war on terror' gave him an opportunity to reassert his belief in international law, in particular his support for the ICC in order to deal with terrorism in the most effective way possible. In the 2009 peace proposal Ikeda reaffirms the potential of the idea of humanitarian competition as a new paradigm towards the future.

The main issues: nuclear disarmament, UN Reform, peace in East Asia and the environment

Nuclear disarmament

By 1957 Ikeda had become Toda's leading disciple, and he took his mentor's declaration of 8 September to heart. As mentioned earlier, the Soka Gakkai had already submitted a petition against nuclear weapons in 1975, and Ikeda's proposals to the UN in 1978 and 1982 are devoted to this theme. The first international exhibition organized by the SGI was 'Nuclear Weapons: Threat to our World,' also in 1982. It was the main topic of the first peace proposal in 1983 and is mentioned in each subsequent proposal without exception.

Toda in 1957, and Ikeda since then, have called for an unconditional ban on nuclear weapons, rising above arguments based on power politics, national interests or ideological systems on both sides of the Cold War divide. In the 1950s the split between the pro-Soviet proponents of nuclear disarmament and others spelled the doom of a promising movement against these weapons in Japan. Toda made it clear that his priority was the protection of all human beings without exception, and his 1957 declaration can be considered as an early example of a concern with what would be called 'Human Security' by Mahbub ul Haq 37 years later.[20]

For Ikeda, the point of departure of any attempts towards the abolition of nuclear weapons has to be the transformation of people's thinking: 'Human hands produced nuclear weapons and weaponry systems, and human hands should be able to reduce and eliminate them' (Ikeda 2001b, 199).

As explained in Chapter 3, I consider that the reason why Ikeda, following Toda, makes the abolition of nuclear weapons one of his top priorities is not only because of the potential threat of complete annihilation of life on earth, or the promise of mutually assured destruction, or the massive death and horror that can be caused by a single bomb, but because nuclear weapons are polluting the human mind and destroying the human spirit every day. The theory of deterrence that lies at the heart of the presence of nuclear weapons is part of a culture of fear and mistrust pervading international society. I believe that this is one of the reasons why Toda called these weapons an 'absolute evil,' and called for their abolition. As Ikeda says:

> Trust in nuclear arms is a negation of trust in humanity. The more people trust in arms, the less they trust one another. Ceasing to put their trust in arms is the only way to cultivate mutual trust among peoples (Ikeda 2001b, 187).

Moreover, even if humanity were to eliminate the 25,000 or so nuclear warheads in the world today,[21] nuclear know-how would enable any state (or organization with sufficient means) to build these weapons again in case of major conflict. Since it is not possible to eradicate human knowledge, it is the fundamental evil within people's minds, the desire to dominate and control, that must be held in check.

As a result, Ikeda not only calls for the abolition of nuclear weapons in his proposals, but also for the abolition of all WMDs including chemical and biological ones, and also of conventional weapons, including landmines and small firearms. Ikeda is even calling for the abolition of war as an institution, and proposes to de-institutionalize war. I think that Ikeda's ceaseless efforts for cultural exchanges linking people together can also be placed in this context, based on the expectation that it is more difficult to create abstract enemy images and to agree to kill and hurt people once one has direct experience of them.

In the 2009 peace proposal, Ikeda asserts this point based on Gabriel Marcel's criticism of the spirit of abstraction. I believe one of the goals of Ikeda's activities and support of institutions for cultural exchanges is to enable people to meet in person and thereby overcome the tendency to reduce others to abstract concepts:

> Marcel uses the term 'the spirit of abstraction' to define the essentially destructive process by which our conceptions of things are alienated from concrete realities. He notes, for example, that it is only possible to participate in war if we first deny the individual

character and humanity of the opponent – reducing him or her to an abstract concept such as fascist, communist, Zionist, Islamic fundamentalist, etc. (2009–PP, 2–3).

Ikeda has made many concrete proposals for the abolition of nuclear weapons. Throughout the years, he has consistently called for the expansion of Nuclear Weapons-Free Zones (NWFZ), the strengthening and ratification of the NPT and Comprehensive Test Ban Treaty (CTBT), the mobilization of ordinary people through an 'Ottawa Process'[22] against nuclear weapons, the strengthening of international law to outlaw nuclear weapons through organizations such as the ICJ and the ICC, and more recently the creation of an international nuclear agency for the elimination of nuclear weapons.

Ikeda has great hopes for the expansion of NWFZs. He sees them as the reflection of the will of ordinary people who are able to take their fate into their own hands through solidarity. In 1997 and 1999 he called for the creation of a NWFZ in North East Asia and for a North East Asian Peace Community. The number of NWFZs has grown steadily since the first one was established in 1968.

In 1993, negotiations for a CTBT had started with the full endorsement of the UNGA, and in his 1994 peace proposal Ikeda expressed his support for the idea:

> The first thing we must do is formulate *a treaty that comprehensively bans nuclear testing.* Then, at the NPT review meeting, we must ensure that the nuclear powers strongly reaffirm the ultimate goal of total abolition of nuclear weapons (1994–PP, 30) (Italics added).

In the 1997 peace proposal he expressed satisfaction at seeing the signing of the CTBT in 1996, but warned that it needed to be ratified to be effective. For several years, Ikeda urged the ratification of the CTBT, namely in the 1998, 2000, 2002, 2003, 2004, 2007 and 2009 peace proposals. In 2005 he added a new strategy, namely the creation of an 'international nuclear disarmament agency,' an idea he reiterated in 2007 and 2008.

In the 2008 peace proposal he wrote:

> In my 2007 peace proposal, I called for a transition to a system of security that is not reliant on nuclear weapons, and to this end urged the establishment of an *international nuclear disarmament agency* to ensure the good-faith fulfillment of existing legal commitments to nuclear disarmament (2008–PP, 21–22) (Italics added).

In the 2007 peace proposal he wrote:

> I would like to propose the formation within the UN of an *inter-national nuclear disarmament agency* to coordinate negotiations for a nuclear disarmament treaty. This body should have powers of inspection to ensure that, once in effect, such a treaty is properly implemented (2007–PP, 26) (Italics added).

He then goes on to acknowledge that there are already efforts in that direction with the establishment of the 'Article VI Forum,' a group of states and NGOs demanding the fulfillment of the obligation of nuclear disarmament stipulated in Article VI of the NPT.

In 2009, he reasserts the significance of that article 'which sets out the obligation for good faith negotiations leading to nuclear disarmament' (2009–PP, 18).

In the 2005 proposal he wrote:

> Just as nuclear non-proliferation efforts are monitored by the International Atomic Energy Agency (IAEA), I believe we need an *international nuclear disarmament agency*, a specialized agency to oversee fulfillment of the 'unequivocal undertaking by the nuclear-weapon States to achieve the total elimination of their nuclear arsenals' referred to above [here Ikeda was quoting the final outcome statement of the 2000 NPT Review Conference][23] (2005–PP, 58) (Italics added).

In the 1984 peace proposal Ikeda had already emphasized the necessity for a monitoring system to be implemented by a UN disarmament agency in order to ensure the compliance of states concerning nuclear disarmament.

Also in the 1997 peace proposal, Ikeda expressed his approval of the 1996 ICJ advisory opinion, siding with those who interpret it as a declaration of illegality; namely that the use or threat of nuclear weapons was against international law.[24] He did so again in 1998, and in 1999 added that the use of nuclear weapons and WMD should fall under the competence of the ICC. It is important to note that Ikeda believes in the power of agreements, treaties and international law as one of the best ways to move towards the elimination of nuclear weapons.

A realistic program for the abolition of nuclear weapons must include a strategy for disarmament in general. Even if the complete elimination of all nuclear warheads was to be realized, people would still have the technology to build new weapons. As soon as a serious conflict would flare up again, many countries would be able to build a nuclear device in a matter of months, or even weeks.[25] Specific plans for the abolition of nuclear weapons must therefore be accompanied by strategies for disarmament, and also plans for the abolition of war as an institution.

One of the most striking examples of Ikeda's support for disarmament in general is his analysis of the book *Giving up the Gun: Japan's Reversion to the Sword, 1543–1879* by Noel Perrin (1980) in his 1985 peace proposal. It explains that in 1575 the use of firearms was at its height in Japan. However throughout the Tokugawa regime, Japan operated a return to the sword, a symbol of human spirit and morality that was favored over the more effective but more cowardly firearms. Japan did not develop its firearms during the whole Edo era (1603–1868) and at the same time its capital, Edo (now Tokyo), was the most populated city in the world, and it successfully developed waterworks, sanitation and transportation systems. Ikeda supports Perrin's conclusion that the development of weapons technology has no connection with a society's overall prosperity.

Ikeda also encourages emulation of the example of Costa Rica, which abolished its armed forces in its 1949 constitution. Other countries have followed this example and there is a field of research specializing in countries without armies, led by such scholars as Christophe Barbey (2001).

For the sake of human security, Ikeda recommends the reduction of the international traffic in conventional arms, as well as a worldwide renunciation of war; the deinstitutionalization of war.

In 1984 and 1988 Ikeda proposed the establishment of a Universal Declaration for the Renunciation of War (UDRW) inspired by the Universal Declaration of Human Rights (UDHR). In the 1984 peace proposal he wrote:

> I propose that the United Nations adopt a Universal Declaration Renouncing War. Consensus among nations on such a declaration would be an important breakthrough in actualizing eternal peace. Lest I be criticized for overoptimistically believing the goal can be attained at once, I further propose that, as a first step, nongovernmental organizations (NGOs) begin the process by building up a foundation for the ultimate adoption of a Universal Declaration Renouncing War in the United Nations (1984–PP, 35).

He repeats the same idea in 1988, expressing his support for the idea that war is illegal from the point of view of international law established by the 1928 General Treaty for Renunciation of War as an instrument of National Policy (Kellogg-Briand Pact). He reasserts this idea in the 1991 peace proposal with renewed hope, inspired by the window of opportunity offered by the end of the Cold War.

In the 1999 peace proposal he wrote: 'To make the new millennium an age of peace and hope, we must explore means of deinstitutionalizing war' (1999–PP, 28). He then makes three concrete proposals to that effect, the establishment of a 'Northeast Asia Peace Community,' the creation of a treaty that would expand the arms trade reporting system so that it can cover more kinds of armament and be more effective, and the creation of an 'Ottawa Process' for the abolition of nuclear weapons.

As part of his strategy towards the de-institutionalization of war, Ikeda has consistently affirmed his support for the pacific spirit at the heart of Article 9 of the Japanese Constitution.[26] In 1991 he wrote:

> Hemmed in by the restrictions imposed by the postwar Constitution, some have advocated revision of that document so that Japan could contribute to world security on a par with other leading nations. I cannot agree with this view, however, for I oppose any change in the peace-oriented national policy adhered to since the end of World War II. Far more feasible is another proposal concerning the formation of an organization – distinct from the Self-Defense Forces – specially designed to participate in United Nations peace-keeping operations (PKO) (1991–PP, 15).

He reasserted his support for Article 9 on a number of occasions, for instance in 2001:

> While there is room for multifaceted debate on specific national security policies, I am concerned above all that the principles and spirit of the peace constitution not be eroded. And, for this reason, I feel that Article 9 should not be touched, a view that I have long asserted (2001–PP, 28).

It can be concluded that Ikeda's strategy for the elimination of nuclear weapons, WMDs, conventional weapons and the institution of war itself, mostly takes the form of his support of international treaties and international law, as well as his ceaseless promotion of dialogue and exchanges through the numerous institutions he has created. As mentioned earlier, getting to know people and appreciate their humanity strongly reduces the desire to kill them. Ikeda's support for the UN is also part of this strategy, as well as his proposals for disarmament.

UN reform

As noted already, Ikeda has been a staunch supporter of the UN for a long time. In his 1975 speech at the inauguration of the IBL/SGI he mentioned that he wanted to reply to (then UN Secretary-General) Kurt Waldheim's request that Buddhist ideals and proposals be shared with the UN. About 30 years later, after having consistently expressed and shown his belief in the UN, as public opinion was voicing increasing doubts about the world body due to its inability to prevent the genocides in the former Yugoslavia, in Rwanda and elsewhere, or to stop the Afghanistan and Iraq wars, Ikeda reaffirmed his unequivocal support for the UN in his 2004 peace proposal:

> There are, in certain quarters, persistent questions about the effectiveness or even necessity of the UN. Some aspects of the organization as it stands may indeed be incompatible with the realities of today's world. But with 191 member states, there is no organization more universal than the UN; it is the only body that can truly serve as a foundation for and give legitimacy to international cooperation. In the absence of a realistic alternative, the best course is to strengthen it and make it more effective. The SGI has sought to do this by generating grassroots support for the UN on a global scale (2004–PP, 30).

In the concluding chapter of his work *The Global Commonwealth of Citizens: Toward Cosmopolitan Democracy* (2008), Daniele Archibugi expresses the same conviction that the UN can be successfully reformed:

> An examination has been made [in this book] of the prospect of reforming the UN, an issue that has been on the agenda for all the sixty years of the organization's life without any significant change being introduced yet. However, the UN, the most ambitious and wide-ranging international organization, must be the pivot of a new multilateralism that is able more decisively to incorporate the basic principles of democracy that are encapsulated in the values of non-violence, public control and political equality. Many actions can be undertaken to allow the UN and its specialized agencies to govern globalization in a more effective, participatory and transparent fashion (Archibugi 2008, 281).

The importance of 'grassroots support' has been one of the main themes throughout all the peace proposals. For instance, Ikeda proposed the creation of a 'World citizens association to support the UN'[27] (1982, 1988), the establishment of a 'World citizens charter' (1988) and a 'World Council for the UN' (1990), and has encouraged education for world citizenship to galvanize support for the world body (1994).

Based on the fact that the SGI is itself an NGO, Ikeda has consistently emphasized the importance of NGO support for the UN, and the necessity for NGOs to have direct input in UN affairs, in 1982, 1984, 1989, 1991, 1993, 1998, 1999 (where he suggested starting a grassroots movement, what he calls an 'Ottawa Process'[28] against nuclear weapons), 2000, 2001, 2004 (mentioning the Cardoso report), 2005 and 2006. In the 2009 peace proposal he called for the creation of a post of under-secretary-general for civil society relations: 'This should be a permanent post specifically dedicated to enhancing the standing of NGOs within the UN system and the promotion of partnership with them' (2009–PP, 22–23). The SGI itself is engaged in activities in support of the UN, with which it has a long history of cooperation.

Besides encouraging popular support for the UN, Ikeda has called for the world body to become a place where the interests of people, and not just member states, are represented. He clearly asked that the UN show its human face in 1991, and used the newly coined term 'human security' to promote the same idea in 1995, 1996, 1997 and 2003. He mentioned the idea of a UN People's Assembly (UNPA) in 1997, 2000 and 2001.

One of the main obstacles preventing the UN from becoming a true parliament of humanity is the veto power of the five permanent members of the UN Security Council. Ikeda has repeatedly criticized this flaw (1982, 1987, 1991) and in 1992 he mentioned Galtung's proposal for dividing the UNGA into lower and upper houses. In 1995 Ikeda wrote:

> Similarly, we must conclude that the current state of the United Nations – with the Security Council in a position of pre-eminence and the General Assembly playing a subordinate role – is undesirable. If we are to enhance the qualities of what *should become a parliament of humanity*, I believe we should do all we can to strengthen and further empower the General Assembly (1995–PP, 24) (Italics added).

In the 2000 peace proposal, Ikeda proposed 'the creation of a global people's council that will function as a consultative body to the General Assembly' (2000–PP, 39). In his 2006 proposal for the empowerment of the UN, Ikeda argued, 'First of all, we must constantly recall that a core purpose of the UN is to be *the parliament of humanity*, a venue where all voices can be heard and all perspectives represented' (Ikeda 2006, 4) (Italics added).

In a similar vein, Archibugi also supports the idea of the UN as a parliament of humanity, and argues for the creation of a 'World Parliamentary Assembly,' an old idea that still needs to be implemented:

> The dream of an elected WP [World Parliament] directly representing the peoples of the world rather than their governments is as old as it is ambitious. Electing a WP is an idea that has been championed for decades by the federalist movements, and has received widespread support from NGO's and even from the European and Canadian parliaments and this idea has come back into fashion in recent years (Archibugi 2008, 172).

This section ends by considering some of the ways in which Ikeda's ideas concerning UN reform have seen a certain degree of implementation. Ikeda proposed the launch of several UN decades, and one of them became a reality. The 'Decade of Education for World Citizens' was proposed in 1987 and 1994 and did not happen, but the 'Decade of Action of the World's People for Nuclear Abolition' (2007–PP) is being implemented directly by the Soka Gakkai in collaboration with civil society partners as the People's Decade for Nuclear Abolition.

The 'Decade of Education for Sustainable Development' (2005–14) was suggested in 2002 by the SGI and other organizations, and adopted by UNGA (this fact is mentioned in the 2005 and 2006 peace proposals). In the 2009 peace proposal he wrote: 'The UN Decade of Education for Sustainable Development reaches its midpoint this year, a fact that highlights the need for ordinary citizens to become even more vigorously engaged in education and awareness-raising activities' (2009–PP, 16).

Besides the implementation of this decade, several proposals in favor of peace on the Korean Peninsula were also implemented, as well as Ikeda's calls during the Cold War for a 'Summit Conference of Heads of States' (1978, 1985) which became a reality, as well as his requests for the strengthening of the ICJ and the creation of the ICC (1995, 1998, 1999, 2002, 2003, 2004). Ikeda had been calling for several years for a new 'Environmental Security Council' (1990, 1991, 1992, 1997), then for the appointment of a High Commissioner for the Environment (2002), and the fact that the UNEP was upgraded from programme to agency in 2007 was welcomed by Ikeda and represents a partial implementation of his larger idea (2008–PP).

One idea that never became a reality, and that disappeared from the peace proposals after a few years, was the adoption of a Universal Declaration for Renouncing War (UDRW) (1984, 1988, 1990), as mentioned above. However, the 1999 The Hague Appeal for Peace can be considered a step in the same direction.

In September 1997, on the occasion of the 40th anniversary of Josei Toda's declaration against nuclear weapons, the WFUNA conferred a special award upon Ikeda, recognizing his support of the UN and his contributions to world peace. In the same year, the SGI became an official member of WFUNA. In 1999 Ikeda was appointed honorary advisor of WFUNA.

There are SGI UN liaison offices in New York, Geneva and Vienna, actively committed to the UN process and to promoting public awareness of global concerns. They actively participate in the search for better solutions together with the UN, while networking with many other NGOs.

Peace in East Asia

On 15 August 1945, the emperor of Japan publicly acknowledged defeat while the rest of East Asia celebrated liberation from their oppressor. The imperial program of ruthless colonization that subjugated Okinawa, Taiwan, Korea, parts of China and most countries in Southeast Asia was called the Great Co-prosperity Sphere by the Japanese government. The suffering it had imposed on the people left deep scars throughout Asia and the wounds are not completely healed today.

It is therefore no small accomplishment for Ikeda to have been able to create ties of friendship between Japan and other Asian countries, to such a degree that at the beginning of the twenty-first century Ikeda is widely recognized as one of the main trailblazers of Sino–Japanese friendship and of warm relations between his native country and Korea, Malaysia, Indonesia, the Philippines and other countries in the region. I believe that one of the reasons Ikeda was able to promote peace in East Asia despite the negative image associated with his native country is that his mentor was jailed by the military authorities, and that Ikeda has apologized repeatedly for what Japan has done, has sharply criticized the Japanese invasions and has shown gratitude for the cultural and civilizational gifts that poured in from China and Korea to Japan over centuries of fruitful cultural exchanges.

As mentioned above, today there are at least 15 research centers devoted to Ikeda's ideas in China, and he has received many academic honors from universities throughout the region, especially China and Korea. During their official state visits to Japan in 2007 and 2008, both Prime Minister Wen Jiabao and President Hu Jintao made arrangements to meet Ikeda in person. The point of departure of Ikeda's painstaking and persistent promotion of friendship between Japan and its former colonial victims is the speech he gave in 1968, as mentioned earlier.

In 1974 Ikeda was invited to meet Zhou Enlai and he has visited China ten times since that first trip. Soka University – established by Ikeda in 1971 – was the first in Japan since World War II to officially admit Chinese students sponsored by the Chinese government,[29] in 1975. Ikeda's passion for peace in East Asia has been expressed many times in the proposals.

The theme of peace in East Asia appears in 20 peace proposals, and in eight of the last nine. In 1986 and 1988 he proposed the creation of an Asia–Pacific Organization for Peace and Culture (APOPAC), and in 1994 the establishment of an Asian UN office to complement the United Nations University in Tokyo, a wish he reiterated in 2005. In 1999 he expressed his desire to see the birth of a Northeast Asia peace community based on the European model. Ikeda has consistently called for peace in the Korean Peninsula and has expressed support for reunification between the two Koreas. In 1986 he wrote:

> The reasons for the division are profoundly related to enforced annexation by the Japanese militarists [in 1910] and Japanese colonial rule. Swept up against their will by the orders of Japanese rulers, the Koreans suffered unspeakable misery (1986–PP, 262).

It is due to this kind of statement that the Japanese extreme right has developed a profound dislike of Ikeda and his philosophy of peace. Those still entertaining nostalgic dreams of the colonial Great Co-prosperity Sphere are under the dangerous illusion that Japan's actions brought some degree of happiness to the conquered nations. They are still denying the abuses committed during the Nanjing Massacre, the chemical experiments of Unit 731 and the enslavement of young women for the sexual satisfaction of the Imperial Army's soldiers. To the contrary, while apologizing repeatedly for the past crimes of his compatriots, Ikeda has steadfastly continued to promote friendship and understanding between Japan and its neighbors, and in 2008 he wrote:

> It has been four decades since I first called for the normalization of Sino–Japanese relations, and I welcome with deep gratification the significant steps that China and Japan have taken toward building a solid partnership for the peace, security and development of Asia and the world. (. . .) It is my conviction that if China, South Korea and Japan, together with ASEAN, continue to make tenacious efforts toward cooperation and coordination, it will be possible

to consolidate the enduring infrastructures for peace in East Asia (2008–PP, 35–36).

In the 2009 peace proposal only one line deals with this issue: 'There is continuing concern about the nuclear programs of Iran and North Korea, and I believe that we must make tenacious efforts to *reduce tensions and build confidence in their respective regions* in order to put an end to the destructive spirals of threat and mistrust' (2009–PP, 21) (Italics added).

The environment

The direct links between peace and the environment have only been recognized recently.[30] A growing number of scholars and activists began showing these connections in the 1990s, and this trend captured the world's attention with the conferral of the 2004 Nobel Peace Prize upon Wangari Maathai for her reforestation campaigns and the 2007 Nobel Peace Prize upon Al Gore and the IPCC for their work on climate change. Since the beginning of the twenty-first century, Ikeda and the SGI have been at the forefront of the struggle to preserve the biosphere and efforts to move towards a harmonious symbiosis between people and the rest of nature. The 'Decade of Education for Sustainable Development' (ESD) (2005–14) was proposed by several NGOs including the SGI, adopted by UNGA and implemented in 2005.

In November 2008 the Toda Institute held a conference on environmental issues entitled 'Facing Climate Change with a Renewed Environmental Ethic.' I believe that one reason why environmental issues have appeared in the peace proposals almost every year since 2001 is because of Ikeda and the SGI's sense of responsibility for this issue once they became involved with the preparations for the adoption of the Earth Charter and the launch of the UN Decade of Education for Sustainable Development (ESD). These efforts were briefly mentioned in a 2004 book surveying several spiritual traditions entitled *Religion and Peacebuilding*:

> How can Buddhists remain silent with regard to the loss of habitat, the loss of wildlife, the degradation of the planet? Some Buddhist groups that originated recently do address these issues that are relegated to oblivion by the majority of Buddhist societies. Soka Gakkai is one of these movements that not only embraces a social agenda based on Buddhist ethics but also raises the environmental awareness across various Asian nations (Neumaier 2004, 88).

In 2009, Ikeda expresses his satisfaction with the establishment of the International Renewable Energy Agency (IRENA) and the planned launch of the International Partnership for Energy Efficiency Cooperation (IPEEC), because he believes they can be considered as the embodiment of the idea of humanitarian competition in humanity's efforts to find solutions to the global environmental crisis. He also makes a new proposal:

> I would propose that in the future an international sustainable energy agency be created under the aegis of the UN to further the work of these two organizations – IRENA and IPEEC – so that international cooperation on energy policy may take firm and universal root throughout the global community (2009–PP, 15).

Potential impact and intended audience of the peace proposals and the SGI's activities for coalition building

This section examines some of the links between the themes, issues and concepts presented in the peace proposals and their potential impact on the world, their target audience, and the endeavors by the SGI to implement some of these ideas in collaboration with other organizations.

The *Seikyo Shimbun* of 30 January 2007 announced the implementation of several ideas that had been mentioned by Ikeda in three of his peace proposals (1983, 1987, 1988), showing his commitment to timely issues. The proposal he made in 1983 for the heads of states of the USSR and the US to meet in person was realized in 1985 with the Reagan–Gorbachev dialogue. Two aspects of his 1987 proposal for a 'UN Education Decade for World Citizens' (which contained four themes: the environment, disarmament, development and human rights) became a reality. They took the form of the 'UN Decade for Human Rights Education' (1995–2004), and the 'UN Decade of Education for Sustainable Development' (2005–14). The peace accord reached in Cambodia in 1991 confirmed the validity of the proposal for peace in that country he had made in 1988 (*Seikyo Shimbun* 2007, 3).

However it is not possible to evaluate how much influence Ikeda's proposals had on these events. There is no systematic study about how many of Ikeda's proposals were implemented. This question might be irrelevant in the context of Ikeda's philosophy of peace, since he acknowledges his role as follows:

> I am neither a politician nor a policy specialist. I am sure there is much lacking in my proposals. I continue to write and issue these proposals in my capacity as a private citizen in the hope that they

> will help deepen the debate on critically important issues and aid
> the search for a way out of our present quandary (IPS 2008).

This single-minded consistency is one of the characteristics of Ikeda's implementation of his philosophy of peace, as mentioned in a previous chapter.

The peace proposals are addressed to the whole world, destined to inspire heads of state, policy makers, NGO leaders and ordinary people alike. They are addressed to SGI members, believers of all religions, and people with no religion equally, and to people of all nationalities, including of course Ikeda's compatriots. Sometimes Ikeda makes proposals directly putting Japan on the spot, but in other cases he makes recommendations concerning other countries, for instance in his 1983 proposal for the leaders of the US and the USSR to meet in person.

Ikeda especially wishes to inspire young people: 'I have a very deep faith in the capacities of young people (. . .) in writing these proposals, my greatest hope, my determination and commitment is to sow the seeds of change in young people's hearts' (IPS 2008).

Ikeda's peace proposals are regularly quoted in research journals, such as *Security Dialogue* (PRIO, International Peace Research Institute, Oslo), on the website of the Transnational Foundation for Peace and Future Research (TFF) and other peace research outlets. Hofstra University in New York organized a course using the book *For the Sake of Peace*, which contains several excerpts from the peace proposals among other texts by Ikeda.

Ikeda often calls for ordinary people and world citizens to unite to create a better world, and the SGI often engages in coalition building in favor of nuclear disarmament campaigns, UN reform, environmental concerns and other issues. As an NGO in consultative status with the UN ECOSOC, the SGI has been active in public education, with a focus on peace, human rights and sustainable development. In carrying out its peace activities, SGI has actively participated in various networks of civil society, including the Conference of NGOs in Consultative Relationship with the UN (CoNGO), which facilitates the coordination of a number of NGO committees on specific issues of global concern. At the local level, SGI groups form a wide range of partnerships with local community organizations and educational institutions. SGI participates in committees and networks and contributes to joint endeavors among groups and individuals in pursuit of common objectives, in fields as varied as disarmament, human rights, sustainable development, and interfaith activities[31] through UN liaison offices in New York, Geneva and Vienna.

Moreover, affiliated research institutions such as the Toda Institute and the Ikeda Center for Peace, Learning, and Dialogue (formerly the Boston Research

Center for the 21st Century), which invite scholars and educators to network together during their conferences and publication activities, are engaged in coalition building with experts in specific topics.

For instance in September 2007, in commemoration of the 50th anniversary of Josei Toda's declaration against nuclear weapons, the Toda Institute organized an international conference entitled 'The Challenge of Abolishing Nuclear Weapons' in San Francisco in collaboration with the Nuclear Age Peace Foundation (NAPF), and the conference results were published in the form of a book in July 2009 (Krieger 2009). Participants were from the Middle Powers Initiative (MPI), the International Physicians for the Prevention of Nuclear War (IPPNW) and other groups. This was an additional opportunity for them to network.

Also each year the Soka Gakkai announces a strategic plan in which it names organizations with which it wishes to have collaborative relations that particular year. For instance the 2006 strategic plan clearly indicated the desire to work in collaboration with PRIO, IPPNW, the Earth Charter Committee and the Pugwash Conference, among others. At the local level, national SGI organizations organize numerous activities with other peace organizations, and this also constitutes a flexible form of coalition building.

A comparison between Ikeda's proposals for world peace, the 'Liberal Peace' and 'Cosmopolitan Democracy'

Josei Toda is recorded as saying, 'If you want to realize peace for all humankind, you must make concrete proposals and take the lead translating them into concrete action' (Toda Website). I believe Ikeda has followed the advice of his mentor, trying to be an example by showing initiative and responsibility in his actions for peace. For instance, I think that the main reason why peace in East Asia is one of his priorities, before peace in any other region, is because he has actually been spearheading movements for the friendship between his own country, Japan, and its neighbors. I also believe the reason why he feels comfortable promoting environmental causes since 2001 (in seven peace proposals out of nine, whereas this issue was only mentioned in 1990, 1992 and 1997 before 2001) is because he has seen the tangible results of his endeavors and those of the SGI in this field. I would like to offer the following interpretation: for Ikeda, it is important to bring out one's courage, compassion and wisdom first, then make a concrete plan and try to implement it by taking action towards peace. The first step in his philosophy of peace is indeed inner transformation.

The second step for Ikeda is to recognize that human beings need one another, and that any action towards peace must include some kind of interaction, through discussion, consensus, argument and any other form of '*dia-logos*,' dialogue based on reasoning and language. The third step is to encourage global citizenship, and when appropriate, to design broad guidelines to create a more peaceful society, elements of a global civilization supported by a flexible world democratic framework that would allow each nation and group to blossom. The UN has an essential role to play in this endeavor and needs to be supported, strengthened and improved.

The threat of using nuclear arms or other weapons of mass destruction, the production, stockpiling and deployment of personnel landmines and of any other kinds of weapons, goes against the spirit of dialogue and respect inherent in this plan, and for Ikeda disarmament is an obvious and essential ingredient in the promotion of peace. The concept of interdependence underlying this project must extend to the animal world, the natural environment and the whole biosphere of which human beings are an integral part, if it is to succeed.

In order to highlight what Ikeda's vision for a future inclusive global civilization can contribute to peace theory, it is useful to compare it with the idea of 'Liberal Peace' as defined by Oliver Richmond. According to Richmond, this type of peace is the most dominant one today in theory and practice, and he defines it as follows:

> The liberal peace is defined as that contained within the methodological and objective-oriented peacebuilding consensus where like-minded liberal states, international, regional and local actors coexist in a western-oriented international society in which states are democratic, human rights are observed at an acceptable level, markets are open and transparent, and multilateralism is the norm except in extreme circumstances (Richmond 2007, 121).

The commonalities and incompatibilities found between this definition of Liberal Peace and Ikeda's concept of global civilization as I have defined it in this chapter make it possible to highlight the originality of some aspects of his theory of peace. As this chapter has shown, democratic governance, human rights and multilateralism are also part of his vision. In the peace proposals Ikeda does not mention the requirement of having 'open and transparent markets,' but he has repeatedly stated that all fields of human endeavor, including the economy, should serve the people and lead to social justice.

The global civilization envisioned by Ikeda is not a 'peacebuilding consensus where like-minded liberal states (. . .) coexist in a western-oriented international society,' but an open forum where each civilization, nation and group would have a voice. Moreover, what is completely missing from the

'Liberal Peace' is the emphasis on individual human beings, the concept of inner transformation and the crucial importance of dialogue and of the enhancement of global citizenship to reach agreements about the steps to take toward the development of the future global civilization.

An attempt to place Ikeda's vision in one of the nine categories[32] of peace concepts presented by Richmond (2007, 183–201) shows that the last one, entitled 'Peace as emancipation: counter-discourses' (197) is the most appropriate, since this type of thinking at least takes into account the centrality of dialogical processes:

> In critical and post-structural approaches to IR [International Relations], there has also been an increasing focus on dialogic ethics as a method of dealing with culture while avoiding the extreme of cultural relativism. For example, Jabri's version of this type of conceptualisation focuses on the type of peace that might be achieved through communicative action, based upon Habermasian dialogic relations (Richmond 2007, 197).

Human agency is also included in this type of vision of peace: 'Peace can be seen as a product, to a certain degree at least, of human agency in negotiating co-existing but different forms of peace' (Richmond 2007, 198). While Ikeda's concept of a global civilization has similarities with the idea of the Liberal Peace, the differences are even more striking, and in this context Ikeda's vision is actually a 'counter-discourse,' and offers one type of 'emancipatory notion of peace' – to use Richmond's terms. One of the most crucial differences between the two concepts is that many proponents of the Liberal Peace, especially in their hegemonic ambitions, advocate the use of force and military might to impose it, as was demonstrated in the invasions and occupations of Afghanistan and Iraq in the first decade of the twenty-first century. For Ikeda the ends and the means have to be consistent, and he completely rejects the use of violence in the process of creating a global civilization (2002–PP, 5).

Ikeda's peace proposals contain some hints concerning the kind of criteria needed to evaluate this future global civilization and to detect whether there are some signs today that it is taking shape. Even though the following monitoring process does not appear in the peace proposals, it is worth mentioning here. Ikeda refers to the Buddhist concept of the 'seven principles preventing decline' used by Shakyamuni to describe a truly prosperous civilization (using the example of the Vajjian republics). It is to be noted that these seven criteria have been applied to the development of the SGI by Ikeda in an attempt to ensure the long-term prosperity of the organization. These seven principles have proven successful with the SGI's presence in 192 countries and territories (as of October 2009), and Ikeda recommends them as criteria for checking humanity's progress in the development of a future inclusive global civilization of interdependence and harmony:

1. Do the Vajjians value discussion and dialogue?
2. Do they value cooperation and solidarity?
3. Do they value laws and traditions?
4. Do they respect their elders?
5. Do they respect children and women?
6. Do they respect religion and spirituality?
7. Do they value people of culture and learning, whether they are Vajjians or not? Are they open to such influences from abroad? (Ikeda 2001b, 145).

In this context disarmament, UN reform, regional integration and a sustainable way of stewarding the environment are definitely pressing issues. The Liberal Peace defined by Richmond fails to meet most of these seven criteria, and is especially deficient concerning the last one. Ikeda's concept of global civilization offers a challenge to peace research and activism: how can humanity move towards a type of global governance that will fulfill these criteria?

In Chapter 5, the similarity between the concept of inner transformation and virtue ethics, humanistic psychology and above all Viktor Frankl's life-affirming philosophy was emphasized. In Chapter 6, the relevance of Jürgen Habermas's Communicative Rationality and of Martin Büber's 'I–You' relationship model for an understanding of Ikeda's concept of dialogue was highlighted. Now that the commonalities and incompatibilities between Ikeda's global civilization and the Liberal Peace have been clarified, the striking similarities with Daniele Archibugi's 'Cosmopolitan Democracy,' mentioned above, can be further emphasized.

Many thinkers favoring humane global governance have expressed views similar to those of Ikeda in his peace proposals (Archibugi and Held 1995; Aksu and Camillieri 2002; Held 1995, 2003; Tehranian (in Ikeda and Tehranian) 2003; Falk 1995, 2008; Archibugi 2008; Paupp 2000, 2007, 2009), but in my opinion Archibugi is the closest. He describes the essence of his work *The Global Commonwealth of Citizens: Toward Cosmopolitan Democracy* (2008) in terms that closely match many of the ideas found in Ikeda's proposals:

> The present book presents the proposal for a cosmopolitan democracy, which a group of researchers at the end of the Cold War developed, as the management of different levels of governance. This

proposal takes into account contemporary historical conditions, in which political communities with different historical and cultural backgrounds interact willy nilly with other neighboring and remote political communities. The form of representation of citizens in the global sphere based on the delegation of governance to a territorial state has become insufficient and in many cases an aberration. For this reason *citizens of the world need to be given the possibility of directly participating in global choices* through new institutions that are parallel to and autonomous with respect to those that already exist inside the states. (. . .) *A world parliament would give institutional clout and a say in political and social affairs to those global movements that have appeared on the world political scene* full of enthusiasm and often with a solid baggage of skills (Archibugi 2008, xv) (Italics added).

To summarize the main thesis of this book, I believe that Ikeda's philosophy of peace can be systematized as follows. The starting point is the question 'What can I do for peace,' which can be answered this way.

First, one can enhance one's own courage, wisdom and compassion through inner transformation. Second, one can hold mutually enriching dialogues trying to bring out the best in oneself and others, emphasizing communicative rationality and building trust. Third, one can develop an identity as a global citizen and contribute to the implementation of elements of an inclusive global civilization of harmony and interdependence.

Finally, even when the difficulties encountered during the process of holding meaningful dialogues or enhancing global citizenship seem insurmountable, Ikeda's philosophy of peace offers a way forward. During such times it is crucial to have the self-discipline to focus once more on self-improvement, finding new strength to continue the work for peace, by going back to the starting point of inner transformation.

CHAPTER 8

Ikeda's Contribution to Peace Theory

> We must be realists in our brains while keeping
> the flame of idealism burning in our hearts. That
> is what peace research and peace-oriented action
> are about.
>
> Johan Galtung (Ikeda and Galtung 1995, 18)

> Efforts must start at home, beginning with indi-
> vidual self-examination. A change, a renaissance,
> an awakening in the individual: these are the keys
> to the transformation of the fate of humanity as a
> whole.
>
> Daisaku Ikeda
> (Ikeda and Díez-Hochleitner 2008, 108)

Ikeda's philosophy of peace has been systematized in the preceding chapters and it can now be compared with those of some of the most important
thinkers in the field. Ikeda is not a peace theorist, but rather a spiritual leader
inspiring millions of people, a cultural bridge builder engaging in numerous
dialogues and an activist launching initiatives and creating institutions for
peace and culture. His work brings him closer to practitioners of social justice
and peacebuilding such as Mahatma Gandhi, Martin Luther King Jr., Mother
Theresa and Nelson Mandela than to peace theorists. The main goal of this
book, especially Chapters 5, 6 and 7, was to systematize Ikeda's ideas into a
coherent framework, highlighting the values and principles underlying his
philosophy of peace. This chapter places this framework in the overall context
of peace theory.

Ten years after the end of World War II Theodore F. Lentz published
'Towards a Science of Peace' (1955), in which he asserted his belief in the

power of the positivist scientific method to bring about a better world. A few years later, conflict research was born in the US and peace research in Europe. As Barbara Mitchels explains: 'the initial drive forward occurred in the United States, where Mary Parker Follett, writing about organisations and labour management, advocated a mutual gains approach in negotiations' (Mitchels 2006, 24). In 1954 the British Quaker and economist Kenneth Boulding established the Center for Advanced Study in the Behavioral Sciences at Stanford University with mathematician-biologist Anatol Rapoport and others. In 1957 Boulding and other academics established the *Journal of Conflict Resolution* and in 1959 the Center for Research on Conflict Resolution at the University of Michigan. Conflict research achieved a certain degree of respectability as a new field.

Whereas the Boulding group originally used the word 'conflict,' Johan Galtung placed the word 'peace' at the center of his initiatives. In 1959 he established the International Peace Research Institute in Oslo (PRIO), and in 1964 the *Journal of Peace Research*. The same year he contributed to the founding of the International Peace Research Association (IPRA) with John Burton, Kenneth and Elise Boulding and others.

In 1963 the Australian John Burton established the Centre for the Analysis of Conflict while a Reader in International Relations at University College London. During the 1970s and 1980s other academics including Herbert Kelman, Roger Fisher, William Ury, William Zartman, Elise Boulding and Adam Curle expanded the study of conflict resolution (Mitchels 2006, 26). Other thinkers worthy of mention are John Paul Lederach, Betty Reardon, Gene Sharp and Glenn Paige.

Concepts and definitions

The terms peace theory, peace research, peace studies, peace and conflict studies, conflict resolution and conflict transformation have slightly different meanings and scholars have failed to agree on a common framework to define them. For David Barash and Charles Webel, the umbrella term is peace and conflict studies (2009), Oliver Ramsbotham, Tom Woodhouse and Hugh Miall prefer conflict resolution (2008) and Johan Galtung opts for peace studies. I also consider peace studies as the most general term and have adopted the following conventions regarding the terminology used in this chapter.

First, within peace studies, I distinguish between peace education and peace research, and I focus on the latter. Within peace research, conflict resolution and conflict transformation are competing terms, and here I will follow

Ramsbotham et al. in their widely used work *Contemporary Conflict Resolution* (2008) to decide which should come first:

> We continue to use conflict resolution as the generic term here for three reasons. First, because it was the earliest term used to define the new field (the 1957 *Journal of Conflict Resolution*). Second, because it is still the most widely used term among analysts and practitioners (. . .). Third, because it is the term that is most familiar in the media and among the general public (Ramsbotham et al. 2008, 9).

They see 'conflict transformation as the deepest level of the conflict resolution tradition rather than a separate venture' (8–9) and they consider that 'it [conflict transformation] implies a deep transformation in the institutions and discourses that reproduce violence, as well as in the conflict parties themselves and their relationships. It corresponds to the underlying tasks of structural and cultural peacebuilding' (29).

They clarify their use of this last term as follows:

> We use *peacemaking* in the sense of moving towards settlement of armed conflict (. . .). *Peacekeeping* (. . .) refers to the interposition of international armed forces to separate the armed forces of belligerents (. . .). *Peace-enforcement* is the imposition of a settlement by a powerful third party. *Peacebuilding* underpins the work of peacemaking and peacekeeping by addressing structural issues and the long-term relationships between conflictants (30).

Based on the above, I would like to suggest that Ikeda's philosophy of peace best corresponds to what Ramsbotham et al. call 'cultural peacebuilding,' within the field of conflict transformation which is the 'deepest level of the conflict resolution tradition,' a branch of peace research. A linear representation of this categorization looks as follows:

> Peace Studies → Peace Research → Conflict Resolution →
> Conflict Transformation → Peacebuilding →
> Cultural Peacebuilding → Ikeda's philosophy of peace

The logic of this classification is confirmed by the 'hourglass model' presented by the same authors (Ramsbotham et al. 2008, 12). To understand this model, it is necessary to consider that conflicts have a life of their own, with the two main phases consisting of escalation and de-escalation:

Escalation: Difference → Contradiction → Polarization → Violence → **War**
De-escalation: **War** → Ceasefire → Agreement → Normalization → Reconciliation

To my knowledge, in the middle of a conflict characterized by direct violence (killing, maiming, hurting), Ikeda's philosophy of peace has not yet been used as a method to de-escalate the situation. However, such developments are quite possible in the future. The greater emphasis in Ikeda's philosophy is clearly on the broadest and deepest transformation of the root causes of conflict, but I believe that it is also applicable to active conflict situations.

It already has an important role to play in order to prevent the escalation from simple difference to more serious contradiction when direct violence has not yet broken out, and to reinforce the de-escalation from normalization to reconciliation when violence has subsided. In other words, the practice of Ikeda's philosophy of peace can help stabilize communities and societies and avoid escalation, violence and bloodshed.

I believe it can be helpful to increase the capacity of a society to accept contradictions and differing opinions and to broaden its political space, which is the overall aim of conflict transformation: 'depending on the stage the conflict has reached, as illustrated in the hourglass model (. . .), the overall aim is to work to prevent the narrowing of political space associated with conflict escalation and to encourage the widening of political space associated with conflict de-escalation and transformation' (Ramsbotham et al. 2008, 26–27). The hourglass model is reproduced below. It represents visually the narrowing of options and political space typical of escalation from differences (wide) to war (narrow), and the widening of political space characteristic of de-escalation from war (narrow) to reconciliation (wide).

I believe Ikeda's philosophy of peace has thus far been applied to the zones highlighted in grey, enhancing peaceful conflict transformation especially as cultural (and sometimes structural) peacebuilding, preventing differences from becoming contradictions leading to polarization (for instance his shuttle diplomacy between China, the Soviet Union and the US in 1974–75 described in Chapter 6) and reinforcing agreements to facilitate normalization to achieve reconciliation (one example is the impact of his 1968 speech in favor of normalization of relations with China mentioned in Chapter 7).

Conflict transformation	Difference	Cultural peacebuilding
	Contradiction	Structural peacebuilding
Conflict settlement	Polarization	Peacemaking
	Violence	Peacekeeping
Conflict containment	**WAR**	**War limitation**
	Ceasefire	Peacekeeping
Conflict settlement	Agreement	Peacemaking
	Normalization	Structural peacebuilding
Conflict transformation	Reconciliation	Cultural peacebuilding

(After Ramsbotham et al. 2008, 12)

In addition to this placement of Ikeda's philosophy of peace on the map of peace research and conflict transformation, I will now highlight some differences and similarities with major peace theorists.

The major developments in the field can be divided into four generations with specific roles: the precursors (1918–45), the foundations (1945–65), the consolidation (1965–85) and the reconstruction (1985–2005) (Ramsbotham et al. 2008, 32–54). Here I will focus on a comparison with the main theorists of the second generation (Kenneth Boulding, Johan Galtung and John Burton), of the third generation (Herbert Kelman, Adam Curle and Elise Boulding) and also thinkers whom I consider as original members of both the third and fourth generations (John Paul Lederach, Betty Reardon, Gene Sharp and Glenn Paige).

More space is devoted to a comparison with Johan Galtung's philosophy of peace than with that of any other thinker because he is the most prolific among the founders of the scientific discipline of peace research and also the co-writer of a dialogue with Ikeda entitled *Choose Peace* (2005). Many peace researchers[1] use Galtung's concepts today. Many other thinkers position themselves against some or all of Galtung's theoretical frameworks,[2] thus establishing the importance of his philosophy of peace as a major point of reference.

Galtung has written 141 books and more than 1,000 articles on peace and peace research and here I will use only part of his work, namely the Transcend Method. I consider this as the most appropriate point of comparison, because Galtung has placed special emphasis on the development of institutions, networks and publications based on the Transcend Method since the early 1990s, and I believe it encapsulates the essence of his theoretical work.

The main references concerning this method are *Transcend and Transform: an Introduction to Conflict Work* (2004), *50 Years, 100 Peace and Conflict Perspectives*

(2008a) and the manuals based on the Transcend Method published and used by the United Nations (2000).

Johan Galtung

According to Peter Lawler, who is known to be critical of Galtung, his work is central to the field of peace research:

> A substantive history of peace research would be brief indeed – not to mention duller – if the input of Johan Galtung did not appear throughout. He was there at the beginnings of institutionalized peace research and remains a major contributor today. His writing has generated a unique lexicon utilized by many if not most peace researchers. Inscribed upon his work are all of the debates that have both impelled peace research onward and occasionally scarred it (Lawler 1995, vii).

Adam Curle recognized the crucial influence of Galtung's concepts on his thinking: 'I am intellectually much indebted to him, having assimilated so many of his ideas that I cannot adequately acknowledge them' (Curle 1981, 41).

Galtung's Transcend Method

As mentioned in Chapter 6 above, Galtung was born in 1930, and as an adolescent during World War II in Norway he had to endure the Nazi occupation, including the abomination of having his father, a medical doctor, taken hostage along with many other important Norwegian figures. These experiences had a strong impact on Galtung, who developed a passionate desire for peace.

After establishing the first peace research institute in the world in 1959, the International Peace Research Institute in Oslo (PRIO), he steered this organization towards the establishment of the first academic journal in this new field, the *Journal of Peace Research* in 1964. The same year he contributed to the establishment of the International Peace Research Association (IPRA). He is considered one of the pioneers in the field of peace studies, together with Elise and Kenneth Boulding and several others. Galtung later systematized his philosophy of peace in what he calls the Transcend Method.

For Galtung, since people have desires and needs which are constantly frustrated by the demands of others, contradiction is omnipresent, conflicts are a natural part of life and our best hope to be able to move towards peace is to learn how to deal with conflicts in the most positive and creative ways. The best strategy to deal with a conflict is for the parties to 'transcend' it, changing their perspective in order to be able to see that both oneself and others need to work together to find a solution to the conflict, instead of blaming each other and trying to win the battle. Galtung established an organization bearing the name of his method in the 1990s.

Galtung is known for having introduced, in academia, the distinction between negative peace, usually defined as the absence of war, and positive peace, a situation where all people have their needs fulfilled and enjoy harmonious relationships. For Galtung, 'Negative peace is the absence of violence of all kinds' (Galtung 1996, 31) and 'By positive peace we mean a cooperative system beyond "passive peaceful coexistence," one that can bring forth positively synergistic fruits of the harmony' (Galtung 1996a, 61).

Inspired by his father's profession, Galtung uses a medical metaphor to emphasize the importance of three elements in a peace researcher's toolbox: the capacity to understand a conflict situation, to foresee how it might develop and to offer concrete solutions:

> Peace studies are so similar to health studies that the triangle *diagnosis-prognosis-therapy* can be applied. There is the common idea of a system (of actors, or cells), of well-states and ill-states. The word-pairs 'health/disease' from health studies and 'peace/violence' from peace studies can be seen as specifications of these more general labels (Galtung 1996a, 1).

Galtung's definition of peace by peaceful means is 'the capacity to handle conflicts with empathy, nonviolence and creativity' (Galtung 2000b). These three qualities have been carefully chosen and are directly linked to Galtung's ABC triangle used to analyze conflicts. Galtung asks three questions concerning conflicts: what is the attitude (A) of the parties in conflict? What is their behavior (B)? What is the contradiction (C) causing the conflict? He then suggests that the best *attitude* to deal with the conflict peacefully is empathy, the best *behavior* is nonviolence, and the best way to resolve the *contradiction* is creativity (Galtung 1996b). He also emphasizes that a conflict might turn violent if any of the three components of the triangle takes a turn for the worse:

> A basic problem is that such processes may also start in A or B. One party may have accumulated negative attitudes (aggressiveness) or negative behavioral inclination (a capacity, predisposition for aggression); and when 'something comes along' that looks like a

problem, either A or B, or both, may be activated and hitched on to
the new problem (Galtung 1996a, 72).

For Galtung conflicts are a natural and omnipresent part of human life,
and thus the choice we have is between using violence or not to transform
and solve them. Conflicts can be violent and destructive, but they can be
turned into a positive source of constructive energy depending on the ABC of
the parties involved.

He highlights three types of violence: direct (killing, hurting), structural
(oppression, exploitation) and cultural (ways of thinking influenced by
religion, ideology, language structures, etc.), and defines cultural violence as
'that which legitimizes direct and/or structural violence' (Galtung 2009a). He
provides an elaborate yet succinct description of the three types of violence:

> Direct violence can be divided into *verbal* and *physical,* and violence
> harming the *body*, *mind* or *spirit*. All combinations leave behind
> traumas that may carry violence over time.

> Structural violence divides into *political, repressive* and *economic,*
> *exploitative*; supported by *structural penetration, segmentation, fragmen-*
> *tation* and *marginalization*. In addition, there is also the *horizontal*
> *structural violence* of being too tightly related, and of being too
> loosely or even unrelated. Structures can be too dominant (vertical),
> too tight (horizontal), too much (both/and), and too little (neither
> one, nor the other).

> Cultural violence divides by content: *religion, law and ideology,*
> *language, art, empirical/formal science, cosmology (deep culture)* and by
> carriers: *schools, universities, media* (Galtung 1996a, 31).

Concerning which type of violence causes the others, Galtung thinks that the
three are interdependent, and this is why he uses the term *direct-structural-cul-*
tural (DSC) *triangle.* For instance, structural violence in the form of a repressive
political system could shape an atmosphere of acceptance and justification for
the regime (cultural violence). Also violent demonstrations and riots (direct
violence) could force the government to establish more repressive policies
(structural violence). At the same time, he highlights the following causal flow:

> Generally, a causal flow from cultural via structural to direct violence
> can be identified. The culture preaches, teaches, admonishes, eggs
> on, and dulls us into seeing exploitation and/or repression as normal
> and natural, or into not seeing them (particularly not exploitation)

at all. Then come the eruptions, the efforts to use direct violence to get out of the structural iron cage, and counter-violence to keep the cage intact (Galtung 1996a, 200).

Based on these three types of violence, the distinction between positive and negative peace can be formulated more succinctly: 'Galtung defined "negative peace" as the cessation of direct violence and "positive peace" as the overcoming of structural and cultural violence as well' (Ramsbotham et al. 2008, 11).

Galtung devised a graph with five conflict outcomes between two imaginary adversaries (A1 and A2) each with their own goals (G1 and G2). This system should not be confused with game theory, which only explores options available in a certain reality. Galtung's goal is to bring changes in that reality (Galtung 2009). The five outcome points are: (4, 5) win/lose (victory), or lose/win (defeat), which broaden, deepen and exacerbate the conflict; (3) lose/lose (withdrawal), when both A1 and A2 abandon all claims; (2) win some and lose some on both sides (compromise); and, the ideal outcome, (1) both sides obtaining what they want together (the Transcend point, or the 'Fifth Way'). Galtung's overall system of conflict transformation is called the Transcend Method, the essence of which is represented in the graph below. He writes:

> Transcendence is the outcome that carries the proud title 'creative conflict transformation.' Something new, *sui generis,* usually unexpected, has emerged from the process, meaning that the positive aspect of a conflict has been made use of, the challenge to transcend (hence the term) the underlying contradiction. Both goals are realized, possibly somewhat transformed. There is bliss. Key word: *creativity* (Galtung 1996a, 96).

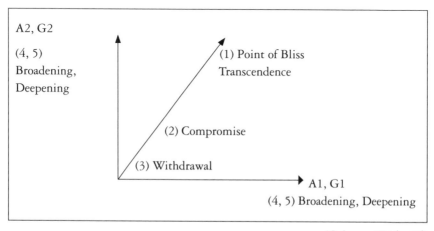

(Galtung 1996a, 96)

With the idea of positive peace, the triangles of attitude-behavior-contradiction (ABC), direct-structural-cultural violence (DSC) and diagnosis-prognosis-therapy (DPT), and with the five conflict outcomes, including the point of transcendence, among many other concepts, Galtung has provided peace studies with a wide and coherent theoretical framework.

Ikeda's system: similarities and differences with Galtung's

One of the main sources of motivation behind this chapter and this research is that I see a strong similarity between Galtung's emphasis on creativity to find the best solution to transform any conflict situation, and Makiguchi, Toda and Ikeda's philosophy of Value-creation, or *soka* in Japanese, which I define as asserting that with courage, wisdom and compassion human beings can create something positive from any situation, conflictual or not. However Ikeda's philosophy of peace cannot be reduced exclusively to the concept of *soka*, and there are some important differences between the system designed by Galtung and what I consider as 'Ikeda's system' introduced in this book.

In the rest of this section, I will mainly quote passages from the dialogue Ikeda and Galtung have written together in order to let some of these harmonies and dissonances resonate.

Galtung and Ikeda first met in December 1984 in Tokyo during a conference on 'Buddhism and Leadership for Peace.' Their meetings led to the publication of the book of dialogues entitled *Choose Peace* in 1995, highlighting agreements and disagreements on a number of points. As shown below, these exchanges help us to see the differences between their philosophies of peace. The point on which they least agree is how to evaluate the usefulness of international human rights, as discussed at the end of this section.

As mentioned in Chapters 5, 6 and 7, I consider that for Ikeda everything starts with the inner transformation of one individual. His definition of peace can be summarized as the capacity to generate courage, wisdom and compassion in order to obtain a higher consciousness that will allow one to hold meaningful dialogues, thereby contributing to the enhancement of global citizenship and the creation of elements of a global civilization of coexistence, harmony and mutual understanding. In similar fashion, Galtung often describes 'development' as human, social and world transformation (Galtung 2009a), and he agrees with Ikeda's general plan for peace, as can be seen from this exchange from their dialogue:

> **Ikeda:** The individual who perseveres along the path of the human revolution attains a realm of eternally indestructible happiness

beyond the life-death cycle. Such a person guides others' innate energy in promising directions and helps them bring forth deeper compassion and wisdom. A tide culminating in the reformation of humanity and our planet is the ultimate goal of the human revolution.

Galtung: Your explanation is clearer than any I have ever heard before (Ikeda and Galtung 1995, 73).

Galtung then asks for clarification concerning the best way to deal with negative energy, and Ikeda's answer seems satisfactory to the Norwegian scholar:

Ikeda: [T]hroughout human history the triumph of the positive has required each individual to conquer his or her own negative aspects and convert them to positive aspects. Though it might seem circuitous, this is actually the shortest, most direct way to the goal, the attainment of which is the reason for the existence of Buddhism and the human revolution (74).

The third step in Ikeda's philosophy of peace, besides inner transformation and dialogue, is the creation of elements of a global civilization, which can be envisioned as a platform or a forum that leaves maximum room for flexibility, rather than a world governance mechanism imposed from above. Unsurprisingly, both agree on this point too:

Ikeda: I agree that the optimum global governing system would be a loose one. Cultural integration, the first of the tasks you assign to a world government, would be unacceptable if it reduced cultural diversity by means of standardization. Interestingly, the post-modernist movement gropes for diversity of identity to replace the universalist monotony of modernism. You and I agree that any attempts to standardize this movement forcibly would be not only contrary to the times, but also doomed to failure (160).

They also agree that the starting point of peace should be an internal revolution:

Ikeda: Gandhi saw that the socialist formula, in which first priority went to the reformation of the political-economic system, was an inversion. He realized that human beings are the true starting point and that, to be long-lasting, all external revolutions must arise from internal revolutions. The more violent the times, the more unflinchingly human beings must direct their searching gazes inward. This is the eternal theme to which he would have us all return.

Galtung: I agree entirely. What you say has a great message for left-wing people who, in their hatred of capitalism and the military establishment, either forget or never develop compassion for the victims of revolutions (64).

Galtung explains the process of inner transformation in a secular humanist way, removing the problem of the specificity of religious practice from the dialogue:

Galtung: The inner dialogue – or meditation – is also a highly self-educating process that may take many forms. A person may meditate seated in front of a wall in a Buddha position. But it is equally possible to meditate while walking, bicycling, or traveling by land or sea. The changing sea-, land- and city-scapes that appear, alter and vanish from consciousness as one travels by train or ship inspire and supply metaphors for thoughts and ideas (15).

Galtung and Ikeda agree that peace is not only the absence of war, and that the concept of positive peace is essential. Beginning in 1967, Galtung has published a large amount of work on positive peace. He is considered as one of the leaders in the introduction of this concept into peace theory, as mentioned earlier.

For Galtung the proper focus of peace studies is the omnipresence of contradictions, due to the incompatibility of goals between people or groups of people. What really matters is how we handle these contradictions, the crucial factor being whether or not violence is used when conflicts arise (Galtung 2008b). For Ikeda, besides contradictions and the opportunity to transform them peacefully, there are many other essential elements in life which are conducive to peace, such as friendship, love, harmony, the creation of value and leading a meaningful life; and contradiction is not considered as an all-pervading reality but as one of the numerous situations one can face. This is an essential difference between the two perspectives.

In a lecture at Harvard University in 1991 entitled 'The Age of Soft Power,' Ikeda asserts that 'we must not limit ourselves to the phenomenal level where hostility and conflict (. . .) undeniably exist,' and that an awareness of the concept of interdependence or dependent origination is crucial in our efforts towards peace:

> Shakyamuni was once asked the following question: 'We are told that life is precious. And yet all people live by killing and eating other living beings. Which living beings may we kill and which living beings must we not kill?' To this simple expression of doubt, Shakyamuni replied, 'It is enough to kill the will to kill.'

> Shakyamuni's response is neither evasion nor deception, but it is based on the concept of dependent origination. He is saying that, in seeking the kind of harmonious relationship expressed by respect for the sanctity of life, *we must not limit ourselves to the phenomenal level where hostility and conflict (in this case, which living beings it is acceptable to kill and which not) undeniably exist.* We must seek harmony on a deeper level – a level where it is truly possible to 'kill the will to kill.' More than objective awareness, we must achieve a state of compassion transcending distinctions between self and other. We need to feel the compassionate energy that beats within the depths of all people's subjective lives where the individual and the universal are merged (Ikeda 1996c) (Italics added).

For Galtung, contradictions can be an excellent source of creativity and energy:

> Deep inside every conflict lies a contradiction, something standing in the way of something else. A problem, in other words. And what could serve better as a *force motrice* for any actor, individual or collective, than a problem demanding to be solved? (Galtung 1996a, 70).

Peace studies in general and conflict resolution/transformation in particular have generated many models based on Galtung's assumption that all life is made of contradiction. I believe that Ikeda offers an alternative view of peace. (The table at the end of this section presents a summary of the major similarities and differences between the two systems.) As mentioned above, the starting point of Ikeda's rationale is the concept of dependent origination (Skt *pratitya-samutpada*) which in this work has been translated as interdependence:

> The doctrine of causal origination amounts to an ethos of symbiosis [*kyosei*, also translated as harmonious coexistence] – an ethos that

ought to be shared by all peoples. In an address delivered to the Chinese Academy of Social Sciences, I defined the ethos of symbiosis as 'a psychological tendency to favor harmony over opposition, unity over division, "we" over "I"; a belief that human beings should live together harmoniously with each other and with nature, support each other and flourish together.' Only when it is seen by all to be such an ethos will the doctrine of causal origination have the power to serve effectively as a basis for global solidarity (Ikeda and Galtung 1995, 94).

In 1973, Christian theologian John Macquarrie had already pointed out the importance of conflict, one of the most common outcomes of contradiction, in his essay entitled *The Concept of Peace*, placing conflict in the context of 'wholeness,' which bears similarities with Ikeda's 'symbiosis' or harmonious coexistence.

I have consistently maintained that peace is more primordial than war in the human condition, yet this affirmation has to be understood in such a way that it recognizes also the reality of conflict, even the necessity and value of conflict. I have in fact also urged that conflict can be creative. But conflict must be included within wholeness. A wholeness which did not include conflict would be a frozen condition, a kind of death lacking dynamism and the possibility of new development. On the other hand, conflict that has broken away from the goal of wholeness has become quite negative and destructive, and can no longer serve the cause of a more fulfilled humanity (Macquarrie 1973, 34).

Macquarrie also mentions the concept of interdependence as the main reason why peace should become one of the main goals for Christians:

One good reason for giving to peace the paramount place among the Christian virtues is just the indisputable fact that in the contemporary world the lives of all people are bound together in an interdependence closer and more evident than has ever been known before (1).

Whereas 'Galtungian' peace studies requires abundant research and writing on specific problems that need particular treatments, 'Ikedian' peace studies in its present form would spend more time on a general therapy. In Ikeda's system, the general *diagnosis* is that people are suffering from the ill effects of human greed, anger and foolishness (the three poisons), the *prognosis* is that it is going to get worse unless each person makes efforts towards self-reformation, and the *therapy* is to generate more courage, wisdom and compassion to attenuate or eradicate the effects of the three poisons, to hold more meaningful dialogues and to contribute to the development of elements of a global civilization through enhanced global citizenship.

Galtung's emphasis on establishing elaborate diagnoses of cultural and structural violence has generated abundant criticism of specific countries' foreign or domestic policies, the negative role of greedy corporations, and the violence inherent in the globalization of materialistic values and practices. Huge volumes of such writings by Galtung and many others attest to this fact.

Ikeda rarely dwells on such considerations. He repeatedly denounces and apologizes for the crimes against humanity committed by the Japanese military during the first half of the twentieth century, and deplores the lack of progress of humanity concerning global issues such as nuclear disarmament, UN reform, the destruction of the environment and some other themes. His Buddhist diagnosis goes to the very heart of the matter, and therefore leaves specific analysis and diagnosis to others. This is reminiscent of the emphasis of his mentor Toda on the root causes of the nuclear threat, which was discussed in Chapter 3.

A full engagement towards the threefold approach of inner transformation, dialogue and global citizenship does require an awareness of the situation of the world and of the actual suffering of millions of people. However, it is not dependent on the severe criticisms and detailed diagnoses required by Galtung's DPT triangle. Using the examples of Gandhi and Havel, Ikeda makes clear that a serious commitment to human happiness will allow one to create value without dwelling too much on diagnoses and prognoses:

> Because it is of pivotal importance to the Gandhian philosophy of nonviolence, a few words must be said about the distinctive traits of Gandhi's brand of optimism. First, it is not relativism determined by objective analyses of circumstances. Instead it is an unconditional, indestructible faith in humanity, a faith born of justice, nonviolence and penetrating self-observation.

> Vaclav Havel manifests a radiant optimism similar to the kind typified by Mahatma Gandhi. He has always maintained the faith evident in some remarks in his book *Disturbing the Peace*: 'Hope is not prognostication. It is an orientation of the spirit, an orientation

of the heart . . . It is not the conviction that something will turn
out well, but the certainty that something makes sense, regardless
of how it turns out' (Ikeda and Galtung 1995, 56).

However, Galtung and Ikeda agree that peace research requires synergy
between the human capacities for hope and for criticism. Galtung says
that 'We must be realists in our brains while keeping the flame of idealism
burning in our hearts' (Ikeda and Galtung 1995, 18), and Ikeda expresses his
complete agreement.

Galtung's three qualities of empathy, creativity and nonviolence have similarities and differences with Ikeda's triad of courage, wisdom and compassion.
Compassion is close to empathy, and this can be considered a similarity. For
Ikeda, creativity is also very important, and it is the basis of the capacity
to create value, which has given its name to the Soka Gakkai. However, for
Ikeda creativity is the result of courage, wisdom and compassion combined,
not one of the three main qualities of human beings. Nonviolence is essential
for Galtung, who is very much inspired by Gandhi, whereas for Ikeda nonviolence is implicit, since there is no courage, compassion or wisdom in the
use of violence. Moreover, dialogue is the opposite of violence, and for Ikeda
the top priority must be the protection of human life: 'Respect for human
rights must be our guide. All peoples must come to realize and assimilate
within themselves the idea of the supreme importance of human life' (Ikeda
and Galtung 1995, 55).

In the systematization of Ikeda's philosophy of peace provided here,
individuals have a choice between courage, wisdom and compassion on the
one hand, and greed, anger and foolishness on the other. By choosing to
bring out the three positive qualities, one will be able to create value and
to communicate with others in the spirit of dialogue. It is in this second
step that Ikeda's opposition to violence is apparent. Creativity is even more
important in the next step, which involves the enhancement of one's commitment to global citizenship and the creation of elements of an inclusive global
civilization.

As a result all six concepts – courage, wisdom, compassion, empathy,
nonviolence and creativity – are present in both systems, but not in the same
position within each system.

For Galtung, the main problem is the omnipresence of contradiction in
life and how we handle situations that could lead to violence. He asserts that
with *empathy* + *nonviolence* + *creativity* one can find the best solutions and
transform any situation peacefully. These three qualities surely require *courage*
and *wisdom*. *Dialogue* is only one of the many peaceful conflict transformation
methods proposed by Galtung.

For Ikeda, the starting point is human life. Then with *courage, wisdom* and *compassion* (*empathy*), one can find the *creativity* to lead a fulfilling life, to hold *dialogues* which are at the opposite of using violence (*nonviolence*), and then use that *creativity* and the mutual enrichment and synergy found in dialogues to create elements of a global civilization.

The place and definition of nonviolence in each system is also different. For Galtung, nonviolence is one of the basic qualities, whereas for Ikeda, it is a natural outcome of a life based on self-development and committed to dialogue. Galtung uses a Gandhian definition of nonviolence, which includes the imperative of using boycotts, demonstrations, direct action and other nonviolent methods in the struggle for peace (see Gene Sharp's '198 Methods of Nonviolent Action,' discussed later in this chapter). The militant aspect of Gandhi's nonviolence mentioned above is not part of Ikeda's system. This can be explained by the fact that Ikeda's emphasis is on inner transformation, and that the concept of structural violence is not essential to his plan for peace.

In the following passage, Ikeda praises the Mahatma's capacity to take concrete action and to mobilize ordinary people as exemplified by the Salt March. This seems to indicate that Ikeda is in favor of mass demonstrations, but he is not. It is only the greatness of Gandhi's spirit that he admires, not the specific protest methods he used:

> The Gandhian combination of idealist and man of practical action finds startlingly vivid manifestation in the famous Salt March of 1930, when Gandhi led thousands of people to the seashore to make their own salt in protest against a cruel tax imposed by the British colonial authorities. (. . .) In standing up nonviolently against wrong and violent governmental practices Gandhi demonstrated the unfailing unity with the ordinary people that was indispensable to his own original way of thinking (Ikeda and Galtung 1995, 57).

However, in many other passages Ikeda shows his skepticism concerning the usefulness of protests and demonstrations:

> During the late 1960s and the early 1970s, students all over the world manifested active nihilism by rejecting all modern values. Their efforts began and ended in destruction and division. Nietzsche himself characterized the nihilist process as destruction brought on by destruction. The impulse to self-destruction generates destructive acts. Often the self depends on generally accepted

value-criteria. When they rejected those criteria, the students were in effect rejecting at least part of their selves. Self-rejection is in a very real sense self-destruction. Social nihilism is restricted to external and externally imposed values. Self-enlightenment to one's own inherent values can halt or reverse the destructive process (94).

Ikeda believes that the inner transformation of one individual brings about better results than external changes to the fabric of society:

[S]ocial-structural changes without a sound philosophical basis produce only limited results. The Buddhist spirit of compassion means empathizing totally with the sufferings of others and being willing to do everything possible to alleviate such suffering. This strikes me as an excellent basis for a philosophy oriented toward ensuring universal human rights (109).

Ikeda quotes American-born British poet T.S. Eliot in a passage in which he made a similar point, from a radio broadcast in February 1937:

[O]ne reason why the lot of the secular reformer or revolutionist seems to me to be the easier is this: that for the most part he conceives of the evils of the world as something external to himself. They are thought of either as completely impersonal, so that there is nothing to alter but machinery: or if there is evil incarnate, it is always incarnate in the other people – a class, a race, the politicians, the bankers, the armament makers, and so forth – never in oneself (Eliot quoted in Ikeda and Galtung 1995, 122).[3]

One finds in this statement by Eliot echoes of Gabriel Marcel's criticism of the spirit of abstraction mentioned in Chapter 7.

Ikeda's lack of interest in organizing large-scale demonstrations, boycotts or other forms of protests is often frustrating for those wishing to apply his philosophy of peace in more dramatic ways than through inner transformation, dialogue and global citizenship. Members of the Soka Gakkai, the SGI and other supporters of Ikeda's philosophy of peace are free to participate in any movement they wish on a private basis, but Ikeda himself neither encourages nor discourages protest. He does not want to see anyone get harmed, and his philosophy does not include the concept of sacrifice, even willingly undertaken self-sacrifice. This lack of presence of large-scale demonstrations and other highly visible forms of protests in Ikeda's philosophy and practice of peace will be further explored in the section on Gene Sharp below.

While lacking enthusiasm for mass demonstrations, Ikeda's philosophy of peace nevertheless includes the active participation of citizens in the construction and reformation of their society. Ikeda has developed a grassroots movement allowing millions of people to improve themselves through inner transformation and dialogue, empowering them to take on the task of transforming the structures of the world by invigorating society in the educational, artistic, cultural, political, and many other spheres. In this sense, Ikeda's philosophy recommends a transformation of both individuals and the society in which they live.

In *Mystics and Militants*, Curle offers an interesting distinction between these two types of peace workers. According to the definitions he offers, Ikeda is both a mystic, 'preoccupied with changing [himself],' and a militant, 'attempting to change institutions' by empowering people to contribute to a better world, and also by establishing new institutions at all levels of society. Arthur Koestler made a similar point in 1945 in *The Yogi and the Commissar and Other Essays*. For Curle, only 'exceptionally aware' peace workers like Gandhi can combine both aspects (Curle 1972, 10).

The most vigorously expressed point of contention between Ikeda and Galtung in their dialogue is their evaluation of the concept of human rights. At least twice, Ikeda feels the need to clarify his disagreement with Galtung. The Norwegian scholar believes that the human rights system 'reinforces the division of the world into states,' but Ikeda does not agree.

> **Galtung:** Instead of chains and cycles of mutual rights and obligations based perhaps on empathy or compassion, these accords are judiciable, legal rules to be guarded by all kinds of governmental and nongovernmental organizations. The construction reinforces the division of the world into states by making them accountable in both directions – upward to the United Nations and downward to their own citizens – and by making them, if not the providers, at least the guarantors of human rights implementation (. . .) (Ikeda and Galtung 1995, 103).

> **Ikeda:** In spite of the objections you raise about the shortcomings of the codex of human rights the West has compiled, I am convinced the time has come for us to revise the view that guaranteeing human rights is a purely domestic national issue. Human rights must be regarded as international and global (104).

Galtung does not relent easily. He renews his attack on what he considers a typically Western construction, while agreeing that the universal aspect of human rights is important:

> **Galtung:** The gist of my critique of human rights is not to take away any rights already achieved, but to add to the list of rights and to give much higher priority to Vasak's third generation [of 'solidarity rights,' for instance the right to common ownership of the human heritage, which operates on a global plane]. In addition, *I believe in universality, but only after dialogues have been conducted and the values of other civilizations have come to be understood* and – to some extent – accepted as contributions as important as those from the West (. . .) (111) (Italics added).

In a reversal of cultural roles, the criticism by the North European scholar of what he considers an institution replete with Western values, such as individualism, fails to change the opinion of the Japanese, who sees in the Universal Declaration of Human Rights (UDHR) a blueprint for universal respect for life:

> **Ikeda:** While appreciating your evaluation and respecting your views that the presently accepted concept of human rights has served to justify Western prejudices and bears the imprint of certain phases of Western history, *I nonetheless believe firmly in the universal value of human rights.* Certainly Western civilization has been guilty of great crimes against indigenous peoples and has a grave responsibility to bear in connection with such horrors as the slave trade and the subjugation of local populations – the Incas, for example. Still, as Arthur M. Schlesinger, Jr. has said, the West has produced its own antidotes. One of the finest of these is the Universal Declaration of Human Rights, which states in its first article that all human beings are born free and are equal in rights and dignity. It can be inferred from this statement that the declaration clearly rejects discrimination against women, children, refugees, the handicapped, foreigners and so on (111–12) (Italics added).

My interpretation of these two passages is that Galtung and Ikeda agree that the universality of human rights is crucial for peace. The difference is that whereas Ikeda believes that the Universal Declaration of Human Rights can serve as the basis to strengthen this universality, for Galtung more work has to be done to design a more global and inclusive system of human rights. This is one of the main themes of his work *Human Rights in Another Key* (1994).

Consistent with the opinions expressed above, Ikeda has been a staunch supporter of the International Court of Justice (ICJ) and the International Criminal Court (ICC), as mentioned in Chapter 7. Ikeda has also expressed his full support for the Earth Charter. This document, as well as the mobilization of large numbers of people from all backgrounds and cultures by the Earth Charter movement, takes into account exactly the kinds of criticisms formulated by Galtung in the dialogue. Support for the Earth Charter can therefore be considered as a way to 'transcend' this disagreement: Galtung's criticisms have been taken into account, and Ikeda has continued his unflinching support for both the UDHR and the Earth Charter. Going back to Galtung's graph, both dialogue partners A1 and A2 have reached their goals G1 and G2.

Finally, Ikeda does not use the five outcome points in his system, because conflict is considered as only one situation among many, and finding peaceful solutions to conflicts is not the only priority of his philosophy. The emphasis is on leading a fulfilling and meaningful life, contributing to the welfare of others, and to the prosperity of humanity in general. This includes, but is not reduced to, the peaceful transformation of conflict. Based on the premise that contradictions between incompatible goals, which are at the source of conflicts, have to be addressed in order to avoid violence, Galtung starts with conflicts and has designed a whole system to transform them peacefully, harnessing their potential for creative energy.

> Conflict releases and builds human and social, individual and collective, energy; the problem is how to channel that energy in constructive rather than destructive directions. Look at the faces, at people's eyes when in conflict: some look dull and apathetic; others' eyes are shining, ready for action. The question is, for what? – the battlefield or to scale peaks of human creativity? (Galtung and Tschudi 2002, 169).

Ikeda's approach starts with one individual human being and one can then imagine waves of happiness starting from this center, expressed through courage, wisdom and compassion, spreading outward through dialogue, with the waves finally affecting society and the world, allowing people who have developed an identity as global citizens to create elements of a global civilization. The following table summarizes the similarities and differences between the two systems.

Concept	Galtung	Ikeda
Starting point for peace	Contradiction, Conflict situation	Human life
Human qualities conducive to peace	Empathy, Nonviolence, Creativity	Courage, Wisdom, Compassion
Importance of Creativity	One of the three basic qualities	A result of the combination of the three basic qualities
Dealing with Violence	Direct: Nonviolence Structural: Creativity Cultural: Empathy	There will be less violence when people practice inner transformation and dialogue and enhance global citizenship
Five outcome points	Essential since contradiction and conflict are at the starting point of the system	Non-essential, only one way to deal creatively with life's challenges
The key to peace	Conflict transformation skills, the Transcend Method	Bringing out the best in self and others through inner transformation, dialogue and global citizenship
Main weakness from the point of view of the other system (not mentioned by Galtung or Ikeda, only a theoretical conclusion by the author of this work)	Too much emphasis on structural violence; nonviolence includes direct action, boycotts and demonstrations, which can turn violent	Not enough emphasis on structural violence; definition of nonviolence too strict, excluding protests, boycotts, demonstrations and other Gandhian tools

Kenneth Boulding

A Quaker and an economist, Kenneth Boulding was born in the UK in 1910 and moved to the US in 1937. He married Elise Bjorn-Hansen in 1941, and together they contributed to the birth and early development of peace and conflict research. As mentioned above, he started the *Journal of Conflict Resolution*, the very first scholarly journal in the field, with Herbert Kelman and others in 1957, and established the Center for Research on Conflict Resolution at the University of Michigan in 1959. Boulding wanted to prevent war by a reform of the international system, which he thought could be achieved by the development of research and information concerning the social situation of various places in the world. He wanted to organize 'social data stations' similar to a network of weather stations in order to collect information about the potential build-up of conflicts (Ramsbotham et al. 2008, 40–41).

For Boulding, countries could behave in two different ways: associative or dissociative. 'The latter involves reliance on military strength and political separation, based on the notion that "good fences make good neighbors." Associative solutions, on the other hand, are efforts to tear down walls, to join together' (Barash and Webel 2009, 288).

In his book *Three Faces of Power* (1989) Boulding also established a distinction between 'threat,' 'economic' and 'integrative' power. Economic power is about bargaining and compromise, whereas integrative power is about long-term, transformative problem-solving. Boulding believes that integrative power, the power of the 'hug,' is fundamental:

> In this volume, I distinguish three major categories, which I have called threat power, economic power, and integrative power – the stick, the carrot, and the hug. These are closely related to another tripartite division: the power to destroy, the power to produce and exchange, and the power to integrate, that is, the power to create such relationships as love, respect, friendship, legitimacy and so on. (. . .) My major thesis in this book is that it is integrative power that is the most dominant and significant form of power, in the sense that neither threat power nor economic power can achieve very much in the absence of legitimacy, which is one of the more important aspects of integrative power (Boulding 1989, 10).

Boulding believes that the way people feel about their memberships in groups is also crucial: 'A major source of the integrative power of a community or organization is the degree to which the personal identity of the members involved is bound up with their perception of the identity of the community or organization as a whole' (173). Reviewing the whole of human history, he is optimistic concerning humanity's tendency and capacity to favor the more peaceful economic and integrative forms of power: 'the increase in the productive and integrative powers of the human race have been much more significant than the increase in its destructive powers, at least up to the present century' (226). He asserts his belief that for thousands of years people have shown much greater propensity for integrative and cooperative activities than for warfare and aggression: 'at least 90 percent of human activity even in the age of civilization was peaceful – plowing, sowing, and reaping, cooking, weaving, and building, making pottery and tools, eating, feasting, singing, worshiping, dancing, having and raising children, and so on' (223).

I see many similarities with Ikeda's values and principles. They both believe in the positive potential of human beings for peace. Boulding's emphasis on the importance of the way people perceive their identity is related to the enhancement of global citizenship, which I think is the most peaceful way to experience belonging. Boulding's concept of integrative power or the 'hug' is reminiscent of Makiguchi's humanitarian competition. I think that for Ikeda, the level of happiness and fulfillment of each individual serves as 'social data stations.' Finally they agree on the importance of reforming the international system, Ikeda emphasizing the role of the UN in this endeavor.

John Burton, Herbert Kelman and the Harvard School

Born in Australia in 1915, John Burton attended the foundation conference of the United Nations in San Francisco. He became the first Honorary Secretary of the Conflict Research Society in London, where he moved in 1963 to work at University College London. In 1966 he became the director of the newly established Centre for the Analysis of Conflict based at University College London (Ramsbotham et al. 2008, 43–44).

He contributed to the development of the 'controlled communication or problem-solving approach' and to the use of the concept of 'second order learning' in conflict transformation. For him Maslow's theory of needs (1954) was fundamental: 'Problem-Solving at the social level – be it the small groups, the nation state or interactions between states – is possible only by processes that take the needs of individuals as the basis for analyzing and planning' (Burton 1979, 80). Burton's approach is still used successfully today, for instance in the form of the 'analytical problem solving' approach:

Analytical problem solving is a social-psychological approach to dealing with deep-rooted, protracted inter-group and international conflicts. Initially developed by Herbert Kelman and John Burton, this technique is based on the human needs theory of conflict, which says that most deep rooted conflicts are caused by one or more person's or group's inability to obtain its fundamental human needs – for instance, identity, security, or recognition. By identifying the underlying needs that are lacking, parties are often able to redefine the conflict in a way that facilitates joint problem solving and collaboration, when such was impossible before. (. . .) Unlike interests, needs are usually mutually-reinforcing, rather than mutually exclusive (Rant Collective 2009).

As Burton wrote, 'the more security and recognition one party to a relationship experiences, the more others are likely to experience [it too]' (Burton 1990, 242).

In general systems theory, 'first order learning' refers to the way people in a society usually react when confronted with certain problems. Those quasi-automatic reactions, conditioned by the culture of a society, are based on what Anatol Rapoport calls 'default values.' In order to transform conflicts successfully, the parties will have to challenge their own assumptions, and remember that they have a choice, a capacity referred to as second order learning. I believe that this implies efforts at inner transformation, and not only technical skills: 'Burtonian problem-solving, seen as paradigm shift rather than workshop technique, is itself firmly at the transformationist end of the conflict resolution spectrum' (Ramsbotham et al. 2008, 47).

Herbert Kelman continued developing the 'problem-solving method' and was the director of the Program on International Conflict Analysis and Resolution at Harvard University from 1993 to 2003. Specializing in the Israeli–Palestinian conflict, he organized workshops between 1974 and 1993 which paved the way for the 1993 Oslo agreements. He believes in the building of new relationships and in facilitated dialogues. A continuation of this work can be found in the mutual gain and win-win approach of Roger Fischer and William Ury at the Harvard Program on Negotiation, whose *Getting to Yes: Negotiating Agreement without Giving In* (1981) became a bestseller.

I think the concept of second order learning is an important aspect of inner transformation. For Ikeda, dialogue is a way to bring out the best in oneself and others and to reach our common humanity. I believe this is the case with Burton's problem-solving method, and that it is similar to Kelman's way of using the concept. However, when it comes to the use of *dialogos* to reach business deals and enhance negotiations, it cannot be considered as an integral part of Ikeda's philosophy of peace when it tilts the balance too much towards Habermas's concept of instrumental/purposive communication.

Adam Curle

Born in 1916, Adam Curle was raised in England and obtained a Diploma in Anthropology at the University of Oxford. In the latter part of World War II, Curle worked for the Civil Resettlement Units (CRU) created by the government to ease the rehabilitation of returning prisoners of war. According to Mitchels,

> The work of the CRUs was innovative and pioneering, and that work, coupled with his earlier life experiences, may have been influential on Adam Curle's understanding of the nature and effects of psychological trauma, and of the positive impact of a holistic and community-based approach to trauma healing (Mitchels 2006, 32).

After teaching at Harvard from 1962 to 1973, Curle was appointed chair of the first department of peace studies at the University of Bradford, effectively establishing peace studies as a new academic discipline in the United Kingdom.[4]

Adam Curle was a Quaker, but he was also very interested in Tibetan Buddhism, and became a personal friend of the Dalai Lama. According to Mitchels:

> Adam is a Quaker, but also profoundly influenced by non-western philosophies, including Tibetan Buddhism. His approach to peacemaking adopts the spiritual values and perceptions of both Quakerism and Buddhism, set in the context of the teachings of modern quantum mechanics and atomic science, sociology and psychology (Mitchels 2006, 35).

The poem 'Indra's Net,' using Buddhist imagery, from *To Tame the Hydra* is one of the many instances where Curle expresses his belief in the 'interconnectedness of all living matter on physical and spiritual levels – the foundation of his philosophy' (Mitchels 2006, 35). Curle shows a profound understanding of the connection between the concept of interdependence or dependent origination (Skt *pratitya-samutpada*) and that of emptiness or latent potentiality (Skt *shunyata*) and how they can contribute to the development of peace:

> First of all I should say that the deconstruction of the self as a completely self-existent, separate entity does not mean that you and I do not exist as recognisable individuals (. . .)

> At each intersection of the endless net
> Of Indra's heaven, according to the myth,
> There is a bead that represents life.
> Each bead reflects every other. (. . .)

We do in fact possess unique individuality, but it is an individuality forged from the flow of energy and wisdom from countless multi-directional sources, playing upon our original inherited endowment; a wonderful paradox of unity in diversity, and endless source of happiness (Curle 1999, 46).

Curle explains the usefulness of the concept of emptiness or latent potentiality from another angle, that of accepting the impermanence of the ego:

> The false identity may be woven around something which is very fallible, such as sporting ability or personal appearance or business acumen. These things become the real me, the essence of our being. When we lose an important match, or our looks, or go bankrupt, it's much more than an upset or a worry. It's a threat to our very being which may lead to what is called an 'identity crisis' (Curle 1995, 70).

He also wrote in an unpublished poem entitled 'Peace':

> Peace is an inner state
> In loving care for anyone in need.
> Its qualities are wisdom
> And compassion (Curle quoted in Mitchels 2006, 22).

He also mentioned these qualities in 'Public Health IV: Reversing the Cycle of Violence,' in terms similar to how I would describe the basic process of inner transformation: 'changing the energy expressed in explosive violence to energy manifested in wise and compassionate action' (Curle 1997, 1).

He wrote about all three qualities which I have identified as essential in Ikeda's philosophy of peace since I consider that strength is equivalent to courage here, and about the crucial Buddhist concept of the Three Poisons in *Another Way*:

> The potential of our nature is frequently blocked and few of us make full use of our latent power of *wisdom, strength and compassion*. We have discussed the virtually universal vicious cycle of the *Three Poisons* which generally is the cause of this failure and the source of much unhappiness and destructive behaviour (Curle 1995, 67) (Italics added).

This awareness of Buddhist concepts gives Curle a common basis with Ikeda. Curle also believed in dialogue, mostly as a therapeutic tool to heal the traumas of war, as one of the most important 'transformative approaches creating radical interpersonal and intrapersonal psychological change' (Mitchels 2006, 51). In the following passage Mitchels describes Curle's emphasis on personal transformation in terms that I believe match almost exactly the starting point of Ikeda's philosophy of peace:

> For Curle, peacemaking links in with the humanistic psychological approaches that aim to encourage internal reflection, questioning personal and external belief systems, empowering individuals to take action to effect personal and social change. He strongly advocates intrapersonal change (Mitchels 1996, 45).

Curle and Ikeda's philosophies are therefore very similar. Curle's theory could be described as a three-step approach made up of inner transformation, dialogue and nonviolent conflict transformation, which includes mediation. It is mostly the third element in Ikeda's theory, the enhancement of global citizenship and the development of elements of a global civilization, which differentiates the two approaches. Again, this points to what is characteristic about Nichiren Buddhism generally, and the Soka Gakkai's approach to Nichiren Buddhism in particular: the focus on engagement with one's immediate environment in expanding concentric circles of empowerment: when one has been able to bring peace to the inner self, one becomes more interested in bringing peace to one's family, community, society, through the use of dialogue and other means. This movement outward is supported by the initial inductive commitment to the meta-objective of world peace and the happiness of all humanity.

Elise Boulding

As mentioned above, Elise married Kenneth Boulding in 1941. She also contributed to the birth and development of the Center for Research on Conflict Resolution, became the first Secretary-General of IPRA in 1964, chair of the Women's International League for Peace and Freedom and editor of the IPRA Newsletter. She introduced several ideas such as imaging the future, the 200-year present and the importance of civil society and of the creation of a global civic culture of peace, as indicated in the title of some of her works, such as *Building a Global Civic Culture: Education for an Interdependent World* (1990) and *Cultures of Peace* (2000). The goal of 'imaging the future' and the '200-year present' is to empower ordinary people to participate in the transformation of the world. In a 2003 interview, Elise Boulding said:

> I'm interested in how people picture the possibilities in their society and in the world. In the peace movement, after World War II ended, I remember going to a conference in Sweden and asking the disarmament experts, 'If we really had disarmament, how would the world function?' Not a single person on that panel had anything that they could say. I realized that the peace movement was working on peace without knowing what a peaceful world would look like. They didn't know what they were working for. It would just be a world with no weapons and no war. But what kind of society would it be? What kind of institutions? (. . .) A favorite concept of mine is the 200-year present, a way of thinking about change. The 200-year present began 100 years ago, with the year of birth of the people who reach their hundredth birthday today. The other boundary of the 200-year present, 100 years from now, is the hundredth birthday of the babies born today. If you take that span, you and I have contact with a lot of people from different parts of that span (Boulding 2003).

Boulding published a book of dialogue with Ikeda in 2006, entitled *Heiwanobunka no kagayaku seikihe* (*Building a Century of a 'Culture of Peace'*)[5] in which she emphasized the importance of education for global citizenship. Ikeda writes:

> Here I am reminded of a dialogue I conducted with the peace scholar Dr. Elise Boulding in which she maintained the importance of providing future generations with arenas where they can fully express their abilities, stressing that we need to create more opportunities for young people to grow into their role as global citizens. She told me she used to recommend the students in her international peace studies class to spend a semester working as interns at a local chapter of an international NGO and actually experience its activities (Ikeda 2006, 10).

Ikeda also mentions her words in connection with inner transformation:

> She [Boulding] emphatically sums up her position: 'We must take control of our lives, because within us is the seed of a new reality – a seed that cannot grow until our lives are our own. It is a reality of ecstasy, made up of love, justice, freedom, peace and plenty.' She

describes a yearning to open the 'seed of joy' in the lives of all people (Ikeda 2000–II, 64–65).

The similarities between the two philosophies are striking. Boulding believes in the potential of human beings to experience justice, freedom and peace, and affirms the concept of inner transformation when she says '[w]e must take control of our lives.' She is also an advocate of education for global citizenship, and recommends imaging the future, just as Ikeda emphasized global visioning in his 2009 peace proposal.

John Paul Lederach

A Mennonite who shares many of the values of the Quakers, John Paul Lederach was influenced by the Brazilian educator Paulo Freire and his famous work *Pedagogy of the Oppressed* ([1968] 1970). Lederach developed the concept of 'peacebuilding from below' and of 'indigenous empowerment' which he defines as follows: '[W]e understand the long-term goal of transformation as validating and building on people and resources within the setting' (1995, 212). For Lederach, for peacebuilding from below to be effective, it must include collaboration between different levels of leadership, including top, middle-level and grassroots leaders. As Oliver Richmond wrote:

> John Paul Lederach, who is widely regarded as having made one of the most important theoretical contributions to the peacebuilding debate, is particularly sensitive to the consent of local actors, particularly civil society actors, to the construction of a specific version of peace. (. . .) [He] proposes three levels of peacebuilding, including an elite 'top-down' approach which involves intermediaries or mediators backed by a supporting government or IO [international organization] and whose goal is to achieve a negotiated settlement. The second level includes problem solving workshops, conflict resolution training, and the development of peace commissions. The third level includes grassroots bottom up approaches (Richmond [2005] 2007, 103–104).

It can be argued that Ikeda's concept of 'inner transformation' is the essence of 'peacebuilding from below,' since each individual is ultimately in charge of their own transformation, the starting point of the process towards world peace. At the same time, Ikeda has held dialogues with people at all levels of Lederach's pyramid, and he believes that good relationships between the top, middle-level and grassroots leaders are essential.

Betty Reardon

Born in 1929 near New York, Betty Reardon is widely recognized as one of the founders of peace education. As mentioned above, within the field of peace studies, peace education and peace research are considered as separate endeavors. However, her pioneering work on feminist peace education is mentioned here due to its seminal influence in the field and also because of some striking similarities between her philosophy of peace and that of Ikeda.

In 1963, she became Director of the Schools Program with the Institute of World Order, where she conducted critical inquiry into war as a system, with the awareness that what needed to change first was people's mindset. Reardon established the Peace Education Center at Teachers College, Columbia University, and also the International Institute on Peace Education in 1982, in order to encourage worldwide networking between peace educators and activists (World People Blog 2006).

In 1999 she was one of the founders and the first Academic Coordinator of the Hague Appeal for Peace Global Campaign for Peace Education, a movement to introduce peace education into schools and other educational settings worldwide. She has served as a consultant to several UN agencies and education organizations and has published widely on peace, human rights education and gender issues (Peace Education Center 2009). Some major publications include: *Sexism and the War System* (1996), *Education for a Culture of Peace in a Gender Perspective* (2001) and *Learning to Abolish War* (2002).

In 'Human Rights as Education for Peace,' she asserts that the Galtungian concepts of positive peace and direct-structural-cultural violence can be best understood through a human rights framework:

> Positive peace, conceptualized by the peace research community to extend the definition of peace beyond the limitation, avoidance or absence of war to include issues of justice, poverty, and freedom, is the concept of peace that is the foundational principle of the Universal Declaration of Human Rights. (. . .)

> Peace research now recognizes several particular forms of violence as the conceptual rubrics under which data are gathered and knowledge derived: physical or behavioral violence including war, (. . .) structural violence (. . .) and cultural violence (. . .). All of these forms of violence can be made most apparent and comprehensible within a human rights framework. Analyzing these forms of violence as violations of particular human rights standards provides a constructive alternative to presenting them as abstract concepts as is often the case in peace education (Reardon 1997).

In 'Toward a Paradigm of Peace' (1992), Reardon establishes a direct link between feminist theory and the concept of inner transformation:

> As a feminist peace educator, I argue that the present paradigm is at once the source and the product of a war system that, for generations, has been transferred from our minds into our experience and from our experience back to our minds. We engage in war and violence because we think violently in images and metaphors of war. If we are to experience an authentic, fulsome peace, we must think peace. If we are to think peace, we need a paradigm of peace (392).

> Among the changes that have to be made for the achievement of such a [paradigm] shift, the most significant ones are within ourselves. The way in which we move toward these inner changes, the way in which we envision and struggle for peace and try to construct that new paradigm, is the most essential means through which we would be enabled to make the larger structural changes required for a peace system (393).

> Thus the journey is really more personally meaningful to us than the destination. What we are about, on a day-to-day basis, is actually how we change paradigms. We must change ourselves and our immediate realities and relationships if we are to change our social structures and our pattern of thought (393–94).

In her emphasis on the primacy of inner transformation and the importance of daily life, Reardon is very close to Ikeda's philosophy. The theme of human rights appears in 12 of the peace proposals, as mentioned in Chapter 7. For instance, Ikeda supports international law and international human rights because they are indispensable for the protection of human life and dignity and because they are necessary elements of a future global civilization of harmony and coexistence.

All the elements of Ikeda's philosophy of peace can be applied by people regardless of gender, and for instance courage, wisdom and compassion are – obviously – inherent in all human beings. The fundamental equality of all people was already asserted in essential components of Ikeda's philosophy of peace, namely the Lotus Sutra and Nichiren Buddhism, as mentioned in Chapter 4; the Dragon King's Daughter was able to reach enlightenment in one instant.

Gene Sharp

In 1983 Gene Sharp founded the Albert Einstein Institution (AEI), 'dedicated to advancing the study and use of strategic nonviolent action in conflicts throughout the world' (AEI 2009a). It is named after the famous physicist because '[i]n his later life, he [Einstein] became enormously impressed with the potential of nonviolent struggle. In 1950, he remarked on a United Nations radio broadcast that, "On the whole, I believe that Gandhi held the most enlightened views of all the political men in our time"' (AEI 2009b).

A political scientist and nonviolence theorist, Gene Sharp is the author of numerous books, including *The Politics of Nonviolent Action* (1973), and *Waging Nonviolent Struggle: Twentieth Century Practice and Twenty-First Century Potential* (2005). His writings have been published in more than 30 languages. His best-known contribution is the list of '198 Methods of Nonviolent Action' found in his 1973 work. The list includes public speeches, group or mass petitions, newspapers and journals, prayer and worship, and singing. For Ikeda these are also quite acceptable ways to communicate, and he uses them regularly. However, the list also includes marches, nonviolent raids, boycott of legislative bodies, mutiny and hunger strike, which I believe Ikeda would never encourage.

Considering that the Soka Gakkai has close to ten million members in Japan, many people concerned about peace, especially in countries where popular mobilization is standard practice, are surprised that the group does not organize large-scale demonstrations. A few possible reasons for this state of affairs are explored here.

Besides the fact that protesting against something external represents a temporary distraction in the process of self-reformation, there might also be a cultural element, which Ikeda sums up succinctly:

> The people of Japan have never struggled to wrest their rights from their rulers. Indeed, they were nearly two centuries later than the French in receiving constitutional guarantees of basic human rights. Even when finally granted, such legal assurances were the result of external, not internal, pressure. They were therefore externally, not internally generated (Ikeda and Galtung 1995, 106).

In Japan, demonstrations fall under the regulations of the traffic control laws, and most people agree that they have to be organized in detail and in collaboration with the local police, who will participate in the event in order to perform their duty of *torishimari*, a mixture of management, control and supervision. Most Japanese do not see as repression of their freedom of expression the fact that they have to report the number of participants, exact route, purpose and all other details to the police well in advance and receive permission. This is considered as a legitimate process necessary to avoid traffic accidents. As a result of this historical and cultural background, demonstrations are not generally considered as an effective or useful method of protest in Japan.

Another explanation could be that the Soka Gakkai uses other, safer ways to bring people together in large numbers and to take a stance. For instance the *Mainichi Shimbun* daily newspaper of 6 November 1994 reported a large meeting organized by the Soka Gakkai the day before. The front page showed a photo of part of a huge crowd of 55,000 people, and the article explained the purpose of the meeting in detail, which was to oppose attempts by the government to curtail freedom of religion (*Mainichi Shimbun*, 1994).

One last reason might be found in the loyalty of Ikeda towards his mentor Toda. In a passage from *The Human Revolution*, responding to questions from members of the Soka Gakkai in January 1947, the latter is reported to have expressed his dislike of strikes and mass demonstrations in no uncertain terms:

> For your sake, I'll gladly march at the head of your demonstration and wave the red flag or whatever, if you need me to. You, yourselves are completely free to do as you wish. But if you think that's going to solve everything, you're fooling yourselves. (. . .) Economic and political struggles ultimately end in compromise. Of course, they're crucial. But trying to solve everything that way is like navigating a rough sea in a tiny boat. (. . .) Incidents like the general strike will recur in the future under many different guises. People will taste first hope and then despair. They'll be confused, not knowing which way to turn (Ikeda 2004c, 194–95).

Ikeda concludes this section of the novel by commenting that Toda was able to stay true to his convictions, unswayed by mass movements affecting society, whether they came from the extreme left or the extreme right:

> While the entire Japanese population trembled at the threat of a general strike, Toda had remained unperturbed, just as during the war, surrounded by a nation of crazed military fanatics, he had not wavered in the slightest (Ikeda 2004c, 196).

Since Gene Sharp's work is devoted to strategic nonviolent action, it is a good example of a philosophy of peace almost incompatible with that of Ikeda.

Inner transformation and the way dialogue has been defined in this book are not emphasized at all, and neither is global citizenship.

Glenn Paige

The founder and president of the nonprofit Center for Global Nonkilling in Honolulu, Glenn Paige has taught at Seoul National University, Princeton and the University of Hawai'i. A Korean War veteran, he wrote *The Korean Decision: June 24–30, 1950* (1968).

An admirer of Gandhism, of Korean Buddhism, and of many other philosophies, Glenn Paige defines his own religion as the faith and practice of 'nonkilling' (Paige 2008), a concept which is fully developed in his book *Nonkilling Global Political Science* ([2002], 2007) which has been translated into more than 30 languages. In the following passage, he lays out his concept of a nonkilling society:

> It is a human community, smallest to largest, local to global, char-
> acterized by no killing of humans and no threats to kill; no weapons
> designed to kill humans and no justifications for using them; and
> no conditions of society dependent upon threat or use of killing
> force for maintenance or change. There is neither killing of humans
> nor threat to kill. This may extend to animals and other forms of
> life, but nonkilling of humans is a minimum characteristic. There
> are not threats to kill; the nonkilling condition is not produced by
> terror (Paige [2002] 2007, 1).

In the second chapter, entitled 'Capabilities for a Nonkilling Society,' Paige argues that:

> The possibility of a nonkilling society is rooted in human experience
> and creative capabilities. The vast majority of human beings have not
> killed and do not kill. Although we are capable of killing, we are not
> by nature compelled to kill. However imperfectly followed, the main
> teaching of the great spiritual tradition is: respect life, do not kill (68).

As stated above in the section on Galtung, Ikeda mentioned the Buddhist principle that '[i]t is enough to kill the will to kill' in a lecture in 1991.

Paige shows the same belief in the human potential for happiness and peace as Ikeda. The path of inner transformation, dialogue and global citizenship is definitely conducive to less killing, and in this sense there is considerable compatibility between the two approaches.

Concluding comments

At the beginning of this chapter Ikeda's philosophy was placed on the map of peace studies as mostly advocating cultural and structural peacebuilding, two essential components of conflict transformation. Ikeda's ideas have not yet been applied to the field of conflict resolution when it comes to peacemaking, peacekeeping or war limitation, but they might have a role to play at these levels too.

Moreover, since all human beings are potentially in conflict with each other, and since there is a lot of violence (cultural, structural and direct) affecting millions of people every day, I consider that Ikeda's philosophy of peace can serve as an overall conflict prevention method, a way of life conducive to better personal relationships, and collectively, to a more harmonious society. In this sense, it belongs fully to the field of conflict resolution.

To conclude this chapter, a table comparing the main concepts of the theorists mentioned above is presented. Concepts were first assigned a number in order of appearance, and those that can be considered as sufficiently equivalent or linked were assigned the same number. Dialogue here has three different meanings: the way Ikeda uses it as an exchange to bring out our common humanity (2a), in conflict transformation sessions to reach an understanding (2b) and in other cases to reach agreements and make deals (3b). Fifteen concepts have been identified:

Ikeda: inner transformation (1), dialogue for bringing out our
common humanity (2a), global citizenship (3), elements of
a global civilization (4), humanitarian competition (5)

Galtung: positive peace (6), structural violence (7), the transcend
point of synergy (8)

Boulding, K.: trust in the human potential (9), reform of the
international system (4), second order learning (1)

Burton and Kelman: dialogue for bringing out our common
humanity (2a), for understanding and conflict transformation (2b)

Fischer, Ury and the Harvard School: dialogue for negotiations and
business deals (2c)

Curle: inner transformation (1), dialogue (2a, 2b)

Boulding, E.: inner transformation (1), global citizenship (2),
    imaging the future (10)

Lederach: bottom-up approach (11)

Reardon: human rights (12), feminist perspective (13)

Sharp: strategic nonviolent action (14)

Paige: nonkilling (15)

This numbering has allowed the creation of the following table comparing the concepts found in the main theories, in which I include Ikeda's philosophy of peace. When it is not possible to determine if a concept is present in a system or not, a question mark is used. It is to be noted for instance that Glenn Paige's idea of 'nonkilling' is so broad and all-encompassing that it is compatible with all other systems. I hope this highly subjective chart will encourage further research.

	1	2a	2b	2c	3	4	5	6	7	8	9	10	11	12	13	14	15
Ikeda	Y	Y	Y	N	Y	Y	Y	Y	N	Y	Y	Y	Y	Y	Y	N	Y
Galtung	Y	Y	Y	N	?	?	?	Y	Y	Y	Y	Y	Y	Y	Y	Y	Y
Boulding, K.	Y	Y	?	?	?	Y	Y	Y	?	?	Y	?	?	Y	?	N	Y
Burton	?	Y	Y	N	N	N	N	Y	?	Y	Y	?	?	?	?	N	Y
Kelman	?	Y	Y	Y	N	N	N	Y	?	Y	Y	?	?	?	?	N	Y
Curle	Y	Y	Y	N	N	N	N	Y	N	?	Y	?	Y	Y	?	N	Y
Boulding, E.	Y	Y	N	N	Y	Y	Y	Y	?	?	Y	Y	Y	Y	Y	N	Y
Lederach	Y	Y	Y	N	N	N	N	Y	?	Y	Y	Y	Y	Y	?	N	Y
Sharp	N	N	N	N	Y	N	N	Y	Y	N	Y	N	Y	Y	?	Y	Y
Paige	Y	Y	Y	Y	Y	Y	Y	Y	Y	Y	Y	Y	Y	Y	Y	Y	Y

Conclusion

The first hypothesis driving this research was that Daisaku Ikeda's philosophy of peace could be systematized into a coherent framework. This was a humbling and challenging task due to the amount of material to be examined, and to the fact that this type of research has never been conducted before. The result of this first phase of the inquiry was the design of the three-pronged approach described in this book.

The next question concerned the originality of this system. The discovery that the three main concepts of Ikeda's philosophy of peace correspond remarkably well to established fields in Western thinking was an unexpected and serendipitous result. As mentioned throughout this book, it is possible to establish strong links between the type of inner transformation Ikeda advocates and virtue ethics as well as humanistic psychology. Dialogue that brings out the best in oneself and others bears striking similarities to the Habermasian concept of communicative rationality and the Büberian idea of 'I–You' relationships. Ikeda's concept of global citizenship, and his proposals to develop elements of a global civilization of harmony and interdependence, find echoes in Archibugi's idea of cosmopolitan democracy. The drawback of such findings is that this might imply that Ikeda's philosophy of peace might have not much new to offer, since each of the three main concepts are not entirely unique when considered separately.

However, what can be considered an original contribution to peace theory is the fact that all three concepts are integrated into one coherent approach. This specific combination of three fields was not found in any other integrated approach to peace, and the best label for this coherent blend of psychology, dialogical skills and cosmopolitanism could simply be 'Daisaku Ikeda's Philosophy of Peace.'

Each of the components is crucial in the process towards peace, but none is sufficient by itself. For instance, inner transformation alone will not allow for the structural changes necessary to protect human life and dignity and build a fairer society, and cosmopolitanism which is not grounded on dialogical practice always runs the risk of being imposed from above, often with dis-astrous consequences. One original contribution of Ikeda to peace theory is therefore the fact that all three elements are interconnected in his philosophy.

Another important idea is the consistent emphasis on life itself and on inner transformation as the starting point for the process towards world peace. This uncompromising stance towards dealing first with what Nussbaum calls 'a clash within the individual self' has crucial consequences in the agency–structure debate concerning societal transformation and peace. For Ikeda, human beings always hold the key to overcoming obstacles to the improve-ment of society and the world, no matter where they are or what they are going through. Ikeda argues that a proactive and self-motivated increase in courage, wisdom and compassion welling up from within will always produce a positive inner change that can then be translated into concrete realizations in the world, and that there is no limit to what people can achieve. However, as mentioned above, the three components are needed together. Inner transformation may be a necessary starting point, but it is not sufficient to achieve peace.

David P. Barash and Charles P. Webel make the same point in *Peace and Conflict Studies* (2009) when they criticize an exclusive reliance on personal transformation as incomplete:

> Peace may begin with each of us, but war, at least, is likely to begin elsewhere, and peace must entail significant changes in the world at large. It may be satisfying – and even necessary – to 'liberate' oneself, but it is not sufficient (Barash and Webel 2009, 481).

However, in the same work they also quote philosopher Martha Nussbaum and implicitly praise her emphasis on self-reformation, her often-quoted response to the 'Huntington thesis':

> The real 'clash of civilizations' is not between 'Islam' and 'the West,' but instead within virtually all modern nations – between people who are prepared to live on terms of equal respect with others who are different, and those who seek the protection of homogeneity and the domination of a single 'pure' religious and ethnic tradition. At a deeper level, as Gandhi claimed, it is *a clash within the individual self,* between the urge to dominate and defile the other and a willingness to live respectfully on terms of compassion and equality, with all the vulnerability that such a life entails (Nussbaum 2007 in Barash and Webel 2009, 215) (Italics added).

Ikeda's philosophy of peace is in agreement with both, on the one hand asserting like Nussbaum that the fundamental struggle for peace takes the form of a 'clash within the individual self,' but on the other hand remarking like Barash and Webel that 'it is not sufficient.'

Whereas for Ikeda inner transformation is the starting point of endeavors towards peace, dialogue is the indispensable axis around which the system of his philosophy of peace revolves. In the following passage, Ikeda shows that in order to be able to hold meaningful dialogues, it is important to exercise self-control and focus on inner transformation when facing the inevitable challenges that appear in the process of dialogical communication. By remembering that the starting point is within, it is possible to lift 'the dialogue to a new level' and to get the dialogue partners to 'walk the path toward peace together.' Ikeda writes:

> During the dialogue that takes place in [Nichiren's treatise] 'On Establishing the Correct Teaching,' the guest grows angry on several occasions when his positions are refuted by the host. The host knows what needs to be said and is prepared to say it, no matter how the guest might react. When the guest becomes enraged, *the host calmly accepts his anger* and, by doing so, wins his heart over, thereby *lifting the dialogue to a new level*. Eventually, the guest comes to understand and appreciate the host's position and the two resolve to *walk the path toward peace together* (Ikeda 2009, 89) (Italics added).

As mentioned throughout this book, for Ikeda there is no clear separation between the spiritual and the rational, or between the religious and the secular. In the following passage concerning the purpose of dialogue, he states his trust in the power of 'humanistic principles' to 'bring individuals together in the cause of realizing peace and happiness for all people.' He continues:

> This kind of open dialogue brims with the conviction that everyone possesses the Buddha nature, even those who may not at first agree with our views. Everyone has different experiences and viewpoints, and each person is unique. When we pursue dialogue grounded in the principles of Buddhism, we don't focus on such differences. Our main aims are to awaken the other person's Buddha nature and to bring individuals together in the cause of realizing peace and happiness for all people based on *humanistic principles*. This is the purpose of dialogue for us (Ikeda 2009, 89) (Italics added).

Equipped with the capacity for both inner transformation and meaningful dialogue, according to Ikeda, people of all backgrounds and walks of life can discuss issues concerning their lives at the local, national and global levels, enhance deliberative and participatory democracy and widen the political space of their societies, a major ingredient for peace and stability. It is then possible to develop an awareness that all people are part of the same world, that we are all global citizens, and overcoming differences, to develop elements of a global civilization of interdependence and harmony.

A Brief Overview of Pacifism and Peace Movements in Japan

The Japanese tradition of organized protest against authority dates back at least to the peasant tradition of the Edo Era, and can be considered as one of the roots of civil society movements in Japan (Tsurumi 1987). A spectacular example is found in the *uchikowashi* – literally 'breaking and smashing,' an outburst of revolt by oppressed villagers who would storm the habitations of the wealthy local leaders and destroy as much property as possible (Durand 2005).

After the 1868 Meiji Restoration, Western ideas streamed into Japan, including concepts such as democracy[1] and liberalism, as well as the importance of individual freedom as a basis for world peace. These ideas became pervasive in Japanese education and politics, while at the same time other imports from the West, colonialism and imperialism, started to take root too, in complete contradiction to the former concepts. The Japanese mind was therefore torn between these extremes, until around 1931, the year of the invasion of Manchuria, when militarism triumphed decisively over pacifism.

One leading Christian peace thinker was Kanzo Uchimura,[2] who established the Mukyokai (Non-church Christians) in 1901 in reaction to the formalism of the established Western churches in Japan (Brock 2006, 189). Uchimura is recognized as one of the most influential figures in the Japanese peace movement:

> In Japanese postwar history a major political preoccupation, and one with which almost the entire academic elite has identified has been the resumption and continuation of the pacifist tradition established in the Meiji period by Protestant Christians. Spearheaded by

Uchimura Kanzo, it was carried on by his disciples in the period after the First World War and the ensuing new social movements of the Taisho period (Zahl [1973] in Schlichtmann 2009, 274).

A loose network of independent Bible study groups, the Mukyokai, which still has about 35,000 members today in Japan, Korea and Taiwan, has been especially appealing to the members of the intelligentsia. Uchimura is famous for his protest against the 1890 Imperial Rescript on Education and his numerous speeches and writings in favor of peace. This is the same Rescript against which the founder of the Soka Gakkai and mentor of Toda, Tsunesaburo Makiguchi (1871–1944), a contemporary of Uchimura, struggled during his entire teaching career. Caldarola makes a clear distinction between the attitude of organized Christianity and that of the Mukyokai:

> From the very beginning of Japanese militarism, the Christian Churches had believed that it was an admirable effort to liberate and unify all the Asian nations. They were persuaded that, in view of the world situation, a holy war could be justified by the achievement of a noble goal, i.e., 'Greater Asia for Common Prosperity' (Caldarola 1973).

The Mukyokai opposed militarism from the start, even after government control over religion became virtually absolute with the passage of the 1939 Religious Bodies Law. In general, established Christian churches welcomed the law, hoping to receive official support and protection during troubled times, but the Mukyokai opposed it based on the tradition of resistance established by Uchimura. The similarity with the Soka Gakkai is striking. The Nichiren Shoshu priesthood adopted an attitude of compromise towards the 1939 law, just like most of the established Christian churches. In sharp contrast, Makiguchi and Toda resisted and were imprisoned, like many Christian protesters, including numerous members of the Mukyokai.

It can be said that from 1931 and the invasion of Manchuria, opposition to the government's militarist policies was systematically rooted out in Japan whenever it tried to appear, and one must wait until the end of World War II to see the rebirth of Japanese peace activism.

A number of interrelated issues explain the blossoming of peace movements in Japan, especially during the 15 years after the war (1945–60), such as the military defeat and occupation, the atomic bombings of Hiroshima and Nagasaki, the death and suffering of millions of Japanese and of many more victims of the Japanese military, and the growing realization of the absurdity of war. The tensions between the implementation of the US–Japan

Security Treaty (Ampo)[3] including the massive presence of US bases in Japan and the spirit and purpose of the pacifist Constitution with its Article 9 are important factors too. Schlichtmann points out that the aim of Article 9 is the abolition of the institution of war, a goal which is in line with the objectives of the United Nations (Schlichtmann 2009, 224–25). The official English translation of Article 9 reads:

> Aspiring sincerely to an international peace based on justice and order, the Japanese people forever renounce war as a sovereign right of the nation and the threat or use of force as means of settling international disputes. (. . .) In order to accomplish the aim of the preceding paragraph, land, sea, and air forces, as well as other war potential, will never be maintained. The right of belligerency of the state will not be recognized (National Diet Library 2009).

Two major changes in society itself must also be taken into account: labor unions gained strong momentum during the rapid industrialization in postwar Japan, and women were allowed to vote for the first time in 1945 – a structural change awakening them to their potential and responsibility as social actors (Yamamoto 2005).

After the defeat, most Japanese people were looking for new values they could believe in, and 'Peace and Democracy' became the mantra of postwar Japan (Dower 2000). With Article 9 of the new Japanese constitution, the population had a legitimate rallying point to promote the new principles, and the protection of this unique statute against proposed revisions has kept many peace movements busy.

The struggle against nuclear weapons also became prominent in Japan, first because of Hiroshima and Nagasaki, but also in the wake of the 1954 Bikini Atoll incident. The crew of a Japanese fishing boat, the *Daigo Fukuryu Maru* (Lucky Dragon No. 5), as well as inhabitants of the Marshall Islands, some US military personnel and hundreds of other Japanese fishing boats, were the victims of US hydrogen bomb tests. Since Japanese women had received the vote in 1945 and had already organized protests against the Korean War (1950–53), they were ready to react quickly to the 1954 Bikini Atoll tragedy (Yamamoto 2005). In 1955 they organized the Hahaoya Taikai (Mothers' Congress), which is one of the historical landmarks in the birth of national and international grassroots efforts to ban nuclear weapons.

As mentioned above, the 1951 Security Treaty between the US and Japan is in direct contradiction with the spirit of Article 9, and the successive renewals of Ampo every ten years since 1960 have been the focus of numerous protests. The initial demonstrations in 1960 were huge, the ones in 1970 substantial, in 1980 tiny and in 1990 almost non-existent. Directly linked to Ampo, the presence of US bases has been the focus of numerous movements and protests.

The most famous of these were the Uchinada and Sunagawa incidents as well as the Girard case. Residents of Uchinada clashed with police in 1952–53 during protests against the use of their coast for firing exercises. In another clash, protesters joined residents in Sunagawa in 1955 to oppose the expansion of the Tachikawa air base. The killing of a Japanese woman during maneuvers by a member of the US military called William S. Girard triggered a third major protest movement (Tanaka 2000). Among other progressive intellectuals, Ikutaro Shimizu was a leading activist in the first anti-base movement in Uchinada and a pioneering thinker who articulated an original concept of society and peace. He is credited with providing one of the main intellectual foundations for the postwar Japanese peace movement which culminated in the 1960 anti-Ampo protests (Kersten 2006).

Yamamoto explains that the labor movement in postwar Japan has been actively involved throughout all these struggles, despite the crackdown by the US authorities that started with the deepening of the Cold War at the end of the 1940s and worsened during the Korean War:

> Many labor leaders played an active role in the nationwide peace movement that emerged in the 1950s. The victories attained in such political battles as the anti-US military base struggle in Sunagawa on the outskirts of Tokyo in the late 1950s and the campaign against the police duties law of 1958 boosted labor's confidence. Such successes made unionists believe another major victory was within their reach at the time of the Ampo struggle of 1960, in which unionists and other activists, together with the Socialist and Communist Parties and student activists, staged massive protests against the Japan–US security treaty. The radicalization of organized labor reached its zenith and some union officials claim labor organizations mustered about 80% of demonstrators around the parliament building, whose number is said to have totaled over 300,000 at the height of the struggle on June 18, 1960 (Yamamoto 2005).

After a flurry of activities and some victories during the first 15 years after World War II, the peace movement in Japan began to lose steam, until the outbreak of the Vietnam War. US involvement started around 1963, building up until the bombing of North Vietnam in 1965. The planes sent to kill hundreds of thousands of Vietnamese civilians were taking off from bases situated in Japan, which became a tacit accomplice in the war. This became the rallying cry of the different peace movements described above. Many of these movements disappeared in 1975, after the end of the war. As Franziska Seraphim (2006) writes concerning Beheiren, the most prominent movement against the Vietnam War which thrived between 1965 and 1975:

> Oda Makoto was a key figure in the Citizen's Federation for Peace in Vietnam, or Beheiren (Betonamu ni heiwa o! shimin rengo), an alliance of groups and individuals who rejected the collective ideology of political organizations for the diversity, spontaneity, voluntarism, and decentralization of a movement promoting 'individual action' against the state on pacifist principles. Between 1965 and 1975, Beheiren kept up an astonishing degree of public involvement via the mass and 'mini' media (e.g. newsletters), demonstrations and teach-ins, and international networks, emphasizing the community of like-minded individuals regardless of the politics of nation-states. The positive energy and commitment radiating from Beheiren's activism as well as the personalities of its leaders had tremendous popular appeal (and elicited equally harsh criticism) (222–23).

There was almost no organized public reaction at the time of the first Iraq war (1991), even though Japan was the largest financial supporter of the attack on Kuwait's invaders. Pacifism is losing its appeal in Japan more and more. For instance, the gang rape of a Japanese schoolgirl by US military personnel in Okinawa in 1995 triggered huge demonstrations and a referendum which forced the Prime Minister at the time to promise the relocation of the Futenma air base, but the overall effect on the US military presence was negligible. More recently the huge demonstrations against the impending second invasion of Iraq on 15 February 2003, which based on the most optimistic estimates totaled two million people in London, three million in Rome and 30 million worldwide, were only able to gather about 5,000 people in Tokyo.

Article 9 is sometimes endangered by the Japanese government's moves to revise the constitution (this was the case in 2008) but there is a well coordinated movement to protect it.[4] Other groups are also engaged in a struggle to force the government to officially recognize the atrocities committed during the colonization and wars in Asia, but the outcome of such actions is far from certain.

Still there are several energetic grassroots organizations for peace and justice in Japan, such as Peace Boat, Peace Depot, Peace On and many others. It is worth mentioning the organization Violence against Women in War – Network Japan (VAWW-NET Japan) which organized a three-day even in Tokyo in December 2000 described as follows by Seraphim (2006):

'An international team of prominent judges heard testimonial and historical evidence about the wartime "comfort women" system from legal teams representing the countries that once suffered under Japan's empire' (4).

Besides the Soka Gakkai, there are several other religious organizations that include peace in their mission statements, for instance the Buddhist group Rissho Kosekai, but none of these religious groups has been as successful as the Soka Gakkai and the SGI in attracting members, or in creating a solid tradition with a large international following.

APPENDIX 2

Josei Toda's Declaration[5] Calling for the Abolition of Nuclear Weapons

(8 September 1957)

Today's 'Festival of Youth' has been blessed with clear, sunny skies free of any trace of yesterday's storm, as if the heavens themselves have responded to your enthusiasm. With a great feeling of joy, I watched the competitors among you display the Soka Gakkai spirit in each event, as the rest of you wholeheartedly applauded their efforts.

Nevertheless, for all the joy I feel today, it is inevitable that the Soka Gakkai will encounter persecution again. I am fully prepared to meet any attack that comes my way personally. Having said that, I would now like to share with you what I hope you will regard as the foremost of my final instructions for the future.

As I have long said, the responsibility for the coming era will be shouldered by the youth. There is no need for me to tell you that *kosen-rufu* [world peace through individual happiness] is our mission. We must absolutely achieve it. But today I would like to state clearly my feelings and attitude regarding the testing of nuclear weapons, a topic that is now being debated heatedly in society. I hope that, as my disciples, you will inherit the declaration I am about to make today and, to the best of your ability, spread its intent throughout the world.

Although a movement to ban the testing of nuclear weapons is now underway around the world, it is my wish to attack the problem at its root, that is, to rip out the claws that are hidden in the very depths of this issue. Thus I advocate that those who venture to use nuclear weapons, irrespective of their nationality or whether their country is victorious or defeated, be sentenced to death without exception.

Why do I say this? Because we, the citizens of the world, have an inviolable right to live. Anyone who tries to jeopardize this right is a devil incarnate, a fiend, a monster. I propose that humankind applies, in every case, the death penalty to anyone responsible for using nuclear weapons, even if that person is on the winning side.

Even if a country should conquer the world through the use of nuclear weapons, the conquerors must be viewed as devils, as evil incarnate. I believe that it is the mission of every member of the youth division in Japan to disseminate this idea throughout the globe.

I shall end by expressing my eager expectation for you to spread this foremost appeal of mine to the entire world with the powerful spirit you have shown in today's sports festival.

APPENDIX 3

The Life and Teachings of Nichiren (1222–82): a Brief Overview

The information in this appendix is mostly based on the entry on Nichiren from the *Oxford Dictionary of Buddhism* (Keown 2003) and on *The Writings of Nichiren Daishonin* (Nichiren 1999).

Nichiren's parents were fisher folk, and since there were no schools in Japan at the time entering the local temple allowed him to receive the best education possible. There he learned to read and write, not only Japanese but also classical Chinese, and to master the art of calligraphy. He sometimes referred to himself as a 'chandala,' a class of untouchables in the ancient Indian caste system: 'Nichiren, who in this life was born poor and lowly to a chandala family' (Nichiren 1999, 303). Keown writes: '[H]e is the only founder of one of the new sects of Kamakura Buddhism not to come from the central provinces around the capital and not to be from an aristocratic family' (2003).

After entering the temple at age 12, he frequently prayed in front of the statue of Bodhisattva *Kokuzo* (Space Treasury) with the wish to become 'the wisest person in Japan' (Nichiren 1999, 175). At 16 he decided to become a priest in order to confirm the validity of his intuitions concerning the meaning of human life. From the ages of 16 to 32 he travelled to the major centers of Buddhist studies in Japan to find out whether some of the writings would confirm his own enlightenment. 'Fully ordained at 16, he went to the capital in 1239 to study at the eminent temples in Kamakura and Kyoto' (Keown 2003).

He confirmed for himself that the teachings of the Lotus Sutra were the closest to what he had in mind. However, he felt something was missing, a practical way to implement the teachings among the realities of daily life. Nichiren became convinced that the only way Buddhism could have real power to transform people's lives was by providing concrete tools allowing everyone to bring out their highest inner potential, manifesting qualities such as courage, compassion and wisdom to confront difficulties and live a dignified existence.

In Japan at the time, there were several popular schools of Buddhism. One of them, the Jodo (Pure Land), also called 'Nembutsu' school, had a mantra (recitation) pronounced *Namu amida butsu* and another, the Shingon (True Words) school, had established mandalas or objects of worship. If Nichiren was to clarify Buddhist philosophy based on his own enlightenment, he would have to add a mantra and a mandala of his own (Matsuda 2009). Since he was convinced that the essence of the Buddhist teachings was to be found in the Lotus Sutra, he established a new mantra, pronounced *Nam-myoho-renge-kyo*, as the daily practice of his Buddhism. 'Nam' is an expression of devotion and 'Myoho-renge-kyo' is the title of the Lotus Sutra in Japanese. This phrase is an expression of praise for the values and principles found in the Lotus Sutra, for cosmic life and for the infinite potential latent in human life. It is also called the *Daimoku* (invocation).

> The Lotus Sutra, as the scripture that directly revealed the totality of Buddhist truth, provided a door, and since its essence was contained within its title, the chanting of this title [Nam-myoho-renge-kyo] could, by itself, unlock the enlightenment that was always already part of the makeup of the human being (Keown 2003).

The mandala Nichiren established is called a *Gohonzon* (object of devotion), and is inscribed mostly with Chinese ideographs (and some medieval Sanskrit script), in contrast to most mandalas at the time, which usually represented legendary figures.

Nichiren returned to his home district in 1253.

> [H]e took the new religious name Nichiren (Lotus of the Sun) and began promoting his views and attacking the teachings of the other schools openly. (. . .) He experienced exile and persecution for his efforts, but accepted it as fulfilment of a passage in the Lotus Sutra itself that said proponents of the true teaching would be persecuted (. . .). Nichiren was sent into exile on Sado Island in 1271, where he remained for three years (Keown 2003).

Nichiren's criticism of their schools angered powerful members of the clergy with connections in the Kamakura government, and as a result he had to endure official persecution from the authorities. He was banished to the Izu peninsula in 1261, and it was after an unsuccessful attempt to have him beheaded at Tatsunokuchi, an execution ground near Kamakura, that he was banished to Sado Island. Nichiren wrote:

> Each of the proponents of the various schools I have mentioned above declares that he beyond all others has grasped the meaning of and is practicing the Lotus Sutra. But none of them have been exiled to the province of Izu as I was in the Kocho era, or exiled to the island of Sado as I was in the Bun'ei era, or been led to the place of decapitation at Tatsunokuchi or faced the countless other difficulties that I have (311).

Overcoming these and other numerous persecutions, 'Nichiren spent his last years on Mt. Minobu, tending to the flock of residents whose swelling numbers gradually transformed his residence from a crude hermitage to a temple, and in the composition of further works' (Keown 2003).

There are many Buddhist groups today claiming Nichiren as their founder. As soon as he passed away in 1282, the six senior priests who had inherited his teachings started to add their own interpretations, and this accounts for the vast differences between the philosophies and practices of the different Nichiren schools in existence today.

The goal of Nichiren Buddhism can be said to be to bring out one's enlightened nature by reciting *Daimoku* in front of the *Gohonzon*. As for more detailed explanations concerning the nature of enlightenment and how one can develop the Buddha nature through chanting, Nichiren left more than 400 writings, mostly letters addressed to individual believers as well as theoretical treatises sometimes addressed to government officials. Nichiren also added a practical twist to Buddhism, emphasizing the necessity for ordinary people to take action in daily life, showing the positive results of one's practice and sharing the teachings with others: 'You must not only persevere yourself; you must also teach others' (386). Keown writes:

> Some scholars have pointed out that both the simplicity of the practice that Nichiren advocated and the vehemence with which he set his views forth stemmed from his humble beginnings and the discrimination he experienced as a young rustic monk thrust into the company of aristocratic scions. However, Nichiren was

also a subtle thinker and the originality of his reshaping of Tendai theology [a Buddhist philosophical system designed by the Chinese scholar T'ien-t'ai or Chih-i (538–97)] deserves attention (2003).

Appendix 4

Daisaku Ikeda's Published Dialogues

(as of 29 October 2009)

In this list, based on 'Dialogue Published' available on the Ikeda Website, dates in parentheses refer to the first time the work was published and show the language the dialogue was originally published in. Titles are in English when available and otherwise in the original language of publication. Languages are in alphabetical order.

1. *Bunmei nishi to higashi* (tentative translation: 'Civilization, East and West')
with Richard Coudenhove-Kalergi
Japanese (1972)

2. *On the Japanese Classics*
with Makoto Nemoto
English, Japanese (1974), Portuguese, Thai

3. *Choose Life: A Dialogue*
with Arnold J. Toynbee
Bengali, Bulgarian, Chinese (traditional), Czech, Danish, English, Filipino, French, German, Hindi, Hungarian, Indonesian, Italian, Japanese (1975), Korean, Laotian, Malay, Nepali, Polish, Portuguese, Russian, Serbian, Sinhalese, Spanish, Swahili, Thai, Turkish, Urdu

4. *Jinsei mondo* (tentative translation: 'On Living')
with Konosuke Matsushita
Chinese (traditional), Chinese (simplified), Japanese (1975), Korean

5. *Ningen kakumei to ningen no joken* (tentative translation: 'Changes within: Human revolution vs. human condition')
with André Malraux
Japanese (1976)

6. *Letters of Four Seasons*
with Yasushi Inoue
Chinese (simplified), English, French, Japanese (1977), Malay, Thai

7. *Dawn After Dark*
with René Huyghe
Chinese (simplified), English, French (1980), Japanese, Portuguese, Spanish, Thai

8. *Before It Is Too Late*
with Aurelio Peccei
Bulgarian, Chinese (traditional), Chinese (simplified), Danish, English, French, German, Indonesian, Italian, Japanese (1984), Korean, Malay, Portuguese, Spanish, Swedish, Thai, Vietnamese

9. *Human Values in a Changing World*
with Bryan Wilson
Chinese (traditional), Chinese (simplified), English, French, Italian, Japanese (1985), Portuguese, Spanish, Thai

10. *Dai san no niji no hashi* (tentative translation: 'The third rainbow bridge')
with Anatoli A. Logunov
Chinese (simplified), Japanese (1987), Russian

11. *Heiwa to jinsei to tetsugaku o kataru* (tentative translation: 'Philosophy of human peace')
with Henry Kissinger
Japanese (1987)

12. *Humanity at the Crossroads*
with Karan Singh
English, Japanese (1988), Thai

13. *Search for a New Humanity*
with Josef Derbolav
Chinese (simplified), English, German (1988), Japanese, Thai

14. *A Lifelong Quest for Peace*
with Linus Pauling
Chinese (traditional), Chinese (simplified), English, Filipino, French, Japanese (1990), Korean, Russian, Spanish, Vietnamese

15. *Tonko no kosai* (tentative translation: 'The radiance of Dunhuang: On beauty and life')
with Chang Shuhong
Chinese (traditional), Chinese (simplified), Japanese (1990)

16. *Sekai shimin no taiwa* (tentative translation: 'Dialogue between citizens of the world')
with Norman Cousins
Japanese (1991)

17. *Taiyo to daichi: Kaitaku no uta* (tentative translation: 'The Sun and the good earth: An ode to pioneering Japanese immigrants')
with Ryoichi Kodama
Japanese (1991), Portuguese

18. *Ode to the Grand Spirit*
with Chingiz Aitmatov
English, German, Japanese (1991), Russian

19. *Ningen to Bungaku o Kataru* (tentative translation: 'Dialogue on humanity and culture')
with Kenji Doi
Japanese (1991)

20. *Space and Eternal Life*
with Chandra Wickramasinghe
English, Japanese (1992)

21. *Kagaku to shukyo* (tentative translation: 'Science and religion')
with Anatoli A. Logunov
Japanese (1994)

22. *Human Rights in the Twenty-First Century*
with Austregésilo de Athayde
English, Japanese (1995), Portuguese

23. *Choose Peace*
with Johan Galtung
English, Italian, Japanese (1995), Korean, Thai

24. *Moral Lessons of the Twentieth Century*
with Mikhail Gorbachev
Chinese (traditional), Chinese (simplified), English, French, German,
Icelandic, Italian, Japanese (1996), Korean, Russian

25. *Taiheiyo no kyokujitsu* (tentative translation: 'Dawn of the Pacific')
with Patricio Aylwin Azócar
Japanese (1997), Spanish

26. *Haranbanjo no Naporeon* (tentative translation: 'The tempestuous life of
Napoleon')
with Philippe Moine, Patrice Morlat and Tadashige Takamura
Japanese (1997)

27. *Kyokujitsu no seiki o motomete* (tentative translation: 'Compassionate light
in Asia')
with Jin Yong
Chinese (traditional), Chinese (simplified), Japanese (1998)

28. *Kodomo no sekai* (tentative translation: 'The path to the land of children')
with Albert A. Likhanov
Chinese (traditional), Chinese (simplified), Japanese (1998), Russian

29. *Utsukushiki shishi no tamashii* (tentative translation: 'A lion's heart')
with Axinia Djourova
Bulgarian, Japanese (1999)

30. *On Being Human: Where Ethics, Medicine and Spirituality Converge*
with René Simard and Guy Bourgeault
Chinese (traditional), English, French, Italian, Japanese (2000)

31. *Global Civilization: A Buddhist–Islamic Dialogue*
with Majid Tehranian
Chinese (traditional), English, French, Italian, Japanese (2000), Persian, Thai

32. *Karibu no taiyo seigi no uta* (tentative translation: 'Dialogue on José Martí,
an apostle of Cuba')
with Cintio Vitier
Japanese (2001), Spanish

33. *Choose Hope*
with David Krieger
English, Italian, Japanese (2001)

34. *Distinct Encounters*
with Rogelio M. Quiambao
English, Japanese (2001)

35. *Sekai no Bungaku o Kataru* (tentative translation: 'Dialogue on world literature')
with Tadashige Takamura and Philippe Moine; Kentaro Nishihara and Rogelio M. Quiambao; Ryohei Tanaka and Hirotomo Teranishi; Tadashige Takamura and Henry Indangasi
Japanese (2001)

36. *Atarashiki jinrui o atarashiki sekai o* (tentative translation: 'Beyond the century: Dialogue on education and society')
with Viktor A. Sadovnichy
Chinese (traditional), Japanese (2002), Russian

37. *Toyo no chie o kataru* (tentative translation: 'Dialogue on Oriental wisdom')
with Ji Xianlin and Jiang Zhongxin
Chinese (traditional), Chinese (simplified), Japanese (2002)

38. *Buddhism: A Way of Values*
with Lokesh Chandra
English, Japanese (2002)

39. *Kibo no seiki e takara no kakehashi* (tentative translation: 'The bridge toward a century of hope')
with Cho Moon-Boo
Japanese (2002), Korean

40. *Planetary Citizenship*
with Hazel Henderson
Chinese (traditional), English, French, Italian, Japanese (2003), Portuguese

41. *Uchu to chikyu to ningen* (tentative translation: 'The cosmos, earth and human beings')
with Alexander Serebrov
Japanese (2004), Russian

42. *Ningen to bunka no niji no kakehashi* (tentative translation: 'A rainbow bridge of humanity and culture')
with Cho Moon-Boo
Japanese (2005)

43. *Indo no seishin* (tentative translation: 'The spirit of India – Buddhism and Hinduism')
with Ved Prakash Nanda
Japanese (2005)

44. *Ningenshugi no dai seiki o* (tentative translation: 'Toward creating an age of humanism')
with John Kenneth Galbraith
Japanese (2005)

45. *A Dialogue Between East and West: Looking to a Human Revolution*
with Ricardo Díez-Hochleitner
English, Japanese (2005), Spanish

46. *Heiwa no bunka no kagayaku seiki e* (tentative translation: 'Building a century of a culture of peace')
with Elise Boulding
Japanese (2006)

47. *Revolutions: To green the Environment, to Grow the Human heart*
with M.S. Swaminathan
English (2005), Italian, Japanese

48. *A Quest for Global Peace*
with Joseph Rotblat
Chinese (traditional), English, German, Italian, Japanese (2006)

49. *Creating Waldens: An East–West Conversation on the American Renaissance*
with Ronald A. Bosco and Joel Myerson
English, Japanese (2006)

50. *Taiwa no bunmei* (tentative translation: 'Toward a civilization of dialogue')
with Tu Weiming
Chinese (traditional), Chinese (simplified), Japanese (2007)

51. *Ningen shugi no hata o* (tentative translation: 'Hoisting the banner of humanism')
with H.C. Felix Unger
Japanese (2007)

52. *A Passage to Peace: Global Solutions from East and West*
with Nur Yalman
English, Japanese (2007)

53. *Yujo no daisogen* (tentative translation: 'Grand Steppes of friendship')
with Dojoogiin Tsedev
Japanese (2007)

54. *Niju-isseiki no heiwa to shukyo o kataru* (tentative title: 'The persistence of religion: Comparative perspectives on modern spirituality')
with Harvey Cox
Japanese (2008)

55. *Bunka to geijutsu no tabiji* (tentative translation: 'A journey on the path of culture and the arts')
with Jao Tsung-I
Chinese (traditional), Japanese (2009)

56. *Tenmongaku to buppo o kataru* (tentative translation: 'A dialogue on astronomy and Buddhism')
with Ronaldo Rogério de Freitas Mourão
Japanese (2009)

APPENDIX 5

List of Acronyms and Abbreviations

AEI	Albert Einstein Institution
APOPAC	Asia–Pacific Organization for Peace and Culture
CoNGO	Conference of NGOs in consultative relationship with the UN
CTBT	Comprehensive Test Ban Treaty
DPJ	Democratic Party of Japan
ECOSOC	Economic and Social Council
ESD	Education for Sustainable Development
IAEA	International Atomic Energy Agency
IBL	International Buddhist League
ICC	International Criminal Court
ICJ	International Court of Justice
IOP	Institute of Oriental Philosophy
IPCC	Intergovernmental Panel on Climate Change
IPEEC	International Partnership for Energy Efficiency Cooperation
IPRA	International Peace Research Association
IRENA	International Renewable Energy Agency
Jpn	Japanese
MPI	Middle Powers Initiative
NAPF	Nuclear Age Peace Foundation
NGO	Non-governmental organization
NPT	Nuclear Non-Proliferation Treaty
NPT PrepCom	Preparatory Committee of the Nuclear Non-Proliferation Treaty
NWFZ	Nuclear Weapons-Free Zones
OECD	Organization for Economic Cooperation and Development
PKO	United Nations Peacekeeping Operations
PP	Peace Proposal
PRIO	International Peace Research Institute, Oslo

SG	Soka Gakkai
SGI	Soka Gakkai International
Skt	Sanskrit
SSOD	Special Session on Disarmament
SUA	Soka University of America
TFF	Transnational Foundation for Peace and Future Research
UDHR	Universal Declaration of Human Rights
UDRW	Universal Declaration for the Renunciation of War
UK	United Kingdom
UN	United Nations
UNDPI	UN Department of Public Information
UNEP	UN Environmental Program
UNESCO	UN Educational, Scientific and Cultural Organization
UNGA	UN General Assembly
UNHCR	Office of the UN High Commissioner for Refugees
UNSC	UN Security Council
UNTAC	UN Transitional Authority in Cambodia
US	United States
USSR	Union of the Soviet Socialist Republics
WFUNA	World Federation of UN Associations
WMD	Weapons of mass destruction
WP	World Parliament
YPC	Youth Peace Conference

Notes

Introduction

1 Soka Gakkai means 'Value-creation Society.' It was established in 1930 as the Soka Kyoiku Gakkai (Value-creating Educational Society), suppressed by the Japanese military government in 1943 and rebuilt after the war as Soka Gakkai. The Soka Gakkai International (SGI) was established in 1975.

2 The Toda Institute for Global Peace and Policy Research was established by Daisaku Ikeda in 1996. Its motto is 'Dialogue of Civilizations for Global Citizenship.' It will be referred to as the Toda Institute in this work from here on.

3 The *Oxford Dictionary of Buddhism* (Keown 2003) states that 'a Bodhisattva forgoes his own final enlightenment until all other beings (. . .) have been liberated.' This can be interpreted as meaning that a Bodhisattva is a person dedicated to the happiness of other people.

Chapter 1

1 This was confirmed during a personal telephone conversation between Ambassador Anwarul Chowdhury and the author on 19 October 2009.

2 See article entitled 'Rep. Johnson Introduces Resolution Concerning Soka Gakkai International President Ikeda's Birthday' from: US Fed News Service, Including US State News. Article date: 7 December 2007. Information retrieved on 2 October 2009 from http://www.highbeam.com/doc/1P3-1394488761.html.

3 See article on the Peking University website, retrieved on 2 October 2009 from http://www.oir.pku.edu.cn/newoir/2005/Article/ShowArticle.asp?ArticleID=4531.

4 See Introduction, note 1.

5 Until around 1960, the membership of the Soka Gakkai was counted in households. This changed later and by the mid-1970s membership was counted by the number of individuals.

6 For instance the exhibition 'Gandhi, King, Ikeda: A Legacy of Building Peace' was on display in the Olin Library, Washington University, St Louis, USA, from 16 to 27 April 2007. The online brochure of the Gandhi-King-Ikeda exhibition is at http://www.morehouse.edu/about/chapel/peace_exhibit/exhibit/download. html and was last retrieved on 9 September 2009.

7 Franziska Seraphim (2006) writes: 'Nonetheless, the Allied trials passed over some major Japanese war crimes, such as (. . .) the government-operated "comfort women system," to which an estimated 100,000 Asian women fell victim. By investigating wartime sexual slavery (. . .) the Women's International Tribunal in 2000 self-consciously picked up where the Tokyo trial had left off.'

8 See 'Tula State L.N. Tolstoy Pedagogical University, Russia, Confers Honorary Professorship.' Retrieved on 9 September 2009 from the Ikeda Website: http://www.daisakuikeda.org/sub/news/2008/april/DI_080402tolstoy-pedag.html.

9 The Dodge Line was a financial and monetary policy drafted in 1948 by Joseph Dodge, then economic advisor for postwar economic stabilization and special US Ambassador to Japan. The policy restricted and regulated Japanese economic activities in order for the country to gain economic independence after World War II.

10 In Japan, the Soka Gakkai is considered part of mainstream society. In China it is praised as a Japanese organization that contributes immensely to Sino–Japanese friendship. In the US it is considered as a benevolent lay Buddhist society that contributes to American society through peace, culture and education. In Italy it is considered as a legally registered religion. It is viewed positively in most countries, with the notable exception of France where the SG is considered least favorably, sometimes called a 'cult' depending on the definition of that term. The author has had many opportunities to experience various reactions of people of these countries towards the Soka Gakkai. For an example of criticism, see Rick Ross's 2004 article disparaging Orlando Bloom for having joined the Soka Gakkai: 'Has Orlando Bloom become the latest celebrity "cult" casualty?' at http://www.cultnews.com/?p=1599. Accessed 7 November 2009.

11 Wilson and Dobbelaere report that 39 percent of the respondents considered that the main benefit of chanting was spiritual and psychological. The rest of the respondents described how they obtained 'material benefits' such as being able to find the right apartment, or the right partner, or overcoming illness, in contrast to the 39 percent who considered the benefits to be in terms of personal growth. See Bryan Wilson and Karel Dobbelaere (1994), *A Time to Chant*. Oxford: Oxford University Press, p. 205.

12 From the mission statement of the Min-On Concert Association retrieved from http://www.min-on.org/about/index.html on 9 September 2009.

13 From the main page of the Tokyo Fuji Art Museum website, accessed on 31 October 2009: http://www.fujibi.or.jp/en/about/index.html.

Chapter 2

1 When the two novels *The Human Revolution* and *The New Human Revolution* are considered together in this book, they are called the *Human Revolution* novels.

2 Kosen-rufu is a Japanese term that literally means to declare and spread widely.

In this work we use the definition adopted by the SGI, which is 'world peace through individual happiness.'

Chapter 3

1 Retrieved from Toda Website, http://www.joseitoda.org/quotations/peace on 12 September 2009.

2 Retrieved from Toda Website, http://www.joseitoda.org/vision/global on 12 September 2009. The Japanese original means something like: 'I want to eliminate the two Chinese ideographs that form the word misery (in Japanese) from the surface of the Earth.' There are several translations of Toda's statement in English, and I have chosen 'I want to rid the world of misery,' which I believe best conveys the meaning of the original.

3 Tsunesaburo Makiguchi (1871–1944) was a Japanese educator who established the Soka Kyoiku Gakkai (Value-creating Educational Society) in 1930 and was imprisoned in 1943 by the military authorities for refusing to compromise his beliefs. He thought the purpose of education was to equip students with the capacity to create something positive, something of value, in any circumstance.

4 One of the most influential Buddhist texts. The *Oxford Dictionary of Buddhism* (Keown 2003) defines it as 'one of the earliest Mahayana scriptures extant, possibly dating from the 1st century BCE.' More information is provided in Chapter 4.

5 In the Lotus Sutra, a Buddhist scripture, a large number of Bodhisattvas emerge from beneath the earth in the 'Emerging from the Earth' (15th) chapter. A Bodhisattva is a person devoted to the happiness of others.

6 Jin'ichi was the name given to Toda at birth. According to Ikeda in *The Human Revolution* (2004a, 54–55), Toda first started to call himself Jogai, meaning 'outside the castle' before meeting Makiguchi, and then changed his name again to Josei, meaning 'castle sage,' once he decided to rebuild the Soka Gakkai in the summer of 1945. See Shiohara 2008b, 149.

7 At that time in Japan, most educated young men kept a diary, convinced that they would succeed by working hard and that it was worth keeping a record of their daily efforts.

8 Shiohara (2008b, 154) gives the full English title of the work as: *An Anatomy of Home Education – Talking about entrance exams for middle level school, and turning our precious children into straight-A students (Katei Kyoikugaku Soron).*

9 In English, to differentiate the two, the title of Toda's novel is *Human Revolution*, whereas Ikeda's work is entitled *The Human Revolution.*

10 Bix (2001) writes: 'A naval officer who assisted Hirohito through many difficult moments of the war was Lt. Comm. Jo Eiichiro. (. . .) Jo was descended from the Kyushu warrior Kikuchi Takefusa, and his samurai background embodied one of the fundamental vindicating events in the history of Japanese national defense.

Kikuchi (. . .) had participated in saving Japan from the Mongol fleet in the thirteenth century, when fortuitous "divine winds" (*kamikaze*) arose to destroy the would-be invaders' (451).

11   The interview with Yoshiharu Suwa on 11 November 2009 was conducted in English by the author and organized by Toru Nishimoto, who also acted as interpreter.

12   When Toda left prison on 3 July 1945, he was not a completely free man and was still on parole. On 4 October the General Headquarters of the US Occupation forces in Japan (GHQ) ordered the Japanese government to repeal the Peace Preservation Law, and they complied on 10 October. On that day Toda became cleared of all charges.

13   According to Hiroshi Aruga (2000), 'The growth of the Soka Gakkai proceeded as if following the pace of the economy – rapidly from 1951 and, from the 1970s until the present, at a more subdued rate' (101). He also mentions that the membership had reached approximately 5,000 households by 1951 (100). I therefore consider the phase of rapid expansion as starting from 1945 with Toda himself.

14   The full text of the declaration appears in Appendix 2.

Chapter 4

1   The *Oxford Dictionary of Buddhism* (Keown 2003) defines this term as follows: 'Four Noble Truths. The four foundational propositions of Buddhist doctrine enunciated by the Buddha in his first sermon (. . .). The first Noble Truth (. . .) is duhkha (. . .), usually translated as "suffering" but often closer in meaning to "flawed" or "unsatisfactory." This states that all existence is painful and frustrating. The second Noble Truth is samudaya or "arising," and explains that suffering arises due to craving (. . .) for pleasurable sensations and experiences. The third Noble Truth is that of "cessation" (nirodha) which states that suffering can have an end (this is nirvana) and the fourth Noble Truth is the Noble Eightfold Path, which consists of eight factors collectively leading to nirvana.'

2   In the same dictionary (see note 1), the term is defined as follows: 'Eightfold Path. The Noble Eightfold Path (. . .) is the last of the Four Noble Truths and is the path that leads (. . .) to nirvana.' The eight elements of the path are then listed as Right View, Right Resolve, Right Speech, Right Action, Right Livelihood, Right Effort, Right Mindfulness and Right Meditation.

3   There is no certainty concerning Shakyamuni Buddha's dates of birth and death. Burton Watson writes: 'Gautama, or Shakyamuni Buddha, the founder of Buddhism, appears to have lived in India sometime around the sixth or fifth century BCE' (Watson 2002, xviii).

4   Keown 2003 (see note 1) defines *pratitya-samutpada* as: 'The doctrine of Dependent Origination, a fundamental Buddhist teaching on causation and the ontological status of phenomena. The doctrine teaches that all phenomena arise in dependence on causes and conditions and lack intrinsic being. (. . .) Early

sources indicate that the Buddha became enlightened under the Bodhi tree when he fully realized the profound truth of Dependent Origination, namely that all phenomena are conditioned (. . .) and arise and cease in a determinate series.'

5 The *Digital Dictionary of Buddhism* (Muller 2009) defines this term as: 'The Three Virtues (Jpn *san-toku*) (Skt *tri -guna, traigunya, guna*). (a) The perfection of the Buddha's causative or karmic works during his three great kalpas of preparation; (b) the perfection of the fruit, or results in his own character and wisdom; (c) the perfection of his grace in the salvation of others.'

6 This concept has found different expressions in several belief systems and is reminiscent of Albert Schweitzer's concept of 'Reverence for Life' and of the Quakers' idea of 'the God within you.'

7 Sutra is a word of Sanskrit origin meaning scripture or discourse in Buddhism.

8 Mahayana Buddhism is one of the two main branches of Buddhism. Mahayana means 'Great Vehicle' in Sanskrit, meaning that this type of Buddhism had broader appeal than the traditional Theravada, which required monastic discipline.

9 A Buddhist principle according to which life and its environment are two phases of a single reality.

10 Kamakura is the name of the city which was the seat of the military government.

11 The Mongols did in fact invade the islands of Tsushima and Iki, which were part of the Japanese archipelago, both times, but they were not able to invade the mainland.

12 There are many types of meditation, and the members of SGI practicing Nichiren Buddhism call it 'chanting,' which entails the recitation of a phrase out loud.

13 In Keown's dictionary (see note 1), the term is defined as follows: 'akusala-mula (. . .). Collective name for the three roots of evil, being the three unwholesome mental states of greed (raga), hatred (dvesa) and delusion (moha). All negative states of consciousness are seen as ultimately grounded in one of more of these three.'

14 King Ashoka (third century BCE) was the third ruler of the Indian Maurya dynasty. The first king to unify India, he began as a ruthless tyrant but later converted to Buddhism and governed in accordance with the Buddhist principles of wisdom and compassion.

15 For instance, when in exile on Sado Island, Nichiren organized the Tsukahara debate. It was the tradition at the time for Buddhist priests to confront each other in debate. This was a serious affair since the loser had to convert to the religion of the winner on the spot. Many Nembutsu believers converted to Nichiren's Buddhism during the Tsukahara debate.

16 Information retrieved on 14 September 2009 from 'A Grassroots Movement,' Ikeda Website: http://www.daisakuikeda.org/main/peacebuild/peace/peace-10.html.

17 In Buddhism, a mandala is an object of worship.

18 Keown's dictionary (see note 1) defines the term Jambudvipa as: 'Name of the southernmost of the four great continents of traditional Buddhist mythology, corresponding to the known world at the time and most probably to be identified with the Indian subcontinent and south-east Asia (. . .).

Chapter 5

1   The last three qualities on Seligman's list are justice, temperance and spirituality/ transcendence (Seligman 2002, 133).

2   See King James's Bible Online, http://www.kingjamesbibleonline.org. Accessed 9 November 2009.

3   The Stanford Encyclopedia of Philosophy defines 'Methodological Individualism' as: 'the claim that social phenomena must be explained by showing how they result from individual actions, which in turn must be explained through reference to the intentional states that motivate the individual actors.' See full entry for this term on: http://plato.stanford.edu/entries/methodological-individualism. Accessed 9 November 2009.

4   The Stanford Encyclopedia of Philosophy explains the meaning of the term 'Functionalism' as follows: 'Functionalism in the philosophy of mind is the doctrine that what makes something a mental state of a particular type does not depend on its internal constitution, but rather on the way it functions, or the role it plays, in the system of which it is a part.' See full entry for this term on: http://plato.stanford.edu/entries/functionalism. Accessed 9 November 2009.

5   See for instance an article by James P. Pfiffner entitled 'Presidential Decision Making: Rationality, Advisory Systems, and Personality' in *Presidential Studies Quarterly*, Vol. 35, 2005, showing the complexity of such decision-making processes.

6   At the time of writing (October 2009) 22 volumes had been published in Japanese and 18 in English. This research covers the first 15 volumes.

Chapter 6

1   The relevant passages from the peace proposals and other documents where Ikeda develops these ideas are mentioned in Chapter 7.

2   Montaigne is mentioned in the 1994, 1995 and 2006 Peace Proposals.

3   Büber 1947, 40.

4   For a full list of the more than 50 dialogues in book form see Appendix 4. The list is also available online on the Ikeda Website: http://daisakuikeda.org/sub/ resources/records/dialog.html. Accessed 14 October 2009.

5   Moreover, whereas dialogues are an accepted literary form in Japan and the rest of East Asia, they are rare in other parts of the world.

Chapter 7

1   Toynbee 1948, 213.

2   The content of this speech is summarized by Ikeda in *Fulfilling the Mission: Empowering the UN to Live up to the World's Expectations* as follows: 'Several years earlier, in September 1968, at a time when there were no official diplomatic relations between China and Japan as no formal peace had been concluded between

them, I had called for the normalization of relations and urged that China be represented in the UN' (Ikeda 2006c, 6).

3 See full text of the declaration in Appendix 2.

4 More than 80 as of September 2009. See full list, retrieved on 22 September 2009 from http://daisakuikeda.org/sub/resources/records/degree/by-country-order.html.

5 More than 15 as of September 2009. See article entitled 'Beijing Normal University, China, Holds Symposium on Daisaku Ikeda's Ideals on Peace and Education,' retrieved on 22 September 2009 from the Ikeda Website: http://www.daisakuikeda.org/sub/news/2008/october/DI_081026beijing.html.

6 Mentioned in the *Seikyo Shimbun* daily newspaper of 6 September 2008, commemorating the 40th anniversary of the 1968 declaration.

7 The reference for this 1975 speech and other speeches related to the peace proposals are given in the Bibliography of this book.

8 Adapted from Ikeda's 1978 text entitled 'A Ten-Point Proposal for Nuclear Disarmament,' the ten points are as follows: the United Nations should:

1. Immediately summon a meeting of top leaders from all nations.
2. Take the initiative in an attempt to find ways of ensuring safe control of atomic energy.
3. Enjoin all nations to a statement promising not to use nuclear weapons.
4. Set up and attempt to expand nuclear-weapons-free zones.
5. Call on the US to submit to the UN an actual plan to bring about a reduction of their nuclear arsenal.
6. Urge countries to halt development of such new weapons as the neutron bomb and Cruise missiles and then take the initiative in drawing up an international agreement to forbid them.
7. Require each nation to submit to the UN an annual report on its military status, including weaponry, military manpower and facilities.
8. Make an appeal for research, debate, advertising and publication activities directed toward total and complete disarmament.
9. Establish at its headquarters a museum showing the horrors of war, and encourage anti-war and pro-disarmament exhibitions.
10. Take steps to provide the economic conditions that will make feasible the nine other proposals and thereby make arms reduction possible.

9 The term 'human security' was coined and popularized by Dr. Mahbub ul Haq in the UNDP's 1994 *Human Development Report*.

10 See 'SGI's Antinuclear Activities' in SGI Quarterly retrieved on 22 September 2009 from http://www.sgiquarterly.org/feature2007Jly-12.html.

11 Whereas the English translation of Ikeda's text uses the word 'hearts,' the Preamble of the UNESCO constitution uses 'minds': 'Since wars begin in the minds of men, it is in the minds of men that the defenses of peace must be constructed.' In Japanese language, the concepts of mind, heart and spirit are often interchangeable. The separation between the intellectual, emotional and spiritual capacities of human beings is not as strong as in the West.

12 Reading, summarizing and analyzing all 27 peace proposals is a daunting task that could discourage students or researchers. As a result, educators or readers wanting to share and study the content of the peace proposals use a book entitled *For the Sake of Peace*, published in 2001 (Ikeda 2001b). However, this work obviously does not contain the ideas of the 2001 to 2009 peace proposals, and it is also a mixture of excerpts from peace proposals, lectures at universities throughout the world and other texts by Ikeda, brought together in a coherent whole. It is nevertheless a valuable learning tool which captures the essence of the first 18 peace proposals. It was one of the reading assignments for the course taught by Professor Michael D'Innocenzo during the spring of 2007 at Hofstra University (New York). The course was entitled 'Gandhi, King, Ikeda: A Legacy of Building Peace.' A description, retrieved on 10 January 2010, can be found at http://www.daisakuikeda.org/sub/news/2007/jan/DI_070130hofstra-univ.html.

13 Said 1994, 12.

14 The phrase 'human security' can already be found in the 1989 and 1994 peace proposals, but obviously not in reference to the technical meaning it acquired in 1994 with Mahbub ul Haq's coining of the term in the UNDP's 1994 *Human Development Report*. The first time Ikeda uses this technical term is therefore in 1995, in the first peace proposal after the 1994 UNDP report.

15 The word 'coexistence' is used often in the peace proposals to indicate coexistence and harmony, but the word has a slightly different connotation in peace studies. It is related to the coexistence of the two blocs on each side of the Iron Curtain during the Cold War, when the US and the USSR were trying to tolerate each other and coexist while being ready to annihilate the other with nuclear or conventional weapons if necessary. The kind of inclusive global civilization Ikeda has in mind is not based on this kind of superficial 'coexistence,' but on harmony and interconnectedness, which does not exclude humanitarian competition.

16 Makiguchi [1903] 1983, 399.

17 Nye 2004, x.

18 Makiguchi [1903] 1983, 399.

19 Technically, the International Criminal Court (ICC) was established in 1998, but it only began functioning in 2002. Therefore most people use the year 2002 as the date of its establishment.

20 Tatsushi Arai, borrowing the vocabulary used by Don Hubert about peace campaigns in the 1990s, sees Toda's declaration as shifting the discourse from *disarmament* (focused on weapons) to *humanitarianism* (focused on people). See 'Appendix A: Confronting the Desire to Arm' in *The Challenge of Abolishing Nuclear Weapons*, edited by David Krieger (2009).

21 David Krieger mentions 'some 26,000 nuclear weapons' (Krieger 2009, 3).

22 In this book, the term 'Ottawa Process' refers to the successful process that led to the Ottawa Treaty, or the Mine Ban Treaty, formally the Convention on the

Prohibition of the Use, Stockpiling, Production and Transfer of Anti-Personnel Mines and on their Destruction, which completely bans all anti-personnel landmines. The petition was launched in 1997 and its successful outcome came to symbolize the capacity of ordinary people to organize themselves and promote international treaties without initially receiving the support of national governments. The term is sometimes applied to similar processes that took place before the actual Ottawa Process started in 1997.

23 See UN Press Release DC/ 2710 of 22 May 2000. 'Nuclear-weapon States Endorse Goal of Total Elimination of Nuclear Arsenals as NPT Review Conference Concludes' (Final outcome statement of the 2000 NPT Review Conference): http://www.un.org/News/Press/docs/2000/20000522.dc2710.doc.html. Accessed 24 October 2009.

24 The key phrase is 'the threat or use of nuclear weapons would generally be contrary to the rules applicable in armed conflict, and in particular the principles and rules of humanitarian law.' The document can be found on the following website, which also includes several controversies concerning the strength and applicability of this advisory opinion: http://www.derechos.org/nizkor/peace/icjopinion/opinion.html. Accessed 24 October 2009.

25 See the chapter by David Krieger entitled 'The Challenge of Abolishing Nuclear Weapons' in the volume of the same title: Some countries, such as Japan, are virtual nuclear powers, possessing the technology and nuclear materials to develop nuclear arsenals in weeks or months (Krieger 2009, 6).

26 The official English translation of Article 9 reads: 'Aspiring sincerely to an international peace based on justice and order, the Japanese people forever renounce war as a sovereign right of the nation and the threat or use of force as means of settling international disputes. (. . .) In order to accomplish the aim of the preceding paragraph, land, sea, and air forces, as well as other war potential, will never be maintained. The right of belligerency of the state will not be recognized' (National Diet Library 2009).

27 This idea is very similar to the concept behind the World Federation of United Nations Associations (WFUNA) established in 1946. Today WFUNA is a global network of people linked together through UN Associations in over 100 member states of the UN, with secretariats in Geneva and New York. It is an NGO which is not part of the UN itself. The national UN Associations (UNA) are NGOs with the mission of enhancing the relationship between the people of a member state and the UN. Japan joined the UN in 1956 and has its own UNA with headquarters in Tokyo. Each prefecture has its own chapter. I think that if there is any difference between Ikeda's idea for a 'World citizens association to support the UN' and the actual WFUNA, it would be that whereas ordinary people can join their national UNA to support the WFUNA, what Ikeda had in mind was the promotion of direct links between citizens throughout the world, and

between them and the UN, without the national association as intermediaries. This would allow them to raise their awareness as 'global citizens' even further.

28   See note 22.

29   Many Chinese students came to Japan before World War II, and after 1945 some Chinese students came to Japan without official support from the Chinese government, on a private basis. The first time Chinese students came to Japan with official recognition from the Chinese government was at Soka University, in 1975. Hirotomo Teranishi, former director of the Soka University International Division, explained in a phone interview (25 August 2008) that the Chinese government had originally sent six Chinese students to another Japanese university, which abruptly cancelled the plan. Hearing this, Ikeda offered to have them study at Soka University instead, and they became the first Chinese students sponsored by the Chinese government to be officially admitted to a Japanese university since the war. Teranishi added that two more students were sent by China in 1978 to Soka University, and four more in 1979, for a total of 12. Hundreds of other students have come from China since then, but through their universities or on a private basis, and not directly through the Chinese government.

30   The emphasis here is on the direct links between peace and the environment. Rachel Carson's *Silent Spring*, published in 1962, was an early warning call concerning environmental issues. Ikeda had also discussed environmental problems earlier. In 1978 he proposed a 'UN for the Environment' in a commemorative lecture. *Before it is Too Late*, his dialogue with Aurelio Peccei published in 1984, also dealt with the environment. In 1992 Ikeda made a declaration regarding the preservation of the Earth's environment. When analyzing the peace proposals, it appears that the environment appears in the 1992 and 1997 proposals, and almost every year since the 2001 proposal.

31   Examples of joint endeavors in which the SGI is involved:

Peace and Disarmament

NGO Committee on Disarmament, Peace and Security, New York: SGI has been a member of the Board of Directors since 2002.

NGO Committee on Disarmament in Geneva: SGI has been a member of the International Bureau of the Committee since 2007.

NGO Committee on Peace, Vienna: SGI has been a member of the Board since 2007.

Global Action to Prevent War: SGI is a member of the International Steering Committee of Global Action to Prevent War.

Human Rights

NGO Committee on Human Rights in Geneva: SGI has been an active member of the Committee since 1997.

NGO Working Group on Human Rights Education and Learning in Geneva: in association with the NGO network of CoNGO, SGI took the initiative in forming an NGO Working Group on Human Rights Education and Learning in Geneva which has been operational since 2006. Currently the SGI representative is the Chair of this NGO Working Group.

Sustainable Development

Action toward adoption of UN Decade of Education for Sustainable Development: in December 2002, the General Assembly adopted the resolution for the UN Decade of Education for Sustainable Development (2005–14). This proposal was originally presented by a Soka Gakkai representative at the Japanese NGO Forum for the World Summit on Sustainable Development (WSSD) in late 2001. This idea was taken up by the Japanese Government, accepted at the WSSD, and approved by the General Assembly in December 2002.

Involvement in the UN Commission on Sustainable Development (CSD): SGI has worked on the promotion of education for sustainable development. In the CSD Education Caucus, SGI has been playing an active role in organizing panel discussions as well as drafting joint statements and other documents. SGI has also contributed to bringing together faith-based organizations active in this area.

Interfaith Activities

Committee of Religious NGOs at the United Nations: the Committee is composed of the representatives of religious, spiritual or ethical NGOs. Since 1972, the Committee has been meeting regularly to share information and insights about issues and events at the United Nations. Serving in the Bureau of the Committee since 1999, the SGI helps organize activities such as monthly briefings. SGI's UN representative in New York served as President of the Committee from 2005–07.

32 Oliver Richmond's nine categories, as listed in *The Transformation of Peace* (2007, 183–201):

Peace as an internal/external binary definition

Peace as hegemonic act of definition

Peace as bottom-up or top-down construction

Temporal concepts of peace

The geography of peace

Levels and agents of peace

A specific logic of peace

The liberal peace and peace-as-governance

Peace as emancipation: counter discourses

Chapter 8

1 See for instance the proponents of the new discipline of 'Peace Journalism' (Ross 2008).

2 The most articulate criticism of Galtung's philosophy was made by Peter Lawler in 1995, in *A Question of Values: Johan Galtung's Peace Research*. The title of this book might indicate that Lawler discovered that Galtung's research was loaded with values, but from the very beginning, Galtung's concept of peace research was designed as a social science with the value of peace and nonviolence at its core, in the same way as health studies are natural sciences with a clear agenda. As Galtung wrote in a recent course description: 'Peace Studies is not a leftist version of international relations, but closer to health studies: an applied science using knowledge to improve the human condition' (Galtung 2009b).

3 This passage from T.S. Eliot can be found in *Christianity and Culture* (1960, 75).

4 The very first departments of peace studies were established just before Curle's arrival in Bradford in the UK, at two other universities. However, they soon disappeared, and as a result the University of Bradford is today considered the pioneer in the field.

5 The dialogue between Ikeda and Elise Boulding was published in Japanese in 2006, but it is not yet available in English (as of November 2009).

Appendices

1 What was introduced in Japan at the time was Western-style democracy, not the capacity of a community or society to grant decisional power to the *demos*. This practice of democracy can be found in all civilizations at different times, and the people of Japan had experienced various forms of indigenous democratic organization for ages before the introduction of Western-style democracy.

2 Useful information about Kanzo Uchimura and Christianity in Japan can be found in Mark R. Mullins (1998), *Christianity Made in Japan: A Study of Indigenous Movements*. Honolulu: University of Hawaii.

3 Ampo is the contraction of the Japanese name for the Security Treaty, taking the first half of the words *anzen* (security) and *hosho* (treaty) which are combined as Ampo. This name is widely used by English-speaking scholars.

4 For instance, a well attended 'Global Article 9 Conference to Abolish War' was held in May 2008 in Tokyo.

5 The declaration was delivered in Mitsuzawa Stadium, Yokohama, Japan, on 8 September 1957. The translation provided here is based on the version published in *A Quest for Global Peace* by Daisaku Ikeda and Josef Rotblat (2007, 124), with two modifications: in the phrases 'the first of my final instructions' and 'this first appeal of mine,' the word 'first' has been changed to 'foremost,' which I believe better reflects the meaning of the Japanese original.

Bibliography

Adorno, Theodor W. [1969] 1976. 'Introduction,' in Theodor W. Adorno et al., *The Positivist Dispute in German Sociology*. New York: Harper & Row.

AEI. 2009a. The Albert Einstein Institute website. Retrieved on 28 September 2009 from http://www.aeinstein.org.

———— 2009b. The Albert Einstein Institute website. Retrieved on 28 September 2009 from http://www.aeinstein.org/organizationsf7bd.html.

Akita Sakigake. 2008. Daily newspaper of 4 September 2008.

Aksu, Esref, and Joseph A. Camilleri (eds). 2002. *Democratizing Global Governance.* London, Palgrave Macmillan.

Anscombe, Elizabeth. 1958. 'Modern Moral Philosophy.' Retrieved on 20 August 2008 from http://www.philosophy.uncc.edu/mleldrid/cmt/mmp.html, originally published in *Philosophy*, Vol. 33 No. 124 (January 1958).

Arai, Tatsushi. 2009. 'Confronting the Desire to Arm: Josei Toda's Declaration for the Abolition of Nuclear Weapons,' in David Krieger: *The Challenge of Abolishing Nuclear Weapons*. New Brunswick, New Jersey and London: Transaction Publishers.

Archibugi, Daniele. 2008. *The Global Commonwealth of Citizens: Toward Cosmopolitan Democracy.* Princeton, New Jersey and Oxford: Princeton University Press.

———— and David Held (eds). 1995. *Cosmopolitan Democracy: An Agenda for a New World Order.* Cambridge: Polity Press.

Arms Control Association. 2006. 'Looking Back: Going for Baruch: The Nuclear Plan That Refused to Go Away.' Accessed on 8 October 2009 from http://www.armscontrol.org/act/2006_06/LookingbackBaruch.

Aruga, Hiroshi. 2000. 'Soka Gakkai and Japanese Politics,' in *Global Citizens: The Soka Gakkai Buddhist Movement in the World*. Oxford: Oxford University Press.

Barash, David P. and Charles P. Webel. 2009. *Peace and Conflict Studies* (2nd edn). London: Sage.

Barbey, Christophe. 2001. *La non-militarisation et les pays sans armee: une realite.* Flendruz, Suisse: APRED.

Bhardwaj, Arya Bhushan. 2006. 'Gandhi's Spiritual Revolution Lives,' in *Peacework: Global Thought and Local Action for Nonviolent Social Change*, Issue 368, September 2006. Retrieved on 20 August 2008 from http://www.peaceworkmagazine.org/gandhi-s-spiritual-revolution-lives.

Bix, Herbert P. 2001. *Hirohito and the Making of Modern Japan*. New York: HarperCollins Publishers. (A hardcover edition was published in 2000. The page numbers in this work refer to the first Perennial edition in paperback.)

Boulding, Elise. 1990. *Building a Global Civic Culture: Education for an Interdependent World*. Syracuse, New York: Syracuse University Press.

———— 2000. *Cultures of Peace: The Hidden Side of History*. Syracuse, New York: Syracuse University Press.

———— 2003. Interview with Julian Portilla for *Beyond Intractability*. Retrieved on 27 September 2009 from http://www.beyondintractability.org/audio/10133/.

Boulding, Kenneth. 1989. *Three Faces of Power*. Newbury Park, California: Sage Publications.

Brock, Peter. 2006. *Against the Draft: Essays on Conscientious Objection from the Radical Reformation to the Second World War*. Toronto: University of Toronto Press.

Büber, Martin. 1947. *Between Man and Man*. Trans. by Ronald Gregor Smith. London: Kegan Paul.

———— [1923] 1996. *I and Thou*. A new translation with a prologue 'I and You' and notes by Walter Kaufmann. New York: Simon and Schuster (a Touchstone book).

Bukh, Alexander. 2009. *Japan's National Identity and Foreign Policy: Russia as Japan's 'other.'* London: Taylor and Francis.

Burton, John. 1979. *Deviance, Terrorism and War: The Process of Solving Unsolved Social and Political Problems*. Oxford: Martin Robertson.

———— 1990. *Conflict: Resolution and Prevention* (Vol. 1 of the Conflict Series). London: Macmillan.

Caldarola, Carlo. 1973. 'Pacifism among Japanese Non-Church Christians.' Retrieved on 7 November 2009 from the website of 'Non-Church Christian Home,' http://www.asahi-net.or.jp/~hw8m-mrkm/nonch/pacif/nonch.pacif.eg.frame.html. Also published by Oxford Journals, *Journal of American Academy of Religions*, 1973; XLI: 506–19.

China Daily. 2008. 'Praise for Man who Called for Friendship,' in *China Daily* 9 May 2008. Retrieved on 10 November 2009 from http://www.china.org.cn/international/Hu2008/2008–05/09/content_15140126.htm.

Compact Oxford English Dictionary. 2008. Entry for 'dialogue.' Retrieved on 18 June 2008 from http://www.askoxford.com/dictionaries/?view=uk.

Crisp, Roger and Michael Slote (eds). 1997. *Virtue Ethics*. Oxford: Oxford University Press. Available online at http://www.questia.com/PM.qst?a=o&d=62733806.

Curle, Adam. 1972. *Mystics and Militants: A Study of Awareness, Identity and Social Action*. London: Tavistock Publications.

—— 1981. *True Justice: Quaker Peacemakers and Peacemaking*. London: Swarthmore Press.

—— 1995. *Another Way: Positive Response to Contemporary Violence*. Charlbury: Jon Carpenter.

—— 1997. 'Public Health IV: Reversing the Cycle of Violence,' in *Medicine, Conflict and Survival 13*. London: Routledge.

—— 1999. *To Tame the Hydra*. Charlbury: Jon Carpenter.

Dalai Lama and Howard C. Cutler. 1998. *The Art of Happiness: A Handbook for Living*. New York: Riverhead Books.

De Ligt, Barthelemy. 1937. *The Conquest of Violence: an Essay on War and Revolution*. London: George Routledge and Sons.

Dobbelaere, Karel. 2000. 'Toward a Pillar Organization?,' in *Global Citizens: The Soka Gakkai Buddhist Movement in the World*. Edited by David Machacek and Bryan Wilson. Oxford: Oxford University Press.

Dower, John W. 1986. *War without Mercy: Race and Power in the Pacific War*. New York: Pantheon Books.

—— 2000. *Embracing Defeat: Japan in the Wake of World War II*. New York: W.W. Norton & Co.

Durand, Frederic. 2005. *Pacifisme dans le Japon d'Apres-Guerre et d'Aujourd'hui* (Pacifism in postwar and contemporary Japan). Unpublished Bachelor's thesis, University of Geneva.

Eriksen, Erik O. and Jarle Weigard. 2003. *Understanding Habermas: Communicative Action and Deliberative Democracy*. London and New York: Continuum.

Falk, Richard. 1995. *On Humane Governance: Toward a New Global Politics – The World Order Models Project Report of the Global Civilization Initiative*. University Park, Pennsylvania: Pennsylvania State University Press.

—— 2008. *Achieving Human Rights*. London and New York: Routledge.

Fischer, Roger and William Ury. 1981. *Getting to Yes: Negotiating Agreement Without Giving In*. New York: Penguin.

Fisker-Nielsen, Anne Mette. 2008. *An Ethnography of Young Soka Gakkai Members' support of the Komeito Political Party*. Unpublished PhD thesis, School of Oriental and African Studies (SOAS), London.

Frankl, Victor. [1959] 2006. *Man's Search for Meaning*. Boston, Massachusetts: Beacon Press.

Freire, Paulo. [1968] 1970. *Pedagogy of the Oppressed*. London and New York: Continuum.

Fukuyama, Francis. 1992. *The End of History and the Last Man*. New York: Free Press.

Galtung, Johan. 1994. *Human Rights in Another Key*. Cambridge: Polity.

——— 1996a. *Peace by Peaceful Means: Peace and Conflict, Development and Civilization*. London: Sage.

——— 1996b. From notes taken by the author during Galtung's course at Soka University in November 1996.

——— 2000a. *Conflict Transformation by Peaceful Means (The Transcend Method): Participants' Manual/Trainers' Manual*. New York and Geneva: United Nations.

——— 2000b. Personal communication with the author.

——— 2004. *Transcend and Transform: an Introduction to Conflict Work*. Boulder, Colorado: Paradigm.

——— 2006. Telephone conversation with the author in January 2006.

——— 2008a. *50 Years, 100 Peace and Conflict Perspectives*. Transcend University Press.

——— 2008b. *50 Years: 25 Intellectual Landscapes Explored*. Transcend University Press.

——— 2009a. Personal correspondence with the author. Email message dated 27 June 2009.

——— 2009b. Course description for 'Foundations of Peace Studies,' offered by Transcend Peace University. Retrieved on 25 September 2009 from http://www.transcend.org/tpu/new/FPS_all.html.

——— and Finn Tschudi. 2002. 'Crafting Peace: On the Psychology of the TRANSCEND Approach,' in *Searching for Peace: The Road to TRANSCEND*. London: Pluto Press.

Gandhi-King-Ikeda Exhibition Brochure. Accessed on 9 September 2009 from http://www.morehouse.edu/about/chapel/peace_exhibit/exhibit/download.html.

Gandhi, Mohandas K. [1913] 1994. 'General Knowledge About Health,' in *The Collected Works of M.K. Gandhi*, Vol. 13, Ch. 153. Originally printed in *The Indian Opinion* on 8 September 1913. New Delhi: The Publications Division.

Giddens, Anthony. [1979] 2007. 'Agency, Structure,' reproduced in Craig Calhoun et al. (eds), *Contemporary Sociological Theory* (2nd edn). Oxford: Blackwell.

Habermas, Jürgen. [1980] 2007. 'Modernity: An Unfinished Project,' in Craig Calhoun et al. (eds), *Contemporary Sociological Theory* (2007) (2nd edn). London: Blackwell.

——— 1981. *The Theory of Communicative Action, Volume 1: Reason and the Rationalization of Society*. London: Beacon Press.

Hahn, Thich Nhat. 1992. *Peace is Every Step: The Path to Mindfulness in Everyday Life*. New York: Bantam.

Havel, Vaclav. 1990. *Disturbing the Peace: A Conversation with Karel Hvizdala*. New York: Knopf.

Held, David. 1995. *Democracy and the Global Order: From the Modern State to Cosmopolitan Governance*. Stanford, California: Stanford University Press.

——— 2003. *Cosmopolitanism: A Defence*. Cambridge: Polity Press.

Hobbes, Thomas. 1651, 1988. *Leviathan*. New York: Prometheus Books.

Horkheimer, Max. [1937] 1972. *Critical Theory*. New York: Herder & Herder.

Hosei University. 2000. 'The Labor Year Book of Japan' (in Japanese). Retrieved on 7 August 2008 from http://oohara.mt.tama.hosei.ac.jp/rn/senji2/rnsenji2-119. html.

Huntington, Samuel. 1993. 'The Clash of Civilizations?,' *Foreign Affairs*, Summer 1993 Vol. 72, No. 3.

—— 1996. *The Clash of Civilizations and the Remaking of World Order*. New York: Simon and Schuster.

Ibsen, Henrik. [1871] 1992. Letter to Georg Brandes, excerpt reproduced in Henrik Ibsen (1992) *Four Major Plays Volume II*. London: Signet Classic.

ICAN. 2008. International Campaign to Abolish Nuclear Weapons (ICAN) website. http://www.icanw.org/1957. Accessed 8 November 2009.

Ikeda, Daisaku. 1975. 'Chairman's Address by Daisaku Ikeda.' Delivered at the First IBL (International Buddhist League) World Peace Conference, held on Guam, January 26, 1975. In *The Soka Gakkai News*, from No. 1 February 25 to No. 18 December 15 1975. Tokyo: Soka Gakkai, pp. 22–23.

—— and Arnold Toynbee. [1976] 1989. *Choose Life*. Oxford: Oxford University Press.

—— 1979. *Glass Children and Other Essays*. New York: Kodansha America.

—— 1980. *My Recollections*. Santa Monica, California: World Tribune Press.

—— 1989–PP. 'Towards A New Globalism' (1989 Peace Proposal). Tokyo: Soka Gakkai.

—— 1990. *The Snow Country Prince*. Illustrations by Brian Wildsmith. English version by Geraldine McCaughrean. Oxford: Oxford University Press.

—— (1990–2008). *Peace Proposals*. Each proposal has been published as an independent text or booklet by the SGI. Tokyo: Soka Gakkai. For other peace proposals, as well as the documents 1975–1982, see the section 'References for the Peace Proposals' below.

—— 1991. *The Cherry Tree*. Illustrations by Brian Wildsmith. English version by Geraldine McCaughrean. Oxford: Oxford University Press.

—— and René Huyghe. [1991] 2007. *Dawn after Dark*. London: I.B.Tauris.

—— 1992. *Over the Deep Blue Sea*. Illustrations by Brian Wildsmith. English version by Geraldine McCaughrean. Oxford: Oxford University Press.

—— and Linus Pauling. 1992. *A Lifelong Quest for Peace: A Dialogue*. Sudbury, Massachusetts: Jones and Bartlett Publishers.

—— [1993] 1996. 'Mahayana Buddhism and Twenty-first-Century Civilization.' A speech delivered at Harvard University on 24 September 1993. In *A New Humanism: The University Addresses of Daisaku Ikeda*. New York and Tokyo: Weatherhill, 1996.

———— 1994–PP. 'Light of the Global Spirit: A New Dawn in Human History' (1994 Peace Proposal). Tokyo: Soka Gakkai.

———— 1995–PP. 'Creating a Century without War through Human Solidarity' (1995 Peace Proposal). Tokyo: Soka Gakkai.

———— and Johan Galtung. 1995. *Choose Peace*. London: Pluto Press.

———— 1995–1. *The New Human Revolution, Vol. 1*. Santa Monica, California: World Tribune Press.

———— 1996a. Speech delivered at Moscow M.V. Lomonosov State University, 17 May 1994: 'The Magnificent Cosmos,' in *A New Humanism: The University Addresses of Daisaku Ikeda*. New York and Tokyo: Weatherhill.

———— 1996b. Speech delivered at Harvard University, Cambridge, 24 September 1993: 'Mahayana Buddhism and Twenty-first-Century Civilization,' in *A New Humanism: The University Addresses of Daisaku Ikeda*. New York and Tokyo: Weatherhill.

———— 1996c. *A New Humanism: The University Addresses of Daisaku Ikeda*. New York: Weatherhill.

———— 1997a. *Songs from my Heart: Poems and Photographs by Daisaku Ikeda*. New York: Weatherhill.

———— 1997b. *Kanta and the Deer*. Illustrated by Christina Sun. New York: Weatherhill.

———— 2000–I. *The Wisdom of the Lotus Sutra, Vol. I*. Santa Monica, California: World Tribune Press.

———— 2000–II. *The Wisdom of the Lotus Sutra, Vol. II*. Santa Monica, California: World Tribune Press.

———— 2001a. Speech delivered at Teachers College, Columbia University, on 13 June 1996: 'Education for Global Citizenship,' in *Soka Education: a Buddhist Vision for Teachers, Students and Parents*. Santa Monica, California: Middleway Press.

———— 2001b. *For the Sake of Peace*. Santa Monica, California: Middleway Press.

———— 2001c. 'The Evil over which we Must Triumph,' in *From the Ashes: A Spiritual Response to the Attack on America*. Emmaus, Pennsylvania: Rodale Press.

———— 2001–7. *The New Human Revolution, Vol. 7*. Santa Monica, California: World Tribune Press.

———— 2002–PP. 'The Humanism of the Middle Way – Dawn of a Global Civilization' (2002 Peace Proposal). Tokyo: Soka Gakkai.

———— and David Krieger. 2002. *Choose Hope*. Santa Monica, California: Middleway Press.

————, René Simard and Guy Bourgeault. 2002. *On Being Human: Where Ethics, Medicine and Spirituality Converge*. Montreal: Montreal University Press.

———— and Majid Tehranian. 2003. *Global Civilization: A Buddhist–Islamic Dialogue*. London: British Academic Press.

—— 2003. *Wonderful Encounters*. Selangor: Penerbit University Kebansaan Malaysia Press in Association with Soka Gakkai Malaysia.

—— et al. 2003–VI. *The Wisdom of the Lotus Sutra, Volume VI*. Santa Monica, California: World Tribune Press.

—— 2003–9. *The New Human Revolution, Vol. 9*. Santa Monica, California: World Tribune Press.

—— 2004a. *The Human Revolution*. Santa Monica, California: World Tribune Press.

—— 2004b. *Fighting for Peace: Poems by Daisaku Ikeda*. Tokyo: Soka Gakkai.

—— 2004c. *Transcend and Transform: an Introduction to Conflict Work*. Boulder, Colorado: Paradigm.

—— and Hazel Henderson. 2004. *Planetary Citizenship: Your Values, Beliefs and Actions Can Shape a Sustainable World*. Santa Monica, California: Middleway Press.

—— and Mikhail Gorbachev. 2005. *Moral Lessons of the Twentieth Century: Gorbachev and Ikeda on Buddhism and Communism*. London: I.B.Tauris.

—— 2006a. *A Youthful Diary: One Man's Journey from the Beginning of Faith to Worldwide Leadership for Peace*. Santa Monica, California: World Tribune Press.

—— 2006b. 'On Attaining Buddhahood in This Lifetime (1): SGI President's New Study Lecture Series: The Fundamental Purpose of Life and a Source of Hope for Humankind,' in *Living Buddhism*, 1 September 2006, p. 77.

—— 2006c. *Fulfilling the Mission: Empowering the UN to Live up to the World's Expectations*. Tokyo: Soka Gakkai.

—— 2006–12. *The New Human Revolution, Vol. 12*. Santa Monica, California: World Tribune Press.

—— 2006–PP. 'A New Era of the People' (2006 Peace Proposal). Tokyo: Soka Gakkai.

—— [2007] 2008. 'Moving beyond the use of military force.' Editorial in *The Japan Times* 11 January 2007. In *Embracing the Future*. Tokyo: The Japan Times.

—— and Joseph Rotblat. 2007. *A Quest for Global Peace*. London: I.B.Tauris.

—— 2007–PP. 'Restoring the Human Connection: The First Step to Global Peace' (2007 Peace Proposal). Tokyo: Soka Gakkai.

—— 2008–15. *The New Human Revolution, Vol. 15*. Santa Monica, California: World Tribune Press.

—— and Ricardo Díez-Hochleitner. 2008. *A Dialogue Between East and West: Looking to a Human Revolution*. London: I.B.Tauris.

—— 2008–PP. 'Humanizing Religion, Creating Peace' (2008 Peace Proposal). Tokyo: Soka Gakkai.

—— 2009a. *Building Global Solidarity Toward Nuclear Abolition*. Retrieved on 12 September 2009 from http://www.daisakuikeda.org/sub/resources/works/props/disarm_proposal.html.

—— 2009b. 'A Life Dedicated to Dialogue,' in *Monthly SGI Newsletter*, No. 314, August/September 2009. Tokyo: Soka Gakkai.

———— 2009c. 'Sustainable development: Transform Self to Heal the Earth,' Global Oneness. Retrieved on 14 September 2009 from http://www.experiencefestival. com/a/Sustainable_development/id/5611539.

———— 2009–PP. 'Toward Humanitarian Competition: A New Current in History' (2009 Peace Proposal). Tokyo: Soka Gakkai.

————, Ronald A. Bosco and Joel Myerson. 2009. *Creating Waldens: An East–West Conversation on the American Renaissance.* Boston, Massachusetts: Dialogue Path Press. Available online and accessed on 7 November 2009 at http://www.ikedacenter.org/books/creating_waldens/foreword.htm.

———— and Lokesh Chandra. 2009. *Buddhism: a Way of Values.* New Delhi: Eternal Ganges Press.

———— and Nur Yalman. 2009. *A Passage to Peace: Global Solutions from East and West.* London: I.B.Tauris.

Ikeda Website. 'Dialogues Published.' Accessed 29 October 2009. http:// daisakuikeda.org/sub/resources/records/dialog.html.

IPS, Inter Press Service News Agency. 2008. 'World Needs a Global Culture of Human Rights, Interview with Daisaku Ikeda President of the Soka Gakkai International.' Retrieved on 17 October 2008 from http://domino.ips.org/ ips%5Ceng.nsf/vwWebMainView/2424BCC2AD247889C125741A00545851 /?OpenDocument.

Japan Society. 2008. 'Rights and Responsibilities: Looking at the Meiji Constitution.' Retrieved on 8 August 2008 from http://aboutjapan.japansociety.org/content. cfm/rights_responsibilities.

Johnson, Hank. 2007. 'Rep. Johnson Introduces Resolution Concerning Soka Gakkai International President Ikeda's Birthday,' from: US Fed News Service, Including US State News. Article date: 7 December 2007. Information retrieved on 2 October 2009 from http://www.highbeam.com/doc/1P3-1394488761.html.

Kanno, Hiroshi. 2004. 'The Modern Significance of the Lotus Sutra,' in *The Journal of Oriental Studies*, Vol. 14.

Katz, Milton S. 1987. *Ban the Bomb: A History of SANE, the Committee for a Sane Nuclear Policy.* New York: Praeger.

Kawada, Yoichi. 2008. Personal exchange with the author at the Institute of Oriental Philosophy, Tokyo, on 30 January 2008.

Kelly, Ann. 2002. 'The Toynbee–Ikeda Dialogue,' in *Art of Living: A Buddhist Magazine* (May).

Keown, Damien. 2003. *Oxford Dictionary of Buddhism.* Oxford: Oxford University Press.

Kersten, Rikki. 2006. 'The Social Imperative of Pacifism in Postwar Japan: Shimizu Ikutaro and the Uchinada Movement,' in *Critical Asian Studies*, Vol. 38, No. 3, September 2006, pp. 303–28, London: Routledge.

King James Bible Online. 2009. http://www.kingjamesbibleonline.org. Accessed 9 November 2009.

King Jr., Martin Luther. 1963. 'I have a dream.' Speech delivered on 28 August 1963 at the Lincoln Memorial, Washington DC, USA. Retrieved on 19 September 2009 from http://www.americanrhetoric.com/speeches/mlkihaveadream.htm.

Kobayashi, Masahiro. 2007. 'Nichiren's Philosophy of Peace,' in *Poetry for World Peace, Harmony and Humanism.* Chennai: Chinmaya Heritage Centre.

Koestler, Arthur. 1945. *The Yogi and the Commissar and Other Essays.* London: Jonathan Cape.

Krieger, David. 2007. Conversation with the author, 9 September 2007.

——— ed. 2009. *The Challenge of Abolishing Nuclear Weapons.* New Brunswick, New Jersey and London: Transaction Publishers.

Lawler, Peter. 1995. *A Question of Values: Johan Galtung's Peace Research.* London: Lynne Rienner.

Lederach, John Paul. 1995. *Preparing for Peace: Conflict Transformation Across Cultures.* New York: Syracuse University Press.

Lentz, Theodore F. 1955. *Towards a Science of Peace: Turning Point in Human Destiny.* London: Halcyon Press.

Macquarrie, John. 1973. *The Concept of Peace* (The Firth Lectures, 1972). London: SCM Press.

Mainichi Shimbun. 1994. Daily newspaper, 6 November 1994.

Makiguchi, Tsunesaburo. [1903] 1983. *Jinsei chirigaku (The Geography of Human Life).* In *Makiguchi Tsunesasburo Zenshu (Complete Works of Tsunesaburo Makiguchi)*, Vols. 1–2 (in Japanese). Tokyo: Daisan Bunmeisha.

——— [1930–31] 1982. *Soka kyoikugaku taikei (The System of Value-creating Pedagogy)*, Vols. I & II. In *Makiguchi Tsunesasburo Zenshu (Complete Works of Tsunesaburo Makiguchi)*, Vol. 5 (in Japanese). Tokyo: Daisan Bunmeisha.

——— [1932–34] 1983. *Soka kyoikugaku taikei (The System of Value-creating Pedagogy)*, Vols. III & IV. In *Makiguchi Tsunesasburo Zenshu (Complete Works of Tsunesaburo Makiguchi)*, Vol. 6 (in Japanese). Tokyo: Daisan Bunmeisha.

Makiguchi Website. May 1939 entry in the timeline. Retrieved on 2 October 2009 from http://tmakiguchi.org/timeline/Buddhistmovement.html. The actual interview is available in Japanese from the same website, retrieved on the same day from http://tmakiguchi.org/sadakokaneko.

Maslow, Abraham. 1954. *Motivation and Personality.* New York: Harper.

Matsuda, Tomohiro. 2009. Personal exchange with the author in Tokyo, 7 July 2009.

Mayer, John R.A. 1998. 'Reflections on the Threefold Lotus Sutra,' in the *Journal of Buddhist Ethics*, Vol. 5. Retrieved on 25 March 2008 from http://jbe.gold.ac.uk/5/mayer981.htm.

McNeill, William. 1989. *Arnold J. Toynbee: A Life.* New York: Oxford University Press.

Menton, Linda K. (ed.). 2003. *The Rise of Modern Japan.* Honolulu: University of Hawaii Press.

Min-On Concert Association Website. 2009. Mission statement. Retrieved on 9 September 2009 from http://www.min-on.org/about/index.html.

Mitchels, Barbara. 2006. *Love in Danger: Trauma, therapy and conflict explored through the life and work of Adam Curle.* Charlbury: John Carpenter.

Montaigne, Michel de. [1580] 2003. *Essays.* Trans. and ed. by M.A. Screech. London: Penguin Books.

Muller, A. Charles (ed.). *Digital Dictionary of Buddhism.* http://buddhism-dict.net. Accessed on 27 October 2009.

Mullins, Mark R. 1998. *Christianity Made in Japan: A Study of Indigenous Movements.* Honolulu: University of Hawaii.

National Diet Library. 2009. Retrieved on 9 September 2009 from http://www.ndl.go.jp/constitution/e/etc/c01.html#s2.

Naval Historical Center. 2008. 'Commodore Perry and the Opening of Japan.' Retrieved on 8 August 2008 from http://www.history.navy.mil/branches/teach/ends/opening.htm.

Neumaier, Eva K. 2004. 'Missed Opportunities: Buddhism and the Ethnic Strife in Sri Lanka and Tibet,' in *Religion and Peacebuilding*, edited by Harold Coward and Gordon S. Smith. Albany, New York: State University of New York Press.

Nichiren. 1999. *The Writings of Nichiren Daishonin.* Tokyo: Soka Gakkai.

Nussbaum, Martha C. 2007. *The Clash Within: Democracy, Religious Violence and India's Future.* Cambridge, Massachusetts: Harvard University Press.

Nye, Joseph S. Jr. 2004. *Soft Power: The Means to Success in World Politics.* New York: Public Affairs.

One Country. 2004. 'Perspective: The Individual and Social Action,' in *One Country: The Online Newsletter of the Baha'i International Community*, Vol. 15, Issue 4 / January–March 2004. Retrieved on 19 August 2008 from http://www.onecountry.org/e154/e15402as_Perspective_Social_Action.htm.

OnWar.com. 2008. 'Russo–Japanese War 1904–1905.' Retrieved on 8 August 2008 from http://www.onwar.com/aced/data/romeo/russojapanese1904.htm.

Ortega y Gasset, José. 1961. *Meditations on Quixote.* Trans. Evelyn Ruff and Diego Marin. New York: Norton.

Paige, Glenn. 1968. *The Korean Decision: June 24–30, 1950.* New York: Free Press.

———— [2002] 2007. *Nonkilling Global Political Science.* Bloomington, Illinois: Xlibris.

—— 2008. Personal conversation with the author in Honolulu, 15 November 2008.

Pauling, Linus. 1958. *No More War*. New York: Dodd, Mead and Co.

Paupp, Terrence. 2000. *Achieving Inclusionary Governance: Advancing Peace and Development in First and Third World Nations*. New York: Transnational Publishers, Inc.

—— 2007. *Exodus from Empire: The Fall of America's Empire and the Rise of the Global Community*. London: Pluto Press.

—— 2009. *The Future of Global Relations: Crumbling Walls, Rising Regions*. New York: Palgrave Macmillan.

Peace Education Center. 2009. Columbia University website, staff index of the Center: http://www.tc.columbia.edu/peaceed/staff/index.htm. Accessed 29 October 2009.

Peking University Website. 2009. Report on the academic symposium in honor of Daisaku Ikeda's birthday. Retrieved on 2 October 2009 from http://www.oir.pku.edu.cn/newoir/2005/Article/ShowArticle.asp?ArticleID=4531.

Perrin, Noel. 1980. *Giving up the Gun: Japan's Reversion to the Sword, 1543–1879*. Boston, Massachusetts: Shambhala.

Pfiffner, James P. 2005. 'Presidential Decision Making: Rationality, Advisory Systems, and Personality,' in *Presidential Studies Quarterly*, Vol. 35.

Plato. 1892. *The Dialogues of Plato translated into English with Analyses and Introductions by B. Jowett, M.A. in Five Volumes*. 3rd edn revised and corrected. Oxford: Oxford University Press.

Radhakrishnan, N. 2006. *The Living Dialogue: Socrates to Ikeda*. New Delhi: Gandhi Media Center.

Ramsbotham, Oliver, Tom Woodhouse and Hugh Miall. 2008. *Contemporary Conflict Resolution* (2nd edn). Cambridge: Polity.

Rant Collective. 2009. 'Conflict Resolution: A Compilation of Notes.' Retrieved on 27 September 2009 from http://rantcollective.net/article.php?id=15.

Reardon, Betty A. 1992. 'Toward a Paradigm of Peace,' *A Peace Reader, Essential Readings on War, Justice, Non-violence and World Order*. Revised edn, edited by Joseph J. Fahey and Richard Armstrong. New York: Paulist Press.

—— 1996. *Sexism and the War System*. Syracuse, New York: Syracuse University Press.

—— 1997. 'Human Rights as Education for Peace,' in *Human Rights Education for the Twenty-First Century*, edited by George J. Andreopoulous and Richard Pierre Claude. Philadelphia, Pennsylvania: University of Pennsylvania Press.

—— 2001. *Education for a Culture of Peace in a Gender Perspective*. Paris: UNESCO.

—— and Alicia Cabezudo. 2002. *Learning to Abolish War: Teaching Toward a Culture of Peace*. New York: Hague Appeal for Peace.

Rees, S. 2003. *Passion for Peace: Exercising Power Creatively*. Sydney: University of New South Wales Press.

Richmond, Oliver P. 2007. *The Transformation of Peace: Rethinking Peace and Conflict Studies*. Basingstoke: Palgrave Macmillan.

Rogers, Carl. [1961] 1995a. *On Becoming a Person: A Therapist's View of Psychotherapy*. Boston, Massachusetts and New York: Houghton Mifflin.

———— [1980] 1995b. *A Way of Being*. Boston and New York: Houghton Mifflin.

Ross, Rick. 2004. 'Has Orlando Bloom become the latest celebrity "cult" casualty?.' Retrieved on 8 August 2008 from http://www.cultnews.com/?p=1599.

Ross, Susan (ed.). 2008. *Peace Journalism in Times of War* (*Peace & Policy* Vol. 13). Piscataway, New Jersey: Transaction.

Said, Edward. 1994. *Culture and Imperialism*. New York: Vintage Books.

Schlichtmann, Klaus. 2009. *Japan in the World: Shidehara Kijuro, Pacifism, and the Abolition of War*, Vol. II.

Seager, Richard. 2006. *Encountering the Dharma: Daisaku Ikeda, Soka Gakkai, and the Globalization of Buddhist Humanism*. Berkeley, California: University of California Press.

Seikyo Shimbun. 2001. 'The High Road to a Century of Peace,' translation based on the 25, 26 and 28 December 2001 *Seikyo Shimbun*. Retrieved on 22 September 2009 from http://www.daisakuikeda.org/sub/resources/interview/interview2/2001seikyo.html.

———— 2007 of 30 January 2007 (in Japanese).

———— 2007 of 22 November 2007, p. 2, 'Conversations with more than 7,000 People'. (Title translated from Japanese by the author.)

———— 2008 of 6 September 2008.

Seligman, Martin. 2002. *Authentic Happiness: Using the New Positive Psychology to Realize Your Potential for Lasting Fulfillment*. New York, London, Toronto, Sydney: Free Press.

Seraphim, Franziska. 2006. *War Memory and Social Politics in Japan, 1945–2005*. Cambridge, Massachusetts and London: Harvard University Press.

SGI Quarterly. 2000. April issue. Retrieved on 19 February 2008 from http://www.sgiquarterly.org/english/Features/quarterly/0004/history.htm.

Sharif, Abu Aaliyah Surkheel. 2006. '*Jihad al-Nafs*: the Greater Struggle.' Retrieved on 18 September 2009 from the muslimmatters.org website at http://muslimmatters.org/2007/11/23/jihad-al-nafs-the-greater-struggle/.

Sharp, Gene. 1973. *The Politics of Nonviolent Action*. Boston, Massachusetts: Porter Sargent.

————2005. *Waging Nonviolent Struggle: Twentieth Century Practice and Twenty-First Century Potential*. Boston, Massachusetts: Extending Horizons Books, Porter Sargent.

Shiohara, Masayuki. 2008a. Personal interview with the author on 19 February 2008.

———— 2008b. 'The Ideas and Practices of Josei Toda: A Successor of Soka Education 1929–1939,' in *Soka Education*, No. 1, March.

Stanford Encyclopedia of Philosophy. 2009a. Entry on Methodological Individualism, http://plato.stanford.edu/entries/methodological-individualism/ accessed 9 November 2009.

———— 2009b. Entry on Functionalism. http://plato.stanford.edu/entries/functionalism/ accessed 9 November 2009.

Stueck, William. 2002. *Rethinking the Korean War: A New Diplomatic and Strategic History.* Princeton, New Jersey: Princeton University Press.

Suwa, Yoshiharu. 2009. Interviewed by the author on 11 November 2009.

Tanaka, Akihiko. 2000. 'The Domestic Context of the Alliances: The Politics of Tokyo.' Retrieved on 10 April 2008 from http://iis-db.stanford.edu/pubs/11376/Tanaka.pdf.

Teranishi, Hirotomo. 2008. Phone interview with the author on 25 August 2008.

Timmons, Mark. 2002. *Moral Theory: An Introduction*. Lanham, Maryland: Rowman and Littlefield.

Tipton, Elise K. 2002. *Modern Japan: A Social and Political History.* London: Routledge.

Toda, Josei. 1929. *Katei Kyoikugaku Soron* (An Anatomy of Home Education). Tokyo: Jobundo.

———— 1930. *Suirishiki Shido Sanjutsu* (A Deductive Guide to Arithmetic). Tokyo: Jobundo.

———— 1957. *Ningen Kakumei* (Human Revolution). Tokyo: Seibunkan Shoten.

Toda Website. http://joseitoda.org.

Tokyo Fuji Art Museum Webpage, accessed 31 October 2009. http://www.fujibi.or.jp/en/about/index.html.

Totani, Yuma. 2008. *The Tokyo War Crimes Trial: The Pursuit of Justice in the Wake of World War II.* Cambridge, Massachusetts and London: Harvard University Press.

Toynbee, Arnold. 1934–61. *A Study of History.* Oxford: Oxford University Press.

———— 1948. *Civilization on Trial.* New York: Oxford University Press.

Tsurumi, Shunsuke. 1987. *A Cultural History of Postwar Japan, 1945–1980.* London: KPI Ltd.

Tzadok, Ariel Bar. 2005. 'The Torah Code of Honor.' Retrieved on 18 September 2009 from http://www.koshertorah.com/PDF/codeofhonor.pdf.

Ushio Publishers. 2000. *Josei Toda* (In Japanese). Tokyo: Ushio.

Watanabe, Kiyoshi. 1983. *Kudakareta Kami – aru fukuinhei no shuki* (Shattered God: The Diary of a Repatriated Soldier). Tokyo: Asahi Sensho.

Watson, Burton [trans.]. 1993. *The Lotus Sutra.* New York: Columbia University Press.

————— [trans.]. 2002. *The Essential Lotus: Selections from the Lotus Sutra*. New York: Columbia University Press.

Weber, Max. [1904–05] 1930. *The Protestant Ethic and the Spirit of Capitalism*. London: HarperCollins.

Wilson, Bryan and Karel Dobbelaere. 1994. *A Time to Chant*. Oxford: Oxford University Press.

Wittner, Lawrence S. 1997. *Resisting the Bomb: A History of the World Nuclear Disarmament Movement 1954–1970*. Stanford, California: Stanford University Press.

————— 2007. 'An Anniversary to Celebrate If You Oppose War.' Posted on the History News Network (HNN) website. http://hnn.us/articles/43037.html. Accessed 8 November 2009.

World People Blog. 2006. 'Betty A. Reardon – USA.' http://word.world-citizenship. org/wp-archive/883. Accessed 27 October 2009.

Yamamoto, Mari. 2005. 'Japan's Grassroots Pacifism,' in *Japan Focus*. Retrieved on 10 April 2008 from http://www.japanfocus.org/products/details/2102.

Zahl, Karl F. 1973. *Die politische Elite Japans nach dem 2. Weltkrieg (1945–1965)* (Japan's Political Elite after WWII). Wiesbaden: Otto Harassowitz, 1973 (vol. 34 of publications by the Institut fur Asienkunde in Hamburg).

References for the Peace Proposals and related documents
(all texts by Daisaku Ikeda)

1975 IBL speech: 'Chairman's Address by Daisaku Ikeda.' Delivered at the First IBL (International Buddhist League) World Peace Conference, held on Guam, January 26, 1975. In *The Soka Gakkai News*, from No. 1 February 25 to No. 18 December 15 1975. Tokyo: Soka Gakkai, pp. 22–23.

1978 Proposal for SSD-I: 'Proposal for Nuclear Disarmament Submitted to Secretary-General Kurt Waldheim on the occasion of the United Nations General Assembly First Special Session on Disarmament May 1978,' in *Proposals on Peace and Disarmament Toward the 21st Century*. Tokyo: Soka Gakkai International, 1991, pp. 5–14.

1982 Proposal for SSD-II: 'A New Proposal for Disarmament and the Abolition of Nuclear Weapons. Presented on the occasion of the United Nations General Assembly Second Special Session on Disarmament June 1982,' in *Proposals on Peace and Disarmament Toward the 21st Century*. Tokyo: Soka Gakkai International, 1991, pp. 15–22.

1983 Peace Proposal: in *Proposals on Peace and Disarmament Toward the 21st Century*. Tokyo: Soka Gakkai International, 1991, pp. 23–30.

1984 Peace Proposal: in *Proposals on Peace and Disarmament Toward the 21st Century*. Tokyo: Soka Gakkai International, 1991, pp. 31–36.

1985 Peace Proposal: in *Proposals on Peace and Disarmament Toward the 21st Century*. Tokyo: Soka Gakkai International, 1991, pp. 37–46.

1986 Peace Proposal: in *Proposals on Peace and Disarmament Toward the 21st Century*. Tokyo: Soka Gakkai International, 1991, pp. 47–58.

1987 Peace Proposal: *Soka Gakkai News*, Feb. 1987, pp. 2–31. Tokyo: Soka Gakkai.

1988 Peace Proposal: *Soka Gakkai News*, March 1988, pp. 8–31. Tokyo: Soka Gakkai.

1989 Peace Proposal: *Soka Gakkai News*, Feb. 1989, pp. 2–23. Tokyo: Soka Gakkai.

1990–2008 Peace Proposals: each published as a separate booklet, Tokyo: Soka Gakkai.

2004–2009 Peace Proposals also available online, last retrieved on 10 November 2009 from http://daisakuikeda.org/main/peacebuild/peace-proposals/pp2009.html.

List of the titles of the Peace Proposals

1983. New Proposals for Peace and Disarmament
1984. A World without War
1985. New Waves of Peace toward the Twenty-first Century
1986. Dialogue for Lasting Peace
1987. Spreading the Brilliance of Peace Toward the Century of the People
1988. Cultural Understanding and Disarmament: The Building Blocks of World Peace
1989. Towards A New Globalism
1990. The Triumph of Democracy: Toward a Century of Hope
1991. Dawn of the Century of Humanity
1992. A Renaissance of Hope and Harmony
1993. Towards a More Humane World in the Coming Century
1994. Light of the Global Spirit: A New Dawn in Human History
1995. Creating a Century without War through Human Solidarity
1996. Toward the Third Millennium: The Challenge of Global Citizenship
1997. New Horizons of a Global Civilization
1998. Humanity and the New Millennium: From Chaos to Cosmos
1999. Toward a Culture of Peace: A Cosmic View
2000. Peace through Dialogue: A Time to Talk: Thoughts on a Culture of Peace
2001. Creating and Sustaining a Century of Life: Challenges for a New Era
2002. The Humanism of the Middle Way – Dawn of a Global Civilization
2003. A Global Ethic of Coexistence: Toward a 'Life-Sized' Paradigm for Our Age
2004. Inner Transformation: Creating a Global Groundswell for Peace
2005. Toward a New Era of Dialogue: Humanism Explored

Index

Japanese names are treated as Western names.

Toda Institute Book Series on Global Peace and Policy
Senior Editor: Olivier Urbain

Bridging a Gulf: Peacebuilding in West Asia
Edited by Majid Tehranian

Democratizing Global Governance
Edited by Esref Aksu and Joseph Camilleri

Dialogue of Civilizations: A New Peace Agenda for a New Millennium
Edited by Majid Tehranian and David Chappell

Managing the Global: Globalization, Employment and Quality of Life
Edited by Donald Lamberton

Reimagining the Future: Towards Democratic Governance
Edited by Joseph Camilleri, Kamal Malhotra and Majid Tehranian

Nuclear Disarmament: Obstacles to Banishing the Bomb
Edited by Jozef Goldblat

Not By Bread Alone: Food Security and Governance in Africa
Edited by Adelani Ogunrinade, Ruth Oniango'o and Julian May

Asian Peace: Security and Governance in the Asia Pacific Region
Edited by Majid Tehranian

Worlds Apart: Human Security and Global Governance
Edited by Majid Tehranian